THE COUPLING CONVENTION

The Coupling Convention

SEX, TEXT, AND TRADITION
IN BLACK WOMEN'S FICTION

Ann duCille

New York   Oxford
OXFORD UNIVERSITY PRESS
1993

Oxford University Press

Oxford   New York   Toronto
Delhi   Bombay   Calcutta   Madras   Karachi
Kuala Lumpur   Singapore   Hong Kong   Tokyo
Nairobi   Dar es Salaam   Cape Town
Melbourne   Auckland   Madrid

and associated companies in
Berlin   Ibadan

Copyright © 1993 by Ann duCille

Published by Oxford University Press, Inc.
200 Madison Avenue, New York, New York 10016

Oxford is a registered trademark of Oxford University Press

Library of Congress Cataloging-in-Publication Data
DuCille, Ann.
The coupling convention : sex, text, and tradition in Black women's fiction /
Ann duCille.
p. cm.   Includes bibliographical references and index.
ISBN 0-19-507972-8 — 0-19-508509-4 (pbk.)
1. American fiction—Afro-American authors—History and criticism.
2. American fiction—Women authors—History and criticism.
3. Feminism and literature—United States—History.
4. Women and literature—United States—History.
5. Man-woman relationships in literature.
6. Afro-American women in literature.
7. Marriage in literature.
8. Love in literature.
9. Sex in literature.
I. Title.
PS374.N4D8   1993
810.9'9287'08996—dc20   93-19916

The lines from "Homage to the Empress of the Blues" are reprinted from *Collected Poems* of
Robert Hayden, edited by Frederick Glaysher, by permission of Liveright Publishing Corporation. Copyright © 1985 by Erma Hayden.

"The Double Standard," pp. 344–346, is reprinted from *A Brighter Coming Day: A Frances
Ellen Watkins Harper Reader.*

9 8 7 6 5 4 3 2 1

Printed in the United States of America
on acid-free paper

For Pearl L. duCille

Acknowledgments

I have been reading the works of black women writers for almost thirty years and teaching them for more than twenty. That I have had the pleasure and privilege of doing so is due, in large measure, to the efforts of black women scholars, critics, and artists who in the seventies, as Barbara Christian says, "plowed the neglected field of Afro-American women's literature when such an act was academically dangerous." These critics and writers—Barbara Christian, Mary Helen Washington, Barbara Smith, Claudia Tate, Hortense Spillers, Frances Smith Foster, Gloria Hull, Patricia Bell Scott, Cheryl A. Wall, Alice Walker, and Toni Morrison, to name only a few—reclaimed (often from obscurity) a literature I now have the luxury of theorizing about with considerably more "safety." Their work has inspired and enabled my own, and it is to these pioneering black women scholars and those who have joined their ranks more recently that I wish to say the first of many thank yous.

Acknowledging that these words do not adequately reflect my indebtedness, I also wish to thank Mari Jo Buhle and Ellen Rooney, both at Brown University, who guided this project from idea to text. Both are inspiring teachers, careful readers, and constructive critics who saw the "larger picture" and made me see it too. My debts to them, however, are not only for the roles they played in reading, coaxing, and critiquing this book but also for their support and friendship throughout the past few years. Sincere thanks go as well to Thadious Davis, Dorothy Denniston, and Michael Harper, whose knowledge of African American literature enhanced and expanded my own. Their encouragement, confidence in me, and faith in my work have been sources of sustenance and inspiration. Others at Brown to whom I am deeply indebted include Bob Lee, George Monteiro, Bernard Bruce, Susan Smulyan, Elizabeth Weed, Paget Henry, and a host of undergraduates who taught me at least as much as I taught them. I cannot leave the Brown contingent without acknowledging the support and guidance of Nancy Armstrong and Leonard Tennenhouse. As

viii   Acknowledgments

mentors, neighbors, and friends they have fed body, mind, and soul literally
as well as figuratively. But long before I had the pleasure of meeting them,
their scholarship beckoned me into the intellectual fray. Nancy's brilliant and
provocative book *Desire and Domestic Fiction: A Political History of the Novel*
showed me how to think unconventionally about the marriage convention.

I am grateful to the Danforth Foundation for a dissertation fellowship,
which facilitated my research immensely. Much of the preparatory work for
this book was undertaken during a fellowship year at Wesleyan University's
Center for the Humanities. For the research fellowship and the intellectual
stimulation it provided, I am grateful to Wesleyan, to the center's director,
Richard Ohmann, and to my fellow researchers, especially Paula Rabinowitz.
I am indebted as well to colleagues and friends at Wesleyan too numerous to
acknowledge individually. To all the unnamed I say a general but no less
sincere "thank you." I must, however, single out Henry Abelove, who believed
in this book even before it was written; Khachig Tololyan, who called the
manuscript to the attention of Elizabeth Maguire at Oxford University Press;
and Indira Karamcheti, who read and reread every word with the discerning
eye of a consummate critic and the tender loving care of a good friend. I also
wish to acknowledge the invaluable research assistance of Deborah Cohler.
The book benefited as well from the kind encouragement of our intercollegiate
feminist writing group, whose members guided me through several versions of
what eventually became chapter 3. Very special thanks go to all six: Indira
Karamcheti and Gertrude Hughes at Wesleyan; Joan Hedrick, Farah Griffin,
and Barbara Sicherman at Trinity; and Laura Wexler at Yale. Others who
read and offered helpful comments on part or all of the manuscript include
William L. Andrews, Hazel Carby, Kevin Gaines, Linda Grasso, Wilson Moses, Louise Newman, Joe Reed, Laura Santigian, and Greta Slobin. I particularly wish to thank Hazel Carby not only for her comments and encouragement but also for the model of her own work, and Laura Santigian, who
willed this book into being as only a good friend can.

Parts of chapters 4 and 5 appeared as "Blues Notes on Black Sexuality: Sex
and the Texts of Jessie Fauset and Nella Larsen" in the *Journal of the History
of Sexuality* 3 (January 1993): 418–44. For their interest in my work I thank
the journal's editors, John C. Fout and Maura D. Shaw Tantillo. For their
faith in this project and for their support and editorial assistance, I thank
Susan Chang, Henry Krawitz, and especially Elizabeth Maguire at Oxford
University Press. I feel particularly fortunate to have found in Liz Maguire an
editor who takes my work seriously and still laughs at my jokes.

Debts of another kind are owed to Janice Allen, Teresa Bill, Ben Jackson,
Anne Hynes, Keith Berger, and Linda, Ron, and Aaron Santigian, all of whom,
above and beyond all else, have given endlessly of the gift of friendship.

Finally, and most emphatically, I wish to thank my family: my younger
brother, Danny duCille (who, although he often says he hates critics, nevertheless has lugged boxes of books from state to state and installed bookshelves in
numerous studies in what is only one of many demonstrations of his love and
support); my older brother, the late Adrian E. duCille, Jr.; my nieces and

nephews—Adrian III, Beverly Ann, Marie Louise, and David duCille—who keep me laughing; and my father, Adrian E. duCille, Sr. My heartiest thanks and deepest appreciation lovingly go to my mother, Pearl L. duCille, to whom this book is dedicated. Her unconditional support and affection have been mainstays throughout my life. As I once said of her in a poem: "way down deep / in the after hour overtime of everything I am / she is." Everything good, that is. The faults, as well as any errors that may remain within these pages, are entirely my own.

Middletown, Conn.   A. duC.
March 1993

Contents

THE COUPLING CONVENTION

Introduction

Conventional Criticism and Unconventional Black Literature

"It is a truth universally acknowledged that a single man in possession of a great fortune must be in want of a wife." This oft-quoted opening line from Jane Austen's *Pride and Prejudice* suggests both the degree to which the marriage plot is indigenous to the genre of the novel and the extent to which the middle and upper classes have historically been preoccupied with matrimony and affairs of the heart and pocketbook.[1] It is a truth not so widely acknowledged, however, that the single everyman in Jane Austen's universal is not only wealthy but white. This study is concerned with what happens when the players change, when the fictive figures "in love and trouble," to use Alice Walker's metaphor, cease to be white men and women of means and property and become black men and women, poor as well as propertied. What happens to the marriage tradition—to Leslie Fiedler's notion of love as "the subject par excellence of the novel," for example—when it is considered in the context of a literature by and about American men and women who for generations were denied the hegemonic, "universal truth" of legal marriage?[2]

Generally thought of as a convention of the white middle class, the marriage plot has received little attention from critics of African American literature.[3] Until recently, love and marriage were all but dismissed as female or, at least, feminized themes little worthy of study when juxtaposed to the masculinized racial and freedom discourse assumed to characterize the African American novel. But while the marriage plot has been coded as white, female, and European, its relationship to the African American novel has always been highly political. Making unconventional use of conventional literary forms, early black writers appropriated for their own emancipatory purposes both the genre of the novel and the structure of the marriage plot.

The Coupling Convention attempts to place these appropriations in historical perspective. I examine the subversive ways in which the marriage convention has been claimed by black women writers in particular, as a trope through

3

which to explore not only the so-called more compelling questions of race, racism, and racial identity but complex questions of sexuality and female subjectivity as well. My aim is to trace a literary history of African American women's novels against the backdrop of the coupling theme, paying particular attention to the diverse sociopolitical crises and conditions of production that have informed and defined that fiction. I argue that at the core of African American women's novels are textualizations not unlike those found in the novel as a "women's medium" more generally: representations of gender relations; celebrations and critiques of the institutions of marriage and family; depictions of female virtue fighting to hold its own against the forces of patriarchal social (dis)order; or, in the words of white feminist scholar Nina Baym, "the story of the formation and assertion of a feminine ego."[4] Part of what this study attempts to do is to examine how these representations and critiques of coupling are mediated by race, class, and time; how the texts of African American women both construct and are constructed by a black feminine ego and a black feminist consciousness; and, ultimately, how these novels reclaim and resexualize the black female body.

While it foregrounds questions of coupling and convention, of sexuality and subjectivity, this project is concerned as well with the critical construction of black women's novels. It explores the ways in which they—like all texts—are produced by their readings, the manner in which these novels become what their interpretations say they are. In this regard, *The Coupling Convention* is perhaps best described as both an exploration of the literature of black women as art and artifact, invention and intervention, and an examination of the production and the reception of that literature. How are black women's texts constructed by their interpretive communities as well as produced by their times? How is it that a text like Zora Neale Hurston's *Their Eyes Were Watching God* (1937), all but dismissed in an earlier era, becomes canonical in ours? Why is it that another text by the same author—Hurston's last novel, *Seraph on the Suwanee* (1948)—remains obscure, dismissed as "inauthentic" even by those who hail Hurston as their great literary foremother?[5] What roles have shifting attitudes toward and representations of marriage played in shaping both the literature and its critical reception?

Historical specificity, then, is a central concern of my analysis of the relationship between the marriage tradition and racial and sexual ideology. For marriage, I argue, is not a transhistorical bourgeois ideal or a linear literary convention but a sign of the times that shifts with the times, the place, and the people. It takes on different social and political meanings for different historical subjects at different historical moments. The multiple meanings black writers have given to marriage, together with their racially charged appropriations of the marriage plot and the sentimental form, make a study of those revisions and appropriations essential.

Writing in 1861, former slave Harriet Jacobs, whose very narrative exposes to ridicule the false values and sexual proclivities of the society that enslaved her, acknowledged both her awareness of the marriage tradition in literature and her own subversion of that tradition. "Reader," she announced, "my story ends with freedom; not in the usual way, with marriage. I and my children are now free!" But Jacobs acknowledged as well the pervasive decadence of the racial and sexual ideology that permitted and perpetuated chattel slavery. "We are as free from the power of slaveholders as are the white people in the north," she continued, "and though that, according to my ideas, is not saying a great deal, it is a vast improvement in *my* condition."[6] So saying, Jacobs identified two issues with which black women writers were to be preoccupied throughout her century and ours: the pervasiveness of patriarchal power and the struggle of black women to claim political freedom and female authority.

For former slaves like Harriet Jacobs and for fictional former slaves like Toni Morrison's Sethe, freedom meant the right to love "big," entitlement to desire: "[T]o get to a place where you could love anything you chose—not to need permission for desire," we are told in *Beloved*, "well now, *that* was freedom."[7] But as Jacobs's second observation suggests, for all people—white as well as black, in the North as well as in the South—freedom to desire was perpetually in jeopardy under a patriarchal system in which women could be "articles of traffic," as Jacobs pointed out, even in the free city of New York.[8]

As its long subtitle suggests, Harriet Wilson's *Our Nig: Sketches from the Life of a Free Black, in a Two-Story House, North, Showing That Slavery's Shadows Fall Even There* (1859) makes a similar point about the ubiquity of the master mentality. Like Jacobs's narrative, Wilson's tale, now recognized as the first published novel by an African American woman, both invokes and inverts the conventions of the sentimental fictive form. "Lonely Mag Smith," Wilson begins conventionally. "Early deprived of parental guardianship, far removed from relatives. . . . As she merged into womanhood, unprotected, uncherished, uncared for, there fell on her ear the music of love, awakening an intensity of emotion long dormant."[9] Wilson goes on to sketch the beginnings of a traditional tale of the unprotected white maiden, seduced, impregnated, and deserted by "charmer" and friends alike, abandoned even by the symbol of her sin and shame when her baby dies three weeks after its birth. But Wilson's tale takes an unconventional turn, for Mag does not die like her infant; nor is she redeemed by marriage to a white man of means and property like other ruined white heroines. Instead, she falls deeper into infamy and disgrace by accepting first the marital protection of one black man and then, when he dies, the common-law protection of another.

The novel establishes that while Mag functions as a faithful and dutiful wife, her motives for marrying the kindhearted African Jim are purely pragmatic: "She cared for him only as a means to subserve her own comfort," we are told (15). A single woman without fortune, food, or shelter, Mag must be in want of a husband, the only means of survival open to her. Rather than elevating her, however, Mag's marriage of (in)convenience to a man of color pulls her "another step down the ladder of infamy" (13). Thus Harriet Wilson uses both material considerations and racial ideology to turn the marriage ideal in on itself. Like Jane Austen and numerous other white women writers, Wilson exposes the valorized institution of marriage as an economic arrangement, but she also expands and particularizes their critiques by showing that, when complicated by racial difference, holy wedlock becomes a source not of redemption or social legitimacy but of disgrace and truly unpardonable sin.

In marrying off her white heroine to a black man, Wilson also inverts the fictional formula invoked by William Wells Brown, among others, in which the mulatta heroine is rescued from slavery by marriage to a benevolently despotic white man. Wilson's inversions and subversions do not stop here, however. She goes on to tell the (autobiographical) tale of Mag's mulatta daughter, Alfrado (Frado), and the abuse she suffers as an indentured servant in the New England household of a Mrs. Bellmont, whose capacity for cruelty and violence rivals that of the worst of southern slaveholders. As a closing commentary on the coupling convention, Frado's eventual marriage to a would-be fugitive slave at the end of the narrative brings none of the protection that this other "peculiar institution" is supposed to afford its helpless, submissive female members. Her mate fails miserably as a husband, and, like so many nineteenth-century white women, the abandoned wife is forced to try her hand at writing a novel as a means of supporting herself and her child.

Incidents in the Life of a Slave Girl and *Our Nig*, as a number of critics have demonstrated, expose the ideological limitations of such concepts as genteel femininity, female virtue, and marital protection.[10] Combining elements of both the slave narrative and the sentimental novel, nineteenth-century black writers like Jacobs, Wilson, and Brown merged an oral tradition rooted in resistance with a literary tradition grounded, at least in part, in what historian Barbara Welter has defined as the cardinal tenets of a "Cult of True Womanhood": piety, purity, submissiveness, and domesticity.[11] But the merger of forms black writers effected in their fiction is far more complex than an easy opposition of resistance and submission implies. Crosscurrents run through both the black slave narrative and the white sentimental novel, suggesting that even "submission" can be an act of defiance. However powerful its prescriptions, "true womanhood" was not an uncontested ideology, and the fiction of white women writers was one site of contestation. The challenge to patriarchal authority written between the lines of some of these women's novels was part of what made the form attractive to early African American writers. But the attraction was mutual and the influence reflexive, for African American narratives of resistance to and escape from chattel slavery gave white women writers a powerful metaphor through which to critique what some of them represented as their own marital slavery.

African American literary history in general and black feminist criticism in particular have taken little note of the multiple, complex, and often contradictory currents of resistance that flow through black writers' appropriations of the "white" marriage plot. This elision is due in part to the tendency to treat black literary texts not as fictive invention but as transparent historical documents, evaluated in terms of their fidelity to "the black experience" and their attention to "authentically black" subject matter. But just whose experience is being claimed as "authentic" when a critic speaks of a distinctly African American or black female experience? Can a critical practice claim *any* black experience without privileging it as *the* black experience, without valorizing it as the master narrative of the race? Is it possible to theorize a critical practice that historicizes experience, acknowledging it as social construction (rather than as objective reality), accessible only through symbolic systems?

Preoccupied with substantiating the claim that black women writers "constitute an identifiable literary tradition" and share a "specifically Black female language" and experience, black feminist criticism has seldom asked such theoretical questions.[12] In fact, it has more often disdained theory, condemning contemporary critical modes such as poststructuralism as white, Western, hegemonic discourses, ideologically antithetical to African American women's culture — as tools of the master which cannot be used to dismantle the master's house.[13] As a praxis, black feminist criticism has taken the important steps of reclaiming lost texts and inserting black women and black women's experience into historically white or predominantly male Anglo- and Afro-American literary traditions. Too often, however, it has done so without fundamentally challenging the assumptions that underpin these traditions or interrogating the notion of tradition itself. In other words, its own defensive posture and normative expectations have defined black feminist criticism as a self-limiting discourse — a discourse whose own interpretive strategies have not allowed it to fully engage the fluidity, multivocality, and contradictory impulses of its fictions.

As a critical strategy underpinning both black literary studies and black feminist criticism, this racial litmus test has misread the aesthetics and the politics of much of the early work of African American authors. These authors' interventions at the level of form as well as content represent an innovative, highly political narrative strategy that African American literary history and black feminist criticism have most often seen as merely imitating the white rhetorical modes of white American writers such as Harriet Beecher Stowe.[14]

African American scholars as critically diverse as literary theorist Houston Baker and feminist critic Barbara Christian are united in the opinion that nineteenth-century black women novelists such as Pauline Hopkins and Frances Harper wrote under the influence of white America, creating inauthentic light-skinned mulatta characters designed to accommodate their white readers' tastes in heroines. Baker argues, for example, that the use of light-skinned figures reflects "an implicit approval of white patriarchy inscribed in the very features of the mulatto character's face."[15] Such judgments persist in literary studies despite the fact that many of these writers specifically addressed their work to black readers. Three of Pauline Hopkins's four novels, for example, were serialized in the *Colored American Magazine*, a black monthly journal whose stated purpose was to make the magazine available to every Negro family.[16] Moreover, as Hazel Carby has pointed out, Frances Harper's immediate audience consisted of black Sunday school students and church people.

For Hopkins and Harper, as for William Wells Brown before them, the use of the mulatta figure was both a rhetorical device and a political strategy. Rhetorically it allowed black writers to explore the proscribed social and sexual relations between the races.[17] Strategically it allowed them to build a visual bridge or a graphic link between the white face of the mulatto and the black body of the slave, not in an effort to cultivate an approving white opinion, as Baker maintains, but in an attempt to insinuate into the consciousness of white readers the humanity of a people they otherwise constructed as subhuman—beyond the pale of white comprehension. Reading these early texts as a kind of "white-faced minstrelsy," as Baker does, severs them from the political, racial, and literary imperatives of their particular historical moments. Such a reading also invokes a defensive critical posture which positions black women's texts *against* the social and literary discourse of white society rather than (as Hazel Carby does) *within* the discourse of black women intellectuals at the turn of the century or, as I argue in chapter 2, within the larger national debates over the political status of women that raged throughout most of the nineteenth century.

In an equally troubling critical move, Barbara Christian chides early-twentieth-century novelist Jessie Fauset for her silence on "the depressing conditions under which most turn-of-the-century blacks lived," asserting that "the problem with Fauset's novels is that she gives us this particular [upper-class] Negro exclusively." In such readings Fauset's heroines are dismissed as decorations, as "proper light-skinned women who unquestionably claim propriety as the highest ideal."[18] Missing the finer parodic points of what I would argue is a powerful critique of middle-class values, including the marriage ideal and its bourgeois accoutrements—a commentary on convention, pretension, genteel femininity, and sexual commodification—Christian concludes that Fauset's heroines

> pursue the values of material success through marriage and inevitably believe that refinement is a reflection of spirituality. As a result, her heroines . . . suffer crises because of a social mishap, either of birth or deportment. Nor does Fauset exercise any critical distance toward the unimportance of her heroines' major crises. She, too, believes that not being able to take up with the "right people" is a tragedy. (43–44)

The attempt to intuit what Fauset believed suggests that in such evaluations it is the critic who fails to maintain a "critical distance." Such readings of this and other nineteenth- and early-twentieth-century texts fail to historicize the very experience and racial consciousness they make the basis of critical interpretations. Consequently marriage is read not as the sign of liberation and civility it was for many nineteenth-century African Americans, nor as the symbol of entrance into the realm of bourgeois American society it became for some early-twentieth-century blacks, nor even simply as a literary device. Rather, the discourse on marriage and marriageability is all but dismissed as the authors' dalliance with the petty preoccupations of white society that have nothing to do with the *real* material conditions of most black Americans. What is at stake in such dismissals is not merely the discourse on marriage but the discourse on race and class: the construction of "black" as a unified category and the erasure of class as a cultural marker.

The idea that an American or an African American literature could be exclusively white or black in its subject matter or in the historical experience it refracts is a notion this study seeks to problematize. For as Barbara Johnson has argued, "Cultures are not containable within boundaries."[19] Even the terms "black" and "white" are fallacious, often implying a "relation of mutual exclusion"—a dichotomy based on the notion of "pure, unified, and separate traditions"—in the face of what are, in fact, complex and interlocking cultural and linguistic phenomena.

In this study I join such scholars as Hazel Carby, Deborah McDowell, Claudia Tate, Thadious Davis, Mae Henderson, Henry Louis Gates, and Cornel West, as well as Barbara Johnson, in arguing that critics of African American literature cannot treat that literature as the discursively familiar, as faithful representations of lived experiences in the social real. Nor can we continue to claim an African American literary tradition as an island, entire unto itself, separate from and uninfluenced by so-called white cultural constructs and Western literary conventions. Intertextuality cannot be defined as movement solely from black text to black text, from one black author to another. Rather, such resonances must be viewed as cutting across racial identities, cultural spaces, and historical moments.

The Coupling Convention is not an act of recovery or reconnaissance. It assumes no single tradition and, in fact, argues against the notion of *a* black tradition, *a* common black female experience, or *a* shared black women's language. I approach the fictions of black women as both artifice and artifact, as indices of power and material relations, as cultural products whose formal structures have inscribed within them the social, political, and economic conditions of the moments in which they were produced and the historical moments they echo. My concern with historical specificity, however, does not assume that current cultural codings are entirely transcendable. The very process of "unreading" that this study attempts, of stripping away what Fredric Jameson calls the "sedimented layers of previous interpretations," is, of course, itself a reading rooted in its own set of interpretive traditions and assumptions. The objects of this attempt to unread the "always-already-read" are, as Jameson says, less the novels themselves than their interpretations and appropriations, including my own appropriations of them through the convention of coupling.[20]

Focusing on the work of selected black women writers from Frances Harper to Zora Neale Hurston, I present in the following chapters a series of readings that explores and, in some instances, attempts to explode the prevailing critical conceptions about that body of work. For all its attempt at alternative readings, however, perhaps the most original contribution this study might make is not its particular slant on how these texts should be read but a commentary on how critical communities constantly "rewrite" them. Readings are not neutral. How we read—even how we define and approach the process of reading—generally reflects where we live politically, ideologically, and intellectually, as well as the nature of our particular interpretive traditions at a given historical moment. Drawing on what postcolonial critic Indira Karamcheti calls the "historicizing, contextualizing lessons of poststructuralism,"[21] I explore how the current moment's deification of certain black women writers (such as Zora Neale Hurston) and the elision of others (such as Jessie Fauset) discursively construct both texts and tradition.

The Coupling Convention is divided into two parts, each focusing on a pivotal point in the shifting representations and meanings of marriage, sexuality, and black womanhood. The first, covering the period from the publication of William Wells Brown's Clotel (1853) to the turn of the century, centers on the nascence of literary activity among black women in the 1890s. Reflecting their authors' concerns with social reform, many novels of this era are characterized by sexual reticence, the literary purification of black womanhood, and the celebration of marriage as a seemingly sexless meeting of like minds and sociopolitical ambitions. Key texts in this time period and thematic vein include Harper's Iola Leroy (1892) and Hopkins's Contending Forces (1900). Other novels, such as Emma Dunham Kelley's Megda (1891), vary the theme somewhat by plotting the union of common Christian spirits. The second part spans the twenty-four-year period between the publication of Jessie Fauset's first novel (1924) and Zora Neale Hurston's last novel (1948). It focuses on a second flowering of novels by African American women — novels characterized by the gradual resexualization of black womanhood reflected in the work of Fauset, Hurston, and Nella Larsen. Hurston's work, especially Seraph on the Suwanee (1948), introduces the figure of the willful wife who resists the traditional dominant-submissive power dynamic of male-female relations.

In chapter 1 I examine the universality of the love story and particularize the marriage or "coupling convention" in terms of African American texts. Through an extended reading of Clotel; or, The President's Daughter, I explore how Brown problematized and subverted the traditional marriage plot and the conventional romantic heroine, in effect giving this study its central paradigm. In chapters 2 and 3 I consider how black women writers at the turn of the century further revised both the marriage plot and the sentimental form to fit their own political and evangelical purposes. Drawing briefly on the prose of Anna Julia Cooper, as well as the fiction of Hopkins and Harper, I explore the ways in which these writers set about "revisioning" the categories of both woman and man as they engaged the racial, social, and intellectual issues of the day, as well as national and international debates about the political status and future of women.

Foregrounding questions of canon and tradition, as well as literary convention and racial and sexual ideology, in part II (encompassing chapters 4, 5, and 6) I consider African American cultural production of the twenties, thirties, and forties and the complex sociocultural conditions that both created the literature of the period and are encoded in it. Chapter 4 sets the historical stage for the chapters that follow by establishing a context for and lens through which to focus on the fiction of Fauset, Larsen, and Hurston. Paying particular attention to the racialism and primitivism of the period, this chapter offers a framework for viewing these writers' works in relation to the classic blues and the so-called Harlem Renaissance. The chapter also examines the ways in which the critical construction of Zora Neale Hurston—what I call "Hurstonism"—has covered over the contributions of such contemporaries as Dorothy West, Fauset, and Larsen.

Chapter 5 focuses on sexuality and female subjectivity in the novels of Fauset and Larsen, as well as the ways in which these authors wrote the black female body into the literary text. Female sexuality and subjectivity are also treated in chapter 6, where they are explored through representations of the willful or resistant wife in Larsen's *Quicksand*, in West's *The Living Is Easy*, and in Hurston's *Their Eyes Were Watching God* and *Seraph on the Suwanee*. The chapter focuses on and offers an extended reading of *Seraph* in an effort to support my argument that, despite its dismissal by both male and female readers, *Seraph on the Suwanee* offers a more intimate analysis of the marital relation and critique of sexual domination than *Their Eyes Were Watching God* and represents an essential, if largely unread, link in the development of the African American woman's novel. Following the model of Hazel Carby, I am concerned in this chapter (as well as in chapters 4 and 5) with recontextualizing Hurston in light of *her* contemporaries and *her* precursors rather than with intertextualizing her in terms of African American women novelists writing today.

Since "feminism" is a historically specific concept that often is not treated as such, I want to shed some light on its use in this investigation. White feminist historian Linda Gordon defines feminism as "a critique of male supremacy, formed and offered in the light of a will to change it."[22] This definition, in effect, isolates masculinism as an independent, dominating power. The history and political presence of women of color, however, argues for a much broader configuration. Nineteenth-century black women activists, for example, were the vanguard embodying a sophisticated interpretation of power relations that recognized—decades before it became intellectually fashionable to do so—the insidious interplay and interdependence of racism and male supremacy. Nevertheless, my use of the term "feminist" is meant to be, as Rita Felski says, descriptive rather than prescriptive.[23] Feminist theoretical and critical strategies have guided my readings of the novels of nineteenth- and early-twentieth-century black women artists.[24] Rather than claiming these works as feminist texts, however, I offer feminist readings of them, focusing on the critiques of male-female relations and patriarchal values embedded in them.

"Patriarchy" is another term used throughout this study. Like feminism, patriarchy is a mutable force often treated transhistorically. For my present purposes, I find Gerda Lerner's definition particularly useful: "Patriarchy in its wider definition means the manifestation and institutionalization of male dominance over women and children in the family and the extension of male dominance over women in society in general."[25] While this definition implies that men hold the greater share of power in society, it does not imply, as Lerner points out, that women are completely without power or resources.

I can think of no wiser words with which to conclude this introduction than the advice of the great Trinidadian scholar, the late C. L. R. James: "[O]ne of the chief errors of thought," James warned, "is to continue to think in one set of forms, categories, ideas, etc., when the object, the content, has moved on, has created or laid premises for an extension, a development of thought."[26] Contemporary theoretical discourses such as poststructuralism have laid the premises for new developments in textual studies. Led by the insights of scholars such as Hazel Carby, Claudia Tate, Michael Awkward, Barbara Johnson, Hortense Spillers, Mae Henderson, Thadious Davis, Henry Louis Gates, and Houston Baker, African American literary criticism is moving beyond the expressive realism in which it was for so long embedded. In its invitation to deconstruct patriarchal authority, contemporary critical theory may be one of the tools that can be appropriated by black feminists to dismantle the master's house. Black feminist criticism must take up new premises, new paradigms, as its practitioners endeavor to theorize African American women's literature out of the margin, into the mainstream—the so-called center. The boundaries that have traditionally defined and circumscribed African American literary criticism and black feminist scholarly inquiry must be deconstructed in a critical practice that no longer merely appends the racial and gendered other to already existing Eurocentric or Afrocentric paradigms but that both interrogates those paradigms and poses new questions across cultures and conventions. I hope that this study will contribute to that process.

1

The Coupling Convention:
Novel Views of Love and Marriage

> "I think you will be happy, Dora, if you love him. All things are possible
> if love is the foundation stone," said Sappho. . . .
> "I like him well enough to marry him, but I don't believe there's enough
> sentiment in me to make love a great passion, such as we read in books.
> Do you believe marriage is the beautiful state it is painted by writers?"
> — PAULINE HOPKINS, *Contending Forces* (1900)

Contending Forces tells a terrible tale of slavery, arson, pillage, lynching,
rape, forced impregnation, and sexual blackmail. It also, as these lines suggest,
is a novel self-consciously aware of the dictates of its romantic form. Accordingly, it tells its horror story through the formula of female virtue pitted
against patriarchal plunder: piety, if not absolute purity, is eventually re-
warded by love and marriage. Is love, then, even in the African American
novel, the "subject par excellence," as Leslie Fiedler maintains?

For at least one black scholar, Afrocentrist Molefi Asante, Fiedler's universal claims for the theme of love are a fallacy, another glaring example of the
hegemony of the European particular. "Traditionally, African writers are not
concerned with the romance variety of literature," Asante claims. "An Afrocentric discussion of literature would guard against this ethnocentric promotion of group universality."[1] Asante's assertion should remind us of the constant need to interrogate the Eurocentric paradigms in which much of our
critical discourse is rooted. It should also remind us, however, of the limitations of any monocentrism. For even if we accept the problematic supposition
that African writers have not been concerned with the theme of romantic love,
African *American* writers have been profoundly concerned with such themes.
The African American novel, like its European and Anglo-American counterparts, has developed around the marriage plot or what I call—because of the
freedom it gives me to move outside the traditional legal and social meanings
of marriage—the "coupling convention."

Speaking schematically, the term "marriage plot," as I use it in this study,
refers to a fictional formula that foregrounds romantic relationships, focuses
on courtship (wanting, wooing, and winning, one might say), and generally
culminates in marriage or at least betrothal. In perhaps the most traditional
versions of the formula, white woman meets white man, sparks fly of one
kind or another, and after several hundred pages of overcoming obstacles,[2]

hero and heroine marry and presumably live happily ever after. I use the phrases "marriage plot" and "marriage story" broadly to describe novels that take mating as text or subtext or that offer an anatomy of a courtship, seduction, marriage, or erotic relationship. I use the term "coupling convention" both to destabilize the customary dyadic relation between love and marriage and to displace the heterosexual presumption underpinning the Anglo-American romantic tradition. I also use the term in conjunction with African American literature to reflect the problematic nature of the institution of marriage for a people long denied the right to marry legally.

Marriage is necessarily a historically complex and contradictory concept in African American history and literature. While modern minds are inclined to view marriage as an oppressive, self-limiting institution, for nineteenth-century African Americans, recently released from slavery and its dramatic disruption of marital and family life, marriage rites were a long-denied basic human right — signs of liberation and entitlement to both democracy and desire. As Claudia Tate has argued:

> Exercising the civil right to marry . . . was as important to the newly freed
> black population as exercising another civil right . . . Negro suffrage. . . .
> To vote and to marry, then, were two civil responsibilities that nineteenth-
> century black people elected to perform; they were twin indexes for measuring
> how black people collectively valued their civil liberties.[3]

This point is punctuated by a number of investigations that document the all-deliberate speed with which newly freed men and women sought to legalize their slave unions. Herbert Gutman's study of the black family, for example, argues that one of the most important social decisions made by ex-slaves was the legal affirmation of their marriages and their families. Using the records of county clerks and justices of the peace, Gutman has documented that in 1866 nearly ten thousand slave marriages were legalized by registration in North Carolina alone. While a newly enacted state law required the registration of slave marriages by the fall of that year, Gutman insists that it was the ex-slaves' own desire to have their unions sanctioned and protected by law that accounts for the large number of registrations. By his reckoning, the high registration rate "indicates the ex-slaves' widespread approval of legal marriage" and their understanding of "some of the 'rules' governing *civil society*" (emphasis added). To reinforce his point, he quotes from the reminiscences of a Reconstruction-era judge from North Carolina, complimenting freedmen and freedwomen on their commitment to each other and to the idea of legal marriage: "Let the marriage bonds be dissolved throughout the State of New York and it may be doubted if as large a proportion of her intelligent white citizens would choose again their old partners."[4]

Gutman's figures and the judge's remark are compelling, but we might question whether in fact the rush to register slave marriages was a matter of choosing again an old mate or claiming the protection of a new right (or rite). We might also question the degree to which the registration process was voluntary. In her study of marriage and the black family, Jessie Bernard treats the institutionalization of marriage after emancipation as a form of social control, enforced at times by military officials who reported cases of men and women "who indulged in marital relations without contracting marital obligations" (11). "After the Civil War," Bernard writes, "there were hundreds of thousands of freedmen milling about in great uncertainty, many with equivocal family status. The task of imposing order on this fluid, almost undifferentiated mass was an enormous one and necessarily shared by institutional agencies of all kinds" (10).

Legislative statutes requiring the registration of slave marriages represent one approach to establishing order. But as Bernard points out, simple declarations that relationships formed under slavery were to be binding often created more problems than they solved. Legislative decrees like North Carolina's left many freedmen open to charges of desertion, bigamy, and adultery, for as slaves they may have had more than one mate. Who, in such cases, was to become the legal partner? Many states ultimately amended their laws, requiring freedmen who had more than one partner to choose one mate among them. In South Carolina, for example, freedmen had until April 1, 1866, to decide which partner would become the legal spouse.[5]

Despite the many complications, thousands upon thousands of newly freed blacks did register their marriages, presumably both in accordance with legislative decrees and by personal choice. As Bernard notes: "[I]n many cases the idea of marriage dignified by a minister appealed to the newly freed Negroes, for it implied equality with whites. Official marriage became a status symbol, and weddings became occasions of great gaiety" (11). Historian Jacqueline Jones adds that the change in the nature of relations between men and women as they moved from slave unions to legal marriages was reflected even in the colorful clothes women wore in their new roles as lawful wives. "Black husbands took pride in buying fashionable dresses and many-colored ribbons, pretty hats and delicate parasols for their womenfolk," Jones writes. "When a freedman walked alongside his well-dressed wife, both partners dramatized the legitimacy of their relationship and his role as family provider."[6] (Interestingly, Jones's observation suggests a patriarchal pride in possession that black women will later come to resist in their fiction.)

The call to bourgeois civility was a loud one to which many newly freed blacks responded by donning the trappings and conventions of "civilized society"—including the hegemonic ideology of monogamous marriage. Bernard's and Jones's observations have significant implications for the bourgeois marriages that will begin to dominate the pages of African American novels in the generations following emancipation. I think, for example, of the detailed attention Nella Larsen gives to clothes and color in *Quicksand* (1928) and the extent to which these elements serve in the text as signifiers of both simmering sexuality and genteel femininity. When read in conjunction with the fictional literature, historical inquiries like those by Gutman, Bernard, and Jones give new import to the function of marriage in early African American texts and to the ways in which nineteenth-century black novelists revised the marriage plot and pressed it into their own literary and social service. These subversive appropriations of plot and form can be found not only in the narratives of nineteenth-century black women writers such as Harriet Jacobs and Harriet Wilson, but in the work of male writers such as William Wells Brown and Charles Chesnutt as well.

Chesnutt's short story "The Wife of His Youth," for example, illustrates graphically the problems inherent in the movement from tenuous slave unions to binding legal marriages. Just as he is about to publicly propose to a beautiful, refined young quadroon of similar social standing and complexion, Mr. Ryder, a light-skinned, freeborn black, now a leading member of the Blue Vein Society (members of the black bourgeoisie so light in complexion that their blue veins show through their pale skin), is approached by an elderly, dark-skinned, toothless former slave woman named 'Liza Jane, looking for Sam, the long-lost husband she helped escape from impending enslavement twenty-five years before. Through her story Ryder recognizes this old woman as "the wife of his youth"; she, however, does not recognize him. Without revealing his identity, Ryder suggests to her that the husband for whom she has been searching for twenty-five years may well have married another woman. "Your slave marriage would not have prevented him," he says, "for you never lived with him after the war, and without that your marriage doesn't count."[7] 'Liza Jane is unperturbed, however, for her *womanly* "fidelity and devotion to those she loves" do not allow for the possibility of such an obstacle to the "happily ever after" that slavery has so long denied her.

In this version of the problematized, racialized coupling convention, the protagonist of Chesnutt's story must choose between the pitiful old woman and his beautiful, young quadroon bride-to-be: between "the old plantation past" and the promises of the future, between moral obligation and romantic desire. He does, by the way, choose "the wife of his youth." It is for him a matter of honor. While "The Wife of His Youth" has most often been read in terms of its attention to the critically valorized theme of slavery, the "peculiar institution's" disruption of the marital union is the crisis around which the plot turns. Chesnutt's deployment of the marriage plot illustrates, on a small scale, the potentially radical purposes to which literary conventions have been put in African American appropriations of the novel and other genres.

In his provocative study, *Tradition Counter Tradition*, Joseph Boone suggests that the same contradictions that have characterized the novel as an at-once radical *and* conventional literary form have also affected its representations of romantic love. Instead of offering a series of "happily ever after" endings, as we might expect of a form so dependent for its subject upon the marriage plot, the genre of the novel has actually generated, in Boone's words, "a system of narrative strategies that have alternately explained, evaded, and (less frequently) exploded the tradition of romantic wedlock embedded in Anglo-American fiction since its beginning."[8] In other words, Boone argues, convincingly, that one aspect of the European and Anglo-American novelistic tradition has served "a powerfully conservative function," romanticizing, valorizing, and exalting the heterosexual institutions of marriage and family. On the flip side of that tradition, however, is an equally persistent counternarrative that has historically challenged, undercut, and at times completely subverted what Boone calls "the evolving hegemony of the marriage tradition" (2). There is, for example, a body of fiction by white women writers (what Nina Baym calls "woman's fiction") that has traditionally rejected the "happily ever after" fictive formula in favor of often-scathing critiques of the failure of marriage as life's master narrative and the failure of men as women's master providers. In his analysis, Boone uses the metaphor of "wedlock" to describe this category of "countertraditional" texts—texts which represent wedded life not as a "hopeful beginning" but as an "emphatic deadend" (141–42).

However, Boone (like Baym) is primarily concerned with Anglo-American fiction.[9] Like many white critics so concerned, he has his own rationale for not including the work of African American writers in his analysis: "[A]s the creation of a white, bourgeois culture," he explains, "the wedlock ideal has simply been most visible in 'white' middle-class fiction written before, say, the 1920s, at which point other voices began to break through the hegemony of dominant literary discourse" (23). Most visible to whom, we might ask? In my reading of American literature, coupling is a dominant convention in such African American novels as Clotel, The Garies and Their Friends (1857), Megda (1891), Hearts of Gold (1896), Four Girls at Cottage City (1898), The House Behind the Cedars (1900), and Contending Forces (1900). In all of these novels, male-female relationships, courtship, coupling, marriage, exogamy, and miscegenation play central roles. What begs to be explored here is how these African American texts—and others like them—inscribe, replot, subvert, exploit, and explode the middle-class wedlock ideal.[10] Perhaps no text provides a better site for such an exploration than William Wells Brown's Clotel, the first novel that might be said to rewrite the romance from a black perspective.

Clotel; or, The President's Daughter

Published in London in 1853, Clotel; or, The President's Daughter: A Narrative of Slave Life in the United States, is a pivotal text in large part because, as the first published novel by an African American, it represents a historical benchmark from which to begin a study of the development of the black novel.[11] Brown's text is particularly important to this project, however, both because of the subversive use it makes of the marriage ideal and because it is so often cited by critics as the progenitor of the nineteenth-century black women's novel. A discussion of the production, construction, and reception of Clotel, as well as its reflexive relationship with nineteenth-century women's fiction (both black and white), seems to me, then, a necessary prerequisite to my study of black women writers and the marriage plot.

While the novel itself has rarely received close textual analysis, many critics have argued (often as a complaint) that with the publication of Clotel, Brown blended the freedom narrative and the sentimental romance into a fictive formula that African American writers were to follow for the next eighty years. A number of critics trace to Brown as well the white-skinned mulatta heroine who functioned as the primary literary representative of black womanhood well into the twentieth century. Barbara Christian, for example, argues that "Brown's description of the mulatta became the model for other black novels," at least until the publication of Ann Petry's *The Street* in 1946.[12] Alice Walker adds that even black writers of the race-proud 1920s such as Fauset, Larsen, and Toomer followed Brown's model and continued to depict black women as "fair-skinned, if not actually *white*-skinned, and in other ways atypical." It is only with the advent of Hurston's Janie Crawford, Walker maintains, "that black women begin to emerge *naturally* in all the colors in which they exist, predominantly brown and black, and culturally African-American."[13]

Such criticisms seem to me ahistorical in the degree to which they chide early African American writers for not being 100 to 150 years ahead of their times. These early authors who, in Brown's case in particular, battled slavery, institutionalized racism, and illiteracy, as well as the discriminatory practices of the publishing industry, are condemned for writing through and against the dominant racial and sexual ideologies of their times, rather than out of the enlightened, feminist vision of ours. Criticisms like Walker's fail to treat literary history as an evolutionary process in which a writer such as Hurston could eventually invent a Janie Crawford precisely because there was a Clotel, a Megda, a Helga Crane.

Brown, like the nineteenth-century women novelists who were to come after him, was concerned with the vulnerability and sexual exploitation of black women, which stand in his work as hallmarks of the deep-seated hypocrisy of a world out of joint—emblems of the barbarism of a "civilized society" that put white lady and "true womanhood" on a pedestal and black slave and black womanhood on the auction block, *even though they looked the same*.[14] The trope of appearance—the metaphor of the mulatta—was an awkward artifice that in some instances inadvertently constructed slavery as the greater tragedy of the nearly white. Its deployment, however, needs to be scrutinized as a political strategy produced by its time, as a means of the particular historical moment, not as an end in itself. Similarly, the focus on female characters and on the feminized subject of matrimony, rather than on male figures and the masculinized theme of manhood rights, must be considered as a claiming of the civil right that marked the difference between slave and free.

Far from simply falling back on an unproblematized sentimentality that "slandered" and "whitewashed" black womanhood, Brown crafted fact and fiction, image and incident, into what I call an "unreal estate," a fictive realm of the fantastic and coincidental, not the farfetched or the fanciful or "magical realism" but an ideologically charged space, created by drawing together a variety of discursive fields—including "the real" and "the romantic," the simple and the sensational, the allegorical and the historical—usually for decidedly political purposes. Often misdiagnosed by critics as sentimental melodrama or badly written realism, the use of the unreal estate is a formal strategy that dominates the African American novel at least until the realism and naturalism of Richard Wright and Ann Petry in the 1940s. In the remaining pages of this chapter, I hope to show how Brown wound together the marriage plot and the mulatta figure in constructing his own politically charged unreal estate.

Clotel as "Unreal Estate"

While it has frequently been labeled sentimental and melodramatic, *Clotel*, as far as I can determine, has never been defined as "woman's fiction." Nevertheless, Brown's "abolitionist" narrative has as much to say on the feminized subject of marriage as it does on the masculinized subject of slavery. In fact, the novel uses the institution of marriage—which Brown defines as "the first and most important institution of human existence"—as a means of exposing the horrors of chattel slavery, as a way of demonstrating the degree to which slavery unraveled the basic social, moral, and ethical fabric of American life for both blacks and whites. "The marriage relation," Brown tells us on the first page of *Clotel*, "the oldest and most sacred institution given to man by his Creator, is unknown and unrecognised in the slave laws of the United States."[15] Brown is, of course, referring to the fact that enslaved Africans were denied the right to legal marriage. Though critics have taken little note of this subversive, political use of the coupling convention, in Brown's antislavery text marriage rites and the right to marry—rather than such "manhood rights" as suffrage, property ownership, or literacy—function as the primary signifiers of freedom and humanity.

In his depiction of the ills and abuses of the peculiar institution, Brown goes on to foreground such issues as the sexual exploitation of African women, the breeding of slaves, the hypocrisy of Southern Christianity, and most particularly, the perfidy of "southern gentlemen," who betray their wives, breed their slaves, and sell their own offspring. The failure of southern "gentlemen" to provide for and protect either their legal white wives or their "black" slave families, along with the separation of those slave families by sale, play particularly dramatic roles in advancing the plot of *Clotel*.

It is with such a sale and forced separation that the novel begins. Among the slaves sold on the auction block upon the death of their owner are Currer, the former mistress of Thomas Jefferson, and her two daughters by Jefferson, Clotel and Althesa. In casting Jefferson as the father of his unfortunate colored heroine, Brown takes considerable license with historical rumor. Widely believed to have fathered at least five children into slavery, the third president of the United States was a favorite target of antislavery activism. His sexual politics not withstanding, the fact that he owned slaves, even as he wrote eloquently of the equality of all *men*, made him a hypocrite in the eyes of most abolitionists. Currer is patterned in part after Sally Hemings, the slave woman most often named as Jefferson's mistress and the mother of his mulatto offspring.[16]

Like Mrs. Bennet in *Pride and Prejudice*, Currer has raised her daughters to be "great ladies," to attract the attention—and ultimately the financial support—of white gentlemen of means and property. Unlike Mrs. Bennet, however, Currer does not have the luxury of plotting marriage for her daughters. The best she can imagine for them is concubinage, for she knows that even as accomplished quadroons, their only hope for a degree of freedom rests with some white gentleman who might take one of them under his wing, emancipate her, and make her, as Brown says, "mistress of her own dwelling" (41).

Sixteen-year-old Clotel is in fact purchased for $1,500 by such a young gentleman, Horatio Green, who does indeed set her up in her own home and by whom she eventually has a daughter, Mary—of course, as they say, "without benefit of marriage." Precisely how "without benefit" she is becomes tragically clear to Clotel when Green decides to solidify his political future through a conventional marriage of convenience to the daughter of a "very popular and wealthy man" on whom his career depends. Ultimately the legal Mrs. Green learns of her husband's affair and demands that Clotel be sold and that Mary be made her personal slave.[17] "With the deepest humiliation," Brown writes, "Horatio Green saw the daughter of Clotel, his own child, brought into his dwelling as a servant," to appease the wrath of a deceived wife determined to punish both the deceiver and the symbol of his deception.

Clotel meets what slaves in the upper South generally considered one of the worst fates imaginable: being "sold down the river" into even harder, harsher forms of slavery, which for women, particularly those as light and lovely as Clotel, often meant sexual commerce of some kind: the "fancy trade," concubinage, or prostitution. For the sake of plot rather than credibility, Clotel is sold as a maid, first to a mistress who makes her cut off her long hair and then to a master who attempts to win her sexual favors with kindness, flattery, and presents. "Trembl[ing] at the sound of every footfall," Clotel miraculously manages to keep her owner at bay by insisting that she left a husband in Virginia and "would never think of taking another" (133). Here Brown suggests but does not confront the sexual vulnerability of his heroine, whom he gives a relatively easy way out of the more likely fate of rape—a lustful but kind and patient master and a timely escape.

Making creative use of her short, "mannish" hair and her light complexion, Clotel eventually escapes with the aid of an industrious dark-skinned slave named William, who finances their getaway with money he has earned "hiring his time."[18] The two make good their flight to Ohio with Clotel posing as white master and William as black slave in much the same fashion as Ellen and William Craft.[19] But while William heads north to Canada, Clotel heads southeast to Virginia, intent on rescuing her daughter, Mary.[20] Still disguised as a white gentleman, she is captured and transported to Washington, D.C., where she is placed in one of the district's "negro pens," from which she also escapes. Hotly pursued, she is cornered on Long Bridge, where, rather than submit anew to slavery, she throws herself into the Potomac, "within plain sight of the President's house and the capital of the Union." "Thus died Clotel," Brown writes, "the daughter of Thomas Jefferson."[21] Seizing the moment to drive home an essential and popular point about America's hypocrisy, Brown continues:

Had Clotel escaped from oppression in any other land, in the disguise in which she fled from Mississippi to Richmond, and reached the United States, no honor within the gift of the American people would have been too good to have been heaped upon the heroic woman. But she was a slave, and therefore out of the *pale of sympathy*. They have tears to shed over Greece and Poland; they have an abundance of sympathy for "poor Ireland;" they can furnish a ship of war to convey the Hungarian refugees from a Turkish prison to the "land of the free and home of the brave." They boast that America is the "cradle of liberty;" if it is, I fear they have rocked the child to death.[22] (emphasis added)

In one of many examples of his ability to manipulate language as well as form, Brown turns the decidedly American metaphor of the cradle of liberty back in on itself and makes it a symbol of confinement, misery, and death.

Among the children *nearly* rocked to death in this cradle of liberty is Mary, the daughter Clotel died trying to rescue. Mary grows up a slave in her father's house, where she falls in love with a fellow servant, a light-skinned mulatto named George. Their plans to couple are interrupted by George's imprisonment for participating in the Nat Turner slave insurrection. Visiting George in jail the night before he is to be hanged, Mary manages to convince her light-skinned lover to trade clothes and places with her and thus escape the hangman's noose. The plan works—for George, anyway; he indeed escapes, making it to Canada, where he works hard and saves money, eventually sending an English missionary to Virginia to buy Mary out of slavery, only to learn that Horatio Green has been compelled by the court to sell his daughter down the river (like her mother) as punishment for her role in George's escape. Heartbroken, George sails for England, where he is taken for white and eventually becomes a partner in the business firm which first employs him as a porter. Mary, meanwhile, is rescued from slavery by a young, white Frenchman who spirits her away from her new mistress and sails with her to Europe, where he makes her his legal wife, Mrs. Devenant. Together they have a son before Devenant conveniently dies, evidently leaving Mary a well-off widow.

This truncated synopsis barely begins to untangle the complex web of obstacles to a "happily ever after" ending this "sentimental," "abolitionist propaganda" presents. I should point out, however, that despite the tragedy that consumes much of the novel, in keeping with convention, *Clotel; or, The President's Daughter* ends with a marriage, seemingly employing the comic device of the happy ending. Many years later Mary and George are reunited in a chance meeting in a graveyard in Dunkirk, and the two are soon "joined in holy wedlock" (199). However, Brown's final words establish pointedly that for this fugitive slave couple, "happily ever after" is only as long as they remain in Europe. "We can but blush for our country's shame," Brown concludes, "that while George and Mary Green, and numbers of other fugitives from American slavery, can receive protection from any of the governments of Europe, they cannot return to their native land without becoming slaves" (200).

This final jab at the ills of American slavery displaces what is seemingly a conventional, comic ending and returns the text to its political, antislavery purpose. Despite the discourse on marriage, Brown's primary interest is not in the marital relation in and of itself but in the marriage rite as a fundamental civil and moral right denied black men and women, for whom holy wedlock is a more "sacred obligation" than it is for the white men who abuse it. The particular, "race-specific" obstacles Brown deploys to disrupt the coupling of men and women who love each other, both within and across racial lines, problematize not the marriage relation itself but the "universal truth" of the traditional marriage story. Brown demonstrates how racial ideology under- mines social convention—how racial ideology, more so perhaps than "race," makes a desire as basic as being "in want of a wife" not a universally acknowl- edged truth but an impossible dream.

As I suggested earlier, not everyone reads Brown's work as generously or sympathetically as I do. Black aestheticist Addison Gayle argues that Brown may be "immediately dismissed as a novelist of style," because of his "reliance on stereotypes" and his acceptance of "Anglo-Saxon values" which made him "incapable of moving The Novel in the right direction."[23] The "right direction" in Gayle's view is toward black nationalism and the radicalism of the Black Arts Movement of the 1960s. Gayle is hardly alone: a number of black femi- nist scholars have been extremely critical of Brown for his representation of black women, among other issues. Barbara Christian, for instance, finds in Brown's novel ample proof that he bought the "myth of the licentious, exotic black woman" that was "so much a part of the consciousness of the South."[24] She notes, in particular, a passage in which Brown writes: "Bottles of ink, and reams of paper, have been used to portray the 'finely cut and well-moulded features,' the 'splendid forms, the fascinating smiles,' and 'accomplished man- ners' of these impassioned and voluptuous daughters of the two races—the unlawful product of the crime of human bondage." Brown goes on to speak of the immorality that pervaded the southern plantation, ending with what for some readers is the slanderous observation that "the greater portion of the colored women, in the days of slavery, had no greater aspiration than that of becoming the finely-dressed mistress of some white man."[25]

That Brown's text foregrounds the "sexualized" white-skinned slave woman is undeniable. However, such passages can be interpreted as slanderous only if one reads over what I would argue is their irony—only if one misreads as *subjects* women whom Brown has carefully represented linguistically as *ob- jects*. As I read them, these words critique rather than condone the myth of the "impassioned and voluptuous" black woman that was indeed a basic part of southern lore. The reference to the immorality that "pervades the domestic circle" is, I would argue, an allusion to the marauding white "gentlemen" who ruthlessly pursue unprotected slave women. Taken out of context, however, these remarks do not reflect the degree to which Brown complicates the notion of consensual union between master and slave, between owner and owned, and the extent to which he indicts not black slave women but the decadent white society that buys and sells them into concubinage. Similarly, the phrase "Bottles of ink, and reams of paper," as well the author's own use of quotation marks around the defining phrases he cites, indicate that he is himself addressing the problem of representation, the positioning of black women as objects of the white male gaze. He is commenting on black women as the subjected subjects of a male discourse of desire that constitutes them as licentious, voluptuous, and passionate (note Brown's use of the term "impassioned" rather than "passionate"). The adjectives used by Christian ("licentious," "lustful," and "exotic") are most emphatically *not* Brown's words. Her terminology endows these women with subject status and gives a different character entirely to the women presented by Brown as victims of their own sexualization and objectification.

Unfortunately, many of these critiques of Brown's representations of black womanhood are based on later, less radical versions of his protest novel — versions which, as Jean Fagan Yellin has noted, are largely denuded of the "rough humor, stark brutality, and pointed debate" that give the original text its vitality.[26] In these later editions, published in the United States rather than England, the heroines are no longer the daughter and granddaughter of Thomas Jefferson but the offspring of an unnamed senator or an ineffectual country gentleman. This important alteration in plot suggests the lengths to which Brown went to present a text that disrupted within "acceptable" limits, a novel that accommodated America's faith in her founding father even as it sought to defend black womanhood through the clumsy (and I think parodic) device of romancing the moral indignation and "womanly sympathy" of white women. Like Harriet Jacobs, Brown "courted" the concern and compassion of white women both by endowing his black female characters with the precious virtues of true womanhood and by textually empathizing with the plight of the poor planter's wife, displaced in her husband's affections by the "unadorned beauty" of her own waiting maid.

Himself a fugitive slave, Brown knew well the horrors of which he wrote in *Clotel*: the terror of being owned, the pain of watching one's mother beaten, of having loved ones sold down the river. As a teenager in Missouri, he saw his own mother sold south when the two of them were captured while attempting to escape.[27] The light-skinned progeny of a white Kentucky gentleman and a slave he claimed was the daughter of Daniel Boone,[28] Brown knew as well the dubious blessing of mixed parentage — blood ties to the big house that might bring exemption from fourteen-hour days in the fields but also the wrath of the mistress, to whom the mulatto slave underfoot was a constant reminder of her husband's infidelity. Through the story of Clotel and Mary, Brown exposes the degree to which the infidelity of white men and the sexual exploitation of black women were institutions in themselves, as much a part of the plantation system as cotton and cane.[29] His novel must be read not simply as an abolitionist exposé, however; it must be read in the larger, dialogic context of nineteenth-century sentimental fiction in which white women writers envisioned white heroines who challenge patriarchal authority and oppressive political systems.

According to Richard Yarborough, "The sentimental novel's common theme of female virtue under siege struck responsive chords in the imaginations of nineteenth-century Afro-American writers as well."[30] These chords resound loudly in Brown's text, which indeed composes its own tale around the popular textualizations of its time. It was not only the theme of besieged virtue that attracted Brown's attention, however. Reading his work in dialogue with such nineteenth-century women's novels as Catharine Maria Sedgwick's *Hope Leslie* (1827) and *The Linwoods* (1835) suggests that Brown was attracted as well by their representations of female independence and civil insurrection.

Such dialogic readings are important for what they say about the interactive nature of so-called black and white traditions as separate entities. It is not, as is often implied in theories of the "speakerly," "signifying" black text, only black novels that talk to each other. Rather, I would argue that almost all texts participate in larger, intercultural dialogues or polylogues in a complex nexus of literary cross-dressing and back talking. The reflexive nature of these literary relationships is as important to address as the relationships themselves; for, if Brown's text talked back to the novels of Harriet Beecher Stowe, Catharine Maria Sedgwick, Lydia Maria Child, and E.D.E.N. Southworth, *all* of these writers also listened to and drew from the Josiah Hensons, Henry Bibbses, Frederick Douglasses, Harriet Jacobses, Mary Princes, and Ellen Crafts of their times.[31]

Digby, one of the male characters in *Hope Leslie*, asserts that "[t]imes are changed. . . . [T]here is a new spirit in the world—chains are broken—fetters are knocked off—and the liberty set forth in the blessed word, is now felt to be every man's birth-right."[32] Concerned with the Puritans' subjugation of America's indigenous populations, Sedgwick's text establishes that however inalienable life, liberty, and the pursuit of happiness may be for white men, such freedom is not the birthright of either white women or native Americans. Using the plight of black women (in white skin) to demonstrate the consequences of misplaced political power, Brown's text takes up this theme and makes the point that in the United States freedom is not the birthright of either black women or black men.

While marital and / or domestic responsibilities are most often the elements that constrict and constrain white women in this particular variety of nineteenth-century sentimental fiction, Brown makes the right to marry the primary signifier of freedom for black women in his text. This at-once metaphorical and literal use of marriage as a liberating rather than confining force is only one of several reversals or inversions Brown effects in his own revision of both the coupling convention and the theme of woman as victim cum victor. The central plot of *Clotel* may echo the tragic tale told by Lydia Maria Child in "The Quadroons," but Brown's revision turns Child's tragic mulattas into two generations of heroic colored women who, rather than dying of broken hearts, use imagination, ingenuity, and courage to outwit their oppressors and secure the freedom of those they love.

Here, too, both historical "fact" and invented fiction supply Brown with fodder for his own literary insurrections. He makes fictive use of the facts of the Crafts' escape from slavery and draws into his narrative numerous other "real life" incidents and experiences, some of which had been widely reported in abolitionist publications and taken up by white writers. Despite his dependence on actual occurrences, Brown is by no means writing realism or even traditional romance. Rather, he constructs in *Clotel* what I defined earlier as an "unreal estate" (and at times an "ideal estate")—a blending of the "real," the "incredible," and, most particularly, the "borrowed."

In examining the poetics of *Clotel*, it is important to note as well the extent to which Brown draws creatively upon already existing literary traditions and narrative strategies in constructing his own. It is not mere coincidence, I suspect, that in the later versions of Brown's novel, Horatio Green becomes Henry Linwood and Clotel becomes Isabelle, reminiscent of Sedgwick's characters Herbert and Isabella Linwood. In keeping with the rhetorical trend of the times (and the concept of the unreal estate), cross-dressing and disguise play key roles in several of Sedgwick's novels, as well as in Brown's text, as characters escape literal and figurative prisons by swapping clothes, races, genders, places, and positions in pursuit of freedom. In *The Linwoods*, the heroine Isabella engineers Herbert Linwood's escape from prison through a black woman servant who changes clothes and places with him, a scene *Clotel* reenacts in Mary's heroic, self-sacrificing rescue of her beloved George. This and numerous other examples of dialogic interaction between black and white traditions—between "minor" and "major" literatures—speak to the almost unspoken among theories of intertextuality and "the black tradition."

According to Henry Louis Gates, "Several of the canonical texts in the Afro-American tradition seem to be related to other black texts primarily in terms of substance or content, whereas they seem to be related to Western texts in terms of form."[33] I would argue, however, that form and content are largely indivisible textual elements that do not readily split along color or cultural lines. *Clotel* makes an important aesthetic intervention at the level of form and language as well as theme and content. Certainly, its content confronts the moral and social problem of slavery; equally important is the fact that its form subverts and rewrites the sentimental genre and its neoclassical diction turns the language of the dominant culture in on itself.

Brown's diction—his use of the "master's tongue"—represents a political strategy that Harryette Mullen has rightly labeled "resistant orality."[34] But while Brown's orality should be read for its poetics as well as its politics, the author's highly appropriative style makes such a formalist reading difficult. *Clotel* has many linguistically powerful passages—wonderfully lyrical moments that sing above the pain and "propaganda" as welcome poems—but we do not always know whom to credit for such moments. Consider, for example, the following:

> The pride of China mixed its oriental looking foliage with the majestic magnolia, and the air was redolent with the fragrance of flowers, peeping out of every nook and nodding upon you with a most unexpected welcome. The tasteful hand of art had not learned to imitate the lavish beauty and harmonious disorder of nature, but they lived together in loving amity, and spoke in accordant tones. (57)

Here Brown paints for his readers a verbal picture of "a perfect model of rural beauty"—a metaphor for racial and marital accord. Word and image, personification and alliteration, combine in challenging black and white to mimic nature, honing harmony out of discord, establishing a peaceful symbiosis of opposites. For all its poetry, however, the passage repeats, altering only slightly (though I think for the better) the opening of "The Quadroons."

What Brown lacked in originality (a common literary failing in the nineteenth century) he made up for in irony. While Gloria Naylor insists that his novel is totally without irony, it seems to me that irony is the rhetorical device on which he most heavily depended. That same compelling facility of language that could craft a poetic phrase (even from someone else's phrase) could shift direction in an instant and turn a metaphor with the cutting edge of irony:

> There she stood, with a complexion as white as most of those who were waiting with a wish to become her purchasers. . . . The auctioneer commenced by saying, that "Miss Clotel had been reserved for the last, because she was the most valuable. . . ." "The chastity of this girl is pure; she has never been from under her mother's care; she is a virtuous creature." "Thirteen." "Fourteen." "Fifteen." "Fifteen hundred dollars," cried the auctioneer, and the maiden was struck for that sum. This was a Southern auction, at which the bones, muscles, sinews, blood, and nerves of a young lady of sixteen were sold for five hundred dollars; her moral character for two hundred; her improved intellect for one hundred; her Christianity for three hundred; and her chastity and virtue for four hundred dollars. (43)

But this biting irony has a softer side—a fondness for parody and double entendre that often gives a smoother edge to otherwise scathing critiques and social commentaries. Not all readers, however, have been able to read between the many faces Brown wears in his novel or to appreciate the full measure of either his irony or his humor.

All of the subsequent versions of Brown's narrative have a lighter touch than the original heavily political protest novel, due in part perhaps to modes of publication and shifting markets.[35] For example, the third version, *Clotelle: A Tale of the Southern States*, was published in 1864 as part of James Redpath's series of "Books for the Camp Fires," whose principal audience was Union soldiers. The names of the characters are changed once again; Mary is now Clotelle, the daughter of a southern gentleman named Henry Linwood rather than the granddaughter of Thomas Jefferson. Clotelle and her husband—now a dark-skinned Negro named Jerome—encounter Linwood, her repentant, guilt-ridden father, in Europe. Linwood at first objects to his daughter's choice of a dark husband, but familiarity, in this instance, breeds content, and Jerome and Linwood are soon "on the most intimate terms."

The novel ends with Linwood's resolve to go back to the United States just long enough to free his slaves and see them safely settled in the North, before returning to France "to end his days in the society of his beloved daughter." This romantic, "all's well that ends well," black-and-white-together conclusion made the novel appropriate reading for Union soldiers, since it carried the message that the South, like the southerner Linwood, would see the error of its ways and be returned to the fold in peace, harmony, and brotherhood.

The final version, *Clotelle; or, The Colored Heroine*, was published in 1867. As Brown notes in the preface to this edition, "With the exception of the last four chapters, this work was written before" the outbreak of the Civil War. In these four brief chapters (covering only nine pages), Clotelle and Jerome return to the United States in the early days of the war. Jerome joins the all-black Union regiment known as the Native Guard and promptly dies what the text takes pains to establish as a noble but needless death: he becomes one of fourteen black soldiers "sacrificed" by a white colonel to enemy fire in a series of futile attempts to retrieve a white captain's long-dead body from the field of battle. "The sad intelligence of Jerome's death" is brought to Clotelle as she ministers to sick and wounded soldiers in the hospitals of New Orleans. Her personal devastation, however, does not long deter her from her work as an "angel of mercy." Having read of the plight of Union soldiers at Andersonville Prison, she goes to Georgia to lend her hand to the soldiers' care. In the midst of nursing the wounded, Clotelle, who the prison guards assume is white, bribes the prison's man of all work to secure the keys to the doors and gates and aids ninety-three Union soldiers in escaping from Andersonville. Her obvious Union sympathies make her a suspect in the escape, and she is forced to flee the area. After the war Clotelle, a widow "possessed with ample means," buys the Poplar Farm, on which she once lived as a slave, and establishes a freedmen's school, resolved to devote the remainder of her life to the education of the newly freed Negro.[36]

It would do a disservice to its textual implications, however, to skim over this final version of Brown's novel without taking note of the peculiar turn taken by the text on its very last page. Clotelle is aided in her flight from Confederate forces by a black couple, Jim and Dinah. In Dinah's words, her husband, Jimmy, "is a free man: he was born free, an' he bought me, an' pay fifteen hundred dollars for me." Implicit in Dinah's statement is her own sense of herself as property, but what is particularly interesting about this passage is the narrative commentary that reflects on and follows up Dinah's disturbing announcement:

> It was true that Jim had purchased his wife; nor had he forgotten the fact, as was shown a day or two after, while in conversation with her. The woman, like many of her sex, was an inveterate scold, and Jim had but one way to govern her tongue. "Shet your mouf, madam, an' hole your tongue. . . . I bought you, an' paid my money fer you, an' I ain't a gwine ter let you sase me in dat way. Shet your mouf dis minit: ef you don't I'll sell you; 'fore God I will. Shet up, I say, or I'll sell you." This had the desired effect, and settled Dinah for the day." (114)

Reading this passage as yet another slap in the face to black womanhood, Alice Walker maintains that Brown presents brown-skinned Dinah as an "object of ridicule" to his readers ("Present," 310). It seems to me, however, that it is not Dinah who is the object of ridicule here but Jimmy—maybe even men as husbands, male authority, or perhaps the previously precious and privileged patriarchal institution of marriage itself. It is worth noting that most of the men in *Clotelle; or The Colored Heroine* fail as mates. Henry Linwood, for example, is much more deceitful and duplicitous in his romantic relations than was his prototype Horatio Green. While Green was presented as an essentially honorable, if ineffectual, man who might have married his colored mistress if the system allowed such a thing, Linwood is cast as a class-conscious cad who "would not have dared to marry a woman of so low an origin, even had the laws been favorable" (30). Of the lies Linwood tells wife and mistress alike Brown writes: "Oh, what falsehood and deceit man can put on when dealing with woman's love!" (32). We also see in this version the consequences for Linwood of his deceit: his ruined political career, his failed marriage, and the remorse that ultimately drives him into a state of mental and physical collapse from which he is rescued by Clotelle's forgiveness and tender loving care.

Misreading the Dinah and Jimmy incident, Alice Walker suggests that Brown was oblivious to the "horrifying impact" of the threat of sale "on a woman formerly sold only by whites" (310). I would argue, however, that the tone and telling details of the text suggest that this final marital scene was carefully crafted by one well aware of the power and gender dynamics with which he played. We hear none of Dinah's alleged nagging, for example, but are instead subjected—in painful, word-for-word detail—to Jim's cruel reminder to his wife that she is his property. This is not an isolated incident but the ritual around which the couple's marital relations revolve and through which the husband "governs" his wife's tongue. Like the white heroines of many nineteenth-century women's novels, black Dinah has discovered that in a society where men dominate women by law and custom, to be married is to be owned. If patriarchy is, as many critics argue, exclusively white in the novels of nineteenth-century black women writers, it seems it is not so in Brown's final fictional work. It is not a protofeminist consciousness that I am attributing to this decidedly male author, however, but a literary one. He recognized and addressed the market for women's fiction, as he had earlier played the markets for first "abolitionist propaganda" and then Civil War narratives.[37] Yet, even as he attempted to play to the tastes of women readers, Brown could not quite resist the masculinist comment that Dinah, "like many of her sex, was an inveterate scold."

As Brown's final fictional commentary on the peculiar institutions of slavery and marriage, the ending of *Clotelle* raises even more questions when taken together with the author's ultimate construction of his heroine as a solitary figure—an *unmarried* woman, seemingly without child. At novel's end, Clotelle, who has outlived two husbands, outsmarted slave catchers, outwitted prison guards, and outdistanced the Confederate army, is completely independent and alone. Unencumbered by child, man, or marital obligations, she returns to the Mississippi valley, resigned to living out the remainder of her life in service to a community she stands *among* but not *of*. Perhaps in this regard Brown's Clotelle has considerably more in common with Hurston's latter-day mulatta heroine Janie Crawford than critics have dared imagine. Both characters survive multiple marriages and mishaps and ultimately return alone to homes that are not really *their* homes to finish out their days amid folk who are not really *their* folk. However hastily appended and unconvincingly rendered the turn, the celebration of marriage that governed Brown's earlier work seems to have become, in the final nine pages of his text, a critique of the institution—an implied indictment that ironically presages the bitter light in which coupling will be cast a century later.

2

Literary Passionlessness and the
Black Woman Question in the 1890s

> The colored woman of to-day occupies, one may say, a unique position in
> this country. In a period of itself transitional and unsettled, her status
> seems one of the least ascertainable and definitive of all the forces which
> make for our civilization. She is confronted by both a woman question
> and a race problem, and is as yet an unknown or unacknowledged factor
> in both.
>
> — ANNA JULIA COOPER, *A Voice from the South* (1892)

Nineteenth-century British thought, as Christina Crosby has noted, is marked
by a fascination with women, the "ceaseless posing of 'the woman question.'"[1]
Much the same holds true on the other side of the Atlantic. However, nineteenth-century American thought is marked as well by the ceaseless posing of
"the race question." Concerned, like most black Americans, with issues of
racial identity and social equality, black female artists and intellectuals writing
at the turn of the century recognized that for them and their sisters the race
question did not exist separate and distinct from the woman question and vice
versa. Their commitment to uplifting the black race, therefore, was inextrica-
bly linked to a commitment to improving the social, cultural, moral, and
material conditions of women. This particularized, gendered sense of racial
purpose and politics often put black women writers at odds with a nationalist,
masculinist ideology of uplift that demanded female deference in the cause of
elevating black men. At the same time, however, racial discrimination within
the woman's movement positioned black women on the outskirts of mainstream suffrage and temperance activism. Central to the literary interventions
of black women writers, then, was the need to redefine who "women" were in
the process of laying claim to womanhood, while also renegotiating gender
relations within their own increasingly patriarchal black communities, as they
claimed the right to participate in the American body politic and to control
the politics of their own bodies.

For many members of the black female intelligentsia of the 1890s, the
institution of marriage was the calling card that announced the civility and
democratic entitlement which they attempted to claim for themselves and the
black masses they saw as their constituencies. Like William Wells Brown,
Harriet Wilson, and Harriet Jacobs before them, these turn-of-the-century
novelists used the coupling convention and the romantic form to address some

of the most compelling sociopolitical issues of their era: the sexual vulnerability of black women, for example, and the lynching of black men. But while their predecessors had used the right to marry to mark the claiming *of* freedom, black women writers of the 1890s invoked the coupling convention to explore the problems of living *in* freedom, in the shadow of slavery and the glaring light of institutionalized racism and discrimination. They used the novelistic form that Pauline Hopkins called the "little romance" to address the big problems black men and women encountered in entering so-called civil society at a moment when perhaps the only civil liberties freely given African Americans were marriage certificates.

Certifying the importance but not necessarily the traditional power dynamics of the institution of marriage, these writers also used the convention of coupling to critique and reorder gender relations. Departing from the popular—though by no means unchallenged—portrait of the proper, submissive Victorian wife, they theorized utopian unions in which empowered black heroines achieve parity with the men they marry and actively participate in the public sphere, usually through social welfare and racial uplift work.

Uniquely concerned with the particularly precarious position of black women, these early authors also deployed the social and literary conventions of the day in advancing a political project that sought to revise, rather than simply inscribe unaltered, the patriarchal standards of female virtue and respectability promoted by the dominant culture. In service to this project, these writers created virtuous, often light-skinned mulatta heroines whose sexual purity reigned on the printed page as a rebuttal to the racist imaging of black women as morally loose and readily accessible. Here, too, however, what critics have often disdained as the white middle-class values and Victorian sexlessness of such idealized colored heroines was both a rhetorical device and a political strategy designed to link black and white womanhood under the protective umbrella of chastity and virtue, even as dominant discourses sought to separate them. The seeming sexlessness of these black heroines must be read in dialogue with the literary, social, and political discourse of the era: as part and product of the particular history of African Americans, of the social constraints of the times, and of what white feminist historian Nancy Cott has defined as the dominant, though by no means monolithic, ideology of female passionlessness.

According to Cott, who coined the term, "passionlessness," or the idea that (white) women lacked carnal ardor, became the central tenet of Victorian sexual ideology, transforming if not completely reversing older notions of women's inherent licentiousness. Because it defined women as moral and spiritual rather than sexual and carnal, the concept of passionlessness gave middle- and upper-class Anglo-American women a degree of power over their bodies, their marriages, and their families, at the same time that it argued for the possibility of an intellectual life. In other words, passionlessness provided the ideological underpinning of claims for female moral superiority that were used to elevate women's status and to expand their possibilities, even as it delimited female social and sexual behavior. Its usefulness as a vehicle for female empowerment, Cott argues, was the major reason that the ideology of passion-lessness was so quickly and widely internalized among white women in the nineteenth century.[2]

However useful and empowering the concept was for white women, passionlessness took on a perhaps even greater ideological force when the so-called passionless subjects were black women whom the dominant culture continued to construct as inherently licentious and "always already sexual." As an element of nineteenth-century fiction, passionlessness necessarily takes on a different political meaning when written in the face of centuries of institutionalized rape and sexual coercion. For early black women writers, literary passionlessness negated a negative: it endowed virtue to the historically virtue-less. In black women's novels, then, the trope of sexual purity must be scrutinized not simply as an inscription of middle-class mores but as a critique that held up to scorn the same hegemonic values it, on some level, inscribed.

The multiple imperatives that shaped black women's fiction in the 1890s have often been misread by scholars who have insisted upon dividing and prioritizing racial and gender identities and color coding social and literary conventions. In this chapter I join such black feminist critics as Hazel Carby and Claudia Tate in theorizing alternative conceptual frameworks through which to analyze a body of fiction that has so often been read merely as assimilating and promoting the values of the dominant culture. Using Pauline Hopkins's *Contending Forces* (1900) and Frances Harper's *Iola Leroy* (1892) as case studies, I argue that the cultural interventions of many of these nineteenth-century novelists were propelled not by an accommodationist desire to assimilate the Victorian values of white society but by a profoundly political, feminist urge to rewrite those patriarchal strictures. For these, after all, were the values of the same social system that had enslaved an entire race, even as it declared the equality of all men — that had systematically raped, defiled, and degraded black women, even as it declared its deference for and defense of true womanhood.

I also attempt in this chapter to establish both a gender sensibility *and* a racial consciousness for nineteenth-century black women writers so often seen as possessing only one or the other. Ann Allen Shockley, for example, is one of many black feminist critics to define the dominant concern of nineteenth- and early-twentieth-century black women writers as "what they [saw] as their strongest oppression — racism."[3] Carolyn Sylvander, Jessie Fauset's principal biographer, similarly maintains that while black women have had to bear the burdens of both race and gender, they have made a "clear and forced choice" to fight racism first and sexism later.[4] In her impressive intercultural study of American women writing between 1890 and 1930, white feminist critic Elizabeth Ammons also insists that the "paramount issue for black women at the turn of the century was race. While they suffered because they were women," she argues, "they suffered more and primarily because they were black: If one or the other of the two issues had to take priority, it had to be race."[5]

Curiously, it seems that only women of color are called upon to sort their suffering and divide and prioritize their racial and gender identities. Politically and socially active white women are rarely, if ever, figured as being preoccupied with the advancement of the Caucasian race, even when their activism is not particularly woman-oriented. As Elizabeth Spelman, a white feminist philospher, has pointed out: "Western feminist theory . . . has implicitly demanded that Afro-American, Asian-American, or Latin American women separate their 'woman's voice' from their racial or ethnic voice without requiring white women to distinguish being a 'woman' from being white."[6] While black women writers of the 1890s were indeed acutely concerned with issues of race, racism, and racial uplift, a closer feminist reading of their fiction reveals that even in the face of slavery, the failures of Reconstruction, the rise of the Ku Klux Klan, and the proliferation of Jim Crow laws, few of these authors confronted racism without also addressing sexism and what sexual vulnerability and male supremacy meant for black women. Rape, for example, is both an impending threat and a devastating reality for the black heroines of Frances Harper and Pauline Hopkins. Their novels indict racism *and* sexism as conspiratorial forces in patriarchal domination, often offering sophisticated analyses of the interplay between racial and sexual ideology.[7]

The assumption that early black women writers were somehow able to split their identities and write within a gender-neutral, race-conscious realm, on the one hand, or within a middle-class, whitewashed space, on the other, has given these writers a kind of "woman without a country" status in feminist and black literary studies. Doubly disadvantaged and twice rejected, these writers have been marginalized within the African American literary tradition for their alleged assimilation of so-called white values and excluded from the canon of white American women novelists because of their assumed preoccupation with matters of race. In other words, not only have black women been marginalized historically by virtue of their race, gender, and material condition, they continue to be peripheralized as historical subjects in contemporary revisionist inquiries.

For example, black women writers are conspicuously absent from *Declarations of Independence* (1990), Barbara Bardes and Suzanne Gossett's pivotal study of the political work of women's fiction in the nineteenth century. The authors do note that a number of black women began writing after the Civil War, but they claim that the primary concern of these writers was "race rather than the political status of women."[8] So saying, these scholars, who purport to use "uncanonized" literary texts to analyze debates over the status and power of women, inadvertently disempower African American women twice over: first by excluding them from their analysis and then by in effect blaming the victims' alleged lack of interest in women's issues for that elision. The paradoxes here are multiple, however. While the white women writers given places of honor in Bardes and Gossett's study were concerned with such privileged political issues as the right of married women to *own property*, the black women writers excluded from their study were concerned with the right of black women not to be *owned as property:* a different take on the status of women, certainly, but one no less political.

Despite their revisionist objectives, studies like *Declarations of Indepen-*

dence fail to consider the different ways in which different women are consti-
tuted under patriarchy and the diverse political responses to oppression these
different constructions produce. Bardes and Gossett are concerned in their
study with public, institutional politics, with textual civil insurrection, with
fictive discussions of woman's rights and novelistic declarations of female
independence. As with notions of feminism that focus narrowly on critiques
of male supremacy, however, the concept of feminist politics as the struggle
for (white) woman's rights—the right to speak, the right to vote, the right of
married women to own property—needs to be expanded to encompass
broader public and private concerns. "Politics" needs to be more broadly
defined to include issues by no means unique to African American women but
by all means central to their particular status and struggles: responses to such
crises as institutionalized rape, racism, and lynching, for example, as well as
to sexual and marital subjugation.

Raped, bred, beaten, and abused in ways often as particular to their gender
as determined by their race, black women, as activists and as writers, have of
necessity been concerned with the political status of women. For them the
woman question has historically been a double-sided dilemma which cuts
across racial and gender identities, even in moments of crisis that seem to make
sex, as Frances Ellen Watkins Harper is widely reported to have remarked, a
"lesser question," momentarily tabled "if only the men of the race could obtain
what they wanted."[9] Placed in historical context, Harper's observation becomes less an advocacy of racial over gender politics than an indictment of
the historical blindness and overt bigotry of woman's rights activists whose
vehement opposition to black male suffrage was often cast in racist terms.
Harper, like many black women intellectuals of her day, realized that the
abolition of slavery had little altered the social and economic conditions of the
majority of black people, who therefore were faced with a compelling need
for political viability. Even in the face of this urgent need, however, black
women by no means easily or universally championed the cause of black male
rather than female suffrage as the most expedient route to political empowerment. Sojourner Truth, for example, originally opposed the ratification of the
Fifteenth Amendment giving black men the vote precisely because it made no
mention of the rights of black women. "If colored men get their rights and not
colored women theirs," she argued, "the colored men will be masters over the
women, and it will be just as bad as it was before."[10] One of few blacks at
the time to openly challenge the "manhood rights" imperative of Frederick
Douglass, Truth focused on the dangers for black women inherent in any
semblance of submission or deference to male power. Even as she reluctantly
lent her support to the cause of universal manhood suffrage, she continued to
insist upon keeping the woman question at the forefront of what Douglass
defined, often in decidedly masculine terms, as the Negro Hour.

As early as 1852 Truth spoke publicly of the black woman's doubly precarious position at the intersection of gender and racial ideologies in an im-
promptu address at the Woman's Rights Convention in Akron, Ohio. In her
oft-quoted query—"Aren't I a woman?"—she drew on her plowing and plant-

ing experiences as a black slave in responding to assertions from white ministers about the inherent inferiority and frailty of the female sex, the superior intellect of men, and the proper place of women:

> That man over there. He say women need to be helped into carriages and lifted over ditches and to have the best place everywhere. Nobody ever helps me into carriages or, over puddles, or gets me a best place. Aren't I a woman? Look at me! Look at my arm! I have ploughed. And I have planted. And I have gathered into barns. And no man could head me. And aren't I a woman? . . . I have borne thirteen children and seen most all sold off to slavery, and when I cried out with a mother's grief, none but Jesus heard me. And aren't I a woman?[11]

Truth extinguished the fire and brimstone of the male ministers with a facility that the privileged status—the "best place"—accorded white women could not. Her remarks are rooted in a profound awareness of the political status of women, but for her "women" was a much broader and far more complex category than it was for most of her white audience. It included those women excluded from Bardes and Gossett's study, women who instead of being helped into carriages were made to plow like mules and reproduce like cattle, without the rights and privileges of either male power or feminine frailty.

While Truth's words have been taken up by white feminists as a battle cry proclaiming the potential power of (white) women, they are actually a scathing indictment of the racist assumptions that place black females outside the category of woman, all the while exploiting their femaleness.[12] These are the same kinds of assumptions that have placed the multifaceted concerns of black women writers outside the category of woman-centered political activism in so many contemporary feminist investigations. This elision seems particularly ironic when we consider that the American male political system has received few assaults from women more vigorous than the antilynching campaign spearheaded by black educator and journalist Ida B. Wells. The force behind this campaign was not only the urge to defend black men against false charges of rape and to protest the heinous crime of lynching but an understanding of the racial, sexual, and political ideologies that underpinned lynch law. Wells and the black women who joined her campaign recognized lynching as part and parcel of the same master mentality and political economy that governed the institutionalized rape of black women and the systematic oppression of black people.[13] The clarity with which black women grasped the connection between the myth of the black male rapist and the myth of the licentious black temptress is evident in both the antilynching campaign itself and the feminist activism of black clubwomen, for whom defending the bodies of black women and the lives of black men was a primary objective.

The campaign against lynching—against sexual imperialism—was waged as well in the literary texts of artists and activists such as Hopkins and Harper. Hopkins, for example, explicitly identifies lynching and concubinage as the subjects of her first novel, *Contending Forces*, and Harper, in naming her heroine Iola—the pseudonym Wells used in her early newspaper articles—and in committing Iola to a life of race work, may have been paying tribute to the antilynching activist. The remainder of this chapter considers the ways in which Hopkins and Harper used the marriage plot and the trope of passionlessness to address both the woman question and the race question, to enlarge the category of woman, and to critique the forces of patriarchy with which black women and all black people were forced to contend at the turn of the century.

Contending Forces: A Romance Illustrative of Negro Life North and South

Like most other novels of the late nineteenth century, *Contending Forces* draws on the conventions of the sentimental romance even as it scrutinizes both the marriage tradition and black life in the 1890s. For Hopkins, a political activist and literary editor of the *Colored American Magazine*, *Contending Forces* is an act of resistance and intervention, as she establishes in her preface: "In giving this little romance expression in print, I am not actuated by a desire for notoriety or for profit, but to do all I can in an humble way to raise the stigma of degradation from my race." Hopkins goes on to delineate the healing, ennobling powers of fiction "as preservers of manners and customs" and as a "record of growth and development from generation to generation."[14] Undoubtedly challenging the authority and racist characterizations of plantation-tradition writers such as Joel Chandler Harris and Charles Nelson Page (and perhaps William Dean Howells as well),[15] Hopkins insists that blacks must find the means by which to define themselves; they alone must "develop the men and women who will faithfully portray the inmost thoughts and feelings of the Negro with all the fire and romance which lie dormant in our history" (14).

Hopkins's was a popular sentiment among African American intellectuals. The social activist and educator Anna Julia Cooper, for example, feminized the issue of self-invention and entitlement in her now-famous pronouncement: "Only the BLACK WOMAN can say 'when and where I enter, in the quiet, undisputed dignity of my womanhood, without violence and without suing or special patronage, then and there the whole *Negro race enters with me.*'"[16] Hopkins's highly politicized contribution to Negro self-invention and the defense of the dignity of black womanhood is by no means a little romance. In a decidedly political maneuver, Hopkins links capitalism, sexism, and racism as the factors behind both the destruction of black families and the disruption of the novel's plotted union. She deploys the coupling convention in addressing the novel's principal themes, which are not love and marriage but the "venomous monster" of lynching and the terrible consequences of concubinage — contending forces which plague the Negro race.

Set in Boston at the turn of the century, *Contending Forces* tells a number of complicated, interrelated tales, including that of Luke Sawyer, a seemingly minor character whose storytelling is actually central to the novel's rhetorical frame. Luke, a newcomer to Boston, tells a gathering of the city's Colored

American League[17] the all-too-familiar horror story of how his parents' industry in building a successful trading business resulted first in threats from less
successful rival white store owners and then in violent mob action. For not
selling out and leaving town quickly enough, Luke's father was lynched, his
mother and sisters raped and whipped to death, and his twin baby brothers
held by the heels and smashed against the walls of the house. Luke, the only
member of his family to survive, was taken in and raised by the Beaubeans,
mulatto neighbors destined to know terror and tragedy of their own.

In Hopkins's "unreal estate," Luke's story refracts and fictionalizes the
actual tragedy in Memphis, Tennessee, that motivated Ida B. Wells's antilynching campaign: in 1892 three of her black male friends, successful shop-
keepers like Luke's father, were arrested for defending their property and
ultimately lynched by a white mob. Like Wells, Hopkins exposes the economic
and political motives behind the lynching of black merchants too successful
for their own survival in a racist economy. Acknowledging the link between
the lynching and disfranchisement of black men and the systematic sexual
assaults on black rather than white women, Hopkins writes rape into her
historical romance. She invents for Luke's telling a second tale, which allows
her to explore more fully the relationship between racial and sexual ideology
and patriarchal oppression. Luke recounts for his audience how Mabelle
Beaubean, the then-fourteen-year-old daughter of the couple who took him in
after the murder of his own family, was kidnapped, raped, and impregnated
by her uncle, her father's white half brother. When confronted by Mabelle's
outraged and grief-stricken father, the uncle, a "southern gentleman" and
Louisiana state senator, dismissed as no crime at all his rape of his colored
niece:

> [W]hatever damage I have done I am willing to pay for. But your child is no
> better than her mother or her grandmother. What does a woman of mixed
> blood, or any Negress, for that matter, know of virtue? It is my belief that
> they were a direct creation of God to be the pleasant companions of men of
> my race. Now, I am willing to give you a thousand dollars and call it square.
> (260–61)

The fact that he is speaking to his brother about his brother's very young
daughter makes no difference to the senator, whose code of honor does not
apply to black women, even (or perhaps especially) those who share his own
white blood. As Luke Sawyer reports, the father's threat of legal action against
his brother resulted in the burning of the Beaubean home and the murder of
all but Mabelle, whom Luke managed to rescue and hide away in a local
colored convent, where, as far as he knows, she died some months later in
childbirth.

Here, as elsewhere in the fiction and the political prose of the period, patho-
logical, systemic acts of racial and sexual imperialism are properly positioned
as part and product of unrestrained patriarchal power and capitalist ideology.
It is no accident, for example, that Hopkins, like Wells, interrogates the eco-
nomics of institutionalized lynching, the racial politics of mob violence, and

the master mentality of southern gentlemen like Beaubean's brother, who even forty years after emancipation can view black women only as property.

Of the many African American novels written between the publication of *Clotel* in 1853 and the turn of the century, *Contending Forces* arguably offers the most complex (if not complete) representation of the intricacies of black American life in the latter 1800s. It presents a multidimensional view of the problems African Americans faced in attempting to claim their rights to life, liberty, and the happiness of romantic pursuit, the challenges they faced in attempting to realize their own versions of the American dream, and the obstacles they encountered in striving to build their own marital and family lives.

Contending Forces is a class-conscious novel which, on the one hand, takes racial uplift to new heights, showcasing the black professional with a roster of black doctors, lawyers, businessmen *and* businesswomen, politicians, ministers, philosophers, and educators. On the other hand, the novel also exposes the reader to the realm of the working class by locating most of its action within the respectable boardinghouse owned and operated by Mrs. Smith, her son, Will, and daughter, Dora, and inhabited by a variety of black men and women, all of whom work for a living.

Mrs. Smith is the mulatta granddaughter of Charles Montford, a white British aristocrat who moved his family and retinue of slaves from Bermuda to North Carolina in the early 1800s to escape the approaching abolition of slavery in the British Isles. The Montford-Smith genealogy is revealed in the first eighty pages of the book, where we learn that once in North Carolina, the Montfords fell prey to the evil plotting of a jealous neighbor, Anson Pollock, whose hatred of Montford and lust for his beautiful wife, Grace, prompted him to conspire against the newcomers. Carefully calculating his every move, Pollock spread the rumor that despite her creamy complexion Grace Montford was of African descent.[18] He then used that allegation as an excuse to kill Montford, whom he accused not only of marrying a Negress but also of plotting a slave rebellion, and to seize both his neighbor's plantation and his neighbor's wife. After her husband's murder, Grace Montford drowned herself to avoid Pollock's sexual assaults. Her two sons were captured by Pollock and turned into the slaves he felt their mother should have been. Charles, Jr., the older of the two, was hired out to a mineralogist—a compassionate Englishman who, impressed by the "lad's appearance, education, and refinement" and touched by his "tragic story," purchased him from Pollock and took him to Europe, where he eventually won a suit against the U.S. government for retribution and return of his family's property. The younger son, Jesse, escaped, making his way to New Hampshire, where he was taken in by a black family whose daughter he married fifteen years later. Mrs. Smith is his daughter.

The novel's controlling sociopolitical critique is encoded in and achieved through the romantic relationship that develops between Mrs. Smith's handsome young son, Will, and the mysterious and hauntingly beautiful Sappho Clark, a boarder at the Smith lodging house. Sappho, who works as a stenographer and typist,[19] is central to *Contending Forces*, both as Dora's friend and Will's love interest and as the conventional, solitary heroine whose already compromised virtue again comes under siege in the midst of the novel, dramatically disrupting the love story on which Hopkins pins her larger concerns with lynching and concubinage. But Sappho, as a romantic heroine, is also deconventionalized by complications of race and history. Boy and girl meet and fall in love in this tale, too, but here the happily-ever-after ending is forestalled by nothing so simple as differences in station, parental disapproval, false pride, or silly prejudice. Racism, rape, incest, impregnation, murder, and patriarchal oppression are the obstacles Hopkins employs to separate her young black lovers.

Sappho has a secret: what she sees as a sin of passion that places her outside the realm of true womanhood and makes her unworthy of the love of a decent man. Through Sappho and her secret, Hopkins confronts the question of revised standards of womanhood: "Do you think, then, that Negro women will be held responsible for all the lack of virtue that is being laid to their charge today?" Sappho at one point asks the older and wiser race woman Mrs. Willis. "I mean," Sappho continues, "do you think that God will hold us responsible for the *illegitimacy* with which our race has been obliged, as it were, to flood the world?" Sappho's question, as we learn later, is a deeply personal one. Mrs. Willis's reply that we are not responsible for wrongs committed under compulsion rings with a sentiment that seems to me very much the message of the time and the text: "We are virtuous or non-virtuous," she tells the troubled Sappho, "only when we have a *choice* under temptation." Africans, Mrs. Willis goes on to point out, were brought to America against their will and therefore under slavery functioned outside a state of morality that implies willpower. "The sin and its punishment lies with the person *consciously* false to his *knowledge* of right," Mrs. Willis concludes (149–50).

Mrs. Willis is, for this moment anyway, the text's *raisonneur* whose words of wisdom are meant to extend to Sappho the right to respectability, bourgeois marriage, and motherhood that her secret past, under the Victorian standards of the day, would necessarily deny her. But Sappho is little comforted by Mrs. Willis's good counsel. When Will Smith proposes marriage, she attempts to warn him away. "[T]here are things which you ought to know," she tells him, "things connected with the past—" Will cuts her off, however, declaring that he has no interest in the past and pleading with her to become his wife. So persuasive are his words that for a moment Sappho, like Tess of the d'Urbervilles, is "carried away by the vehemence of his wooing. All obstacles," Hopkins writes, "seemed, indeed, but trifles before this all-absorbing, passionate, eager warmth of youth's first love" (312). After a "tempest of weeping," Sappho, hoping to indeed put the past behind her, places her hand in Will's and accepts his proposal.

But while Will has no interest in Sappho's past, his best friend, John Langley, is extremely interested in her history. Langley, an ambitious, young colored lawyer who doubles as Will's friend and Dora's fiancé, is imbued with all the deceit, duplicity, and sexual cruelty the author could muster.[20] His presence in the novel enables Hopkins to explore the relationship between racial, sexual, and patriarchal ideologies. Though his personal history is not known for much of the story, Langley just happens to be the great-nephew of Anson Pollock, the same white villain who robbed, enslaved, and murdered Mrs. Smith's white ancestors, the Montfords. He is an example of the ideology of the father (or uncle) being visited upon the son, who in turn visits it upon innocent men and women. He may be as well, however, an example of the era's preoccupation with heredity and genetics. Though he presents himself as a gentleman, Langley is a scoundrel whose perfidy betrays his poor-white and slave origins, creating in the text the same disturbing, potentially racist polemic of identity that Mark Twain's *Pudd'nhead Wilson* (1894) presents: the implication that evil (like intelligence) is hereditary and both class- and race-determined.[21] Langley's evil impulses, Hopkins writes, were the direct result of slavery. "Natural instinct for good had been perverted by a mixture of 'cracker' blood of the lowest type on his father's side with whatever God-saving quality that might have been loaned the Negro by pitying nature" (221). (Perhaps it is the "God-saving quality" of his Negro blood that gives Langley a conscience and entitles him to die repentant, as he does at the end of the novel.)

As licentious as his great-uncle, Langley becomes sexually obsessed with Sappho and plays a major role in unraveling the mystery surrounding her. He exposes her tragic history, which, in keeping with the narrative strategies of the form, must first be confronted, then overcome. His engagement to Dora Smith, his best friend's sister, does not stop Langley from attempting to blackmail Sappho into becoming his mistress when he learns the horrible details of her past. Following Sappho, watching her every move, noting every facial expression, Langley correctly surmises that the story Luke Sawyer told the Colored American League about a fourteen-year-old girl's rape and her family's murder is Sappho's story. Sappho Clark is actually the Beaubeans' daughter, Mabelle, whom Luke Sawyer rescued after her family's murder and took to a colored convent in New Orleans, where she eventually gave birth to a son, whom she turned over to an aunt to raise. To give Sappho Clark a new chance at life in a new identity, the sisters of the convent gave out the story that Mabelle had died in childbirth.

Having pieced together her story, Langley confronts Sappho with the truth and, on the eve of her engagement to Will, attempts to force her into a sexual liaison with him. He assures her that while his own passion for her is steadfast, stronger than honor or reason, the proud Will Smith will quickly forsake her when he learns of her past. Sappho does not quite catch his meaning at first and mistakes his proposition for a proposal of marriage and protection — an error Langley quickly corrects: "Marriage!" he exclaims, "who spoke of marriage? Ambitious men do not marry women with stories like yours!" (320). He gives her a week in which to accept his proposition or face the consequences of having her real identity and history exposed.

Langley's words confirm Sappho's sense of her own unworthiness and send her fleeing from the city, pausing only long enough to reclaim the son she vows never again to deny and to write Will a note revealing Langley's treachery and identifying herself as Mabelle Beaubean, the subject of Luke Sawyer's tragic tale. With apologies to Will for having deceived him, she explains that for his sake she must leave Boston. "[Langley] has made me realize how much such a marriage with me would injure you," her letter reads. "Disgrace shall never touch you or yours through me" (329).

Contrary to Langley's prediction, the Smiths—Ma, Will, and sister Dora— are unanimous in their concern, sympathy, and unimpeached affection for Sappho. "To think [Sappho] should believe us capable of feeling anything for her but sympathy!" Ma Smith exclaims. "You must find her, Will, and bring her back home." Ma's sentiments are echoed by Dora, who immediately removes Langley's engagement ring from her finger and asks Will to return it. Will, too, is anxious to find Sappho, pausing only long enough to find Langley. The ensuing confrontation reflects the different patriarchal ideologies under which the two men operate. For Will, even in his outrage, is the positive patriarch, the genuine gentleman, defending the honor of his fiancée and his sister and protecting *his* womenfolk from harm. Langley, on the other hand, is a complete cad, an example of patriarchy at its worst. Asked why he has deliberately sought to humiliate Dora, the woman he asked to be his wife, he replies:

> I did not intend to humiliate Dora, for men do many like things which never come to the ears of the woman they call wife. Accidentally I learned Miss Clark's story. . . . You will thank me when you know all. She is beautiful. . . . Am I different from other men who have made like proposals to a *fille de joie*? (338)

Langley's words recall those of Senator Beaubean, who viewed his incestuous assault of his niece as "no crime at all." His speech also allows Hopkins to once again distinguish between the unbridled lust of bad patriarchy (Langley's passion "stronger than honor or reason") and the controlled lustlessness of good patriarchy (the "passionate, eager warmth" of Will Smith's love). Restrained from further challenging the villain by the timely arrival of family friend Dr. Lewis (who, by the way, has long been in love with Dora himself), Will flings Dora's engagement ring in Langley's face and orders him out of the Smith lodging house by nightfall. With his mother's and sister's blessings, he turns his full attention toward finding the woman he loves. But even with the hired help of the best detectives in Boston, Sappho is not to be found.

In keeping with the romantic form, the lovers—Will and Sappho—of course find each other again at the end of the novel, by which time the Smiths have been happened upon by a wealthy white cousin who fills in the details of their aristocratic origins, claims them as kin, and helps them secure their rightful inheritance. Thus, the Smiths acquire all the accoutrements of bourgeois society. Invited by wealth, family connections, and skin complexion to, in effect, be white, they still choose to be black and to use some of their newfound riches for the betterment of the black race.[22] Will, who we learn has succeeded brilliantly first at Harvard and then at Heidelberg, plans to build a tuition-free school for Negro youth. Believing that he has lost Sappho forever and resolved that without her "no wife or child would ever be his," he intends to make himself a father to the youth of his race (386). Dora has married Dr. Lewis, who, like his prototype Booker T. Washington, has founded and presides over an industrial college for blacks, and whom she assists in "the upbuilding of their race."[23] Eventually, the Lewises have a daughter whom they name after their beloved Sappho.

It is while visiting his sister and brother-in-law in New Orleans that Will happens upon his niece's namesake—the long-lost Sappho Clark, who has been working as a governess. Through this chance meeting, Sappho is reunited with the Smiths, who gleefully express their love and compassion, assuring her that her past is no impediment to her joining the family as Will's wife. The novel closes with the happy family of Smiths (including Sappho, now Mrs. Will Smith, and her son Alphonse) and Lewises sailing off to Europe to visit their newfound British cousin in a land that, unlike the United States, will allow them to assert their claim to white as well as black identity. "Sappho was happy in contemplating the life of promise which was before her," Hopkins writes in closing. "Will was the noblest of men. Alphonse was to him as his own child. United by love, chastened by sorrow and self-sacrifice, he and she planned to work together to bring joy to hearts crushed by despair" (401).

Contending Forces concludes not only with the marriage at last of Will and Sappho but with the reconstruction of a family, as Will claims Sappho's son as his own and mother and child are welcomed into the extended Smith family. Thus, what Sappho finds at novel's end is not only a husband but reclaimed subjectivity, family, and community, as well as entitlement to romantic love and bourgeois marriage. But as is so often the case in these African American revisions of the marriage plot, matrimony here means not submission and domesticity but partnership in race work. However, Sappho finds something else as well: she finds at last a way to make peace with the past.

According to Claudia Tate, Sappho uses her "scarred womanhood" for "heroic self-transformation," signaled by her change of name from Mabelle Beaubean to Sappho Clark.[24] But I am not entirely convinced that the glass is half full at this point: that this unnaming/renaming is the affirmation, the assertion of a revised Afrocentric text of female virtue, that Tate sees it to be. Mabelle's calling herself Sappho links her metaphorically to the lesbian poet of the same name. But in claiming Sappho she denies not only the sexual dominance of men but the importance of Mabelle—her history, her child—as well. All of these denials of Mabelle ultimately make Sappho Clark not an active "subject of her own desire," as Tate maintains, but—until she marries Will—a fugitive from that desire and a continuing victim of the patriarchal social order that first defiled her and then imposed upon her a sexual standard that condemns her for that defilement.

The text implies, however, that the more damaging condemnation is the one Sappho inflicts upon herself out of her own acceptance of traditional standards of virtue; for even as those who love her search her out to tell her so, she hides from them in shame, fear, and distrust. The words she spoke earlier in the novel ring with an irony the text seems to foreground: "All things are possible," she counseled Dora, "if love is the foundation stone." It seems, however, that Sappho's hard-won understanding of patriarchal power is stronger than her belief in the possibilities of love. When Will chides her for her lack of confidence in his love, she replies: "Ah, Will; I had suffered so much at the hands of selfish men! Can you wonder that I mistrusted you, and felt that you would only despise me when you knew all?" (395–96). Patriarchy is for Sappho not exclusively white, as it seems to be for so many other female characters in nineteenth-century novels, but profoundly male.

In one of the earliest contemporary readings of *Contending Forces*, Richard Yarborough took note of Pauline Hopkins's concern with the "apparent inevitability with which the Afro-American past manifests itself in the lives of blacks."[25] This seems to me to be particularly true of Sappho Clark, whose efforts to escape history in the cloak of a new identity, which includes denying her child, bring added guilt and shame to her, as well as misery to those who love her. It is only when she confronts the past, embracing her son, that she is able to transcend it — that she indeed becomes an "active female-hero" entitled to her own desire.

Without denying Sappho's courage, however, I want to suggest that hers is not entirely a "heroic *self*-transformation." The signal name change, as I read the text, is not from Mabelle Beaubean to Sappho Clark but from Sappho Clark to Mrs. William Smith. This is not to suggest that Sappho's identity is subsumed under the title "Mrs." but rather to acknowledge the role the Smiths play in revising the text of female respectability, in displacing premarital virginity as the primary signifier of female virtue and marriageability. Will Smith and his family are Sappho's coauthors: their loving acceptance of her and her history finally makes Sappho able to love and accept herself. Encoded in the Smiths' response to Sappho's history — their unflinching support and complete understanding — is the text's and the race's "declaration of independence" from impossible standards of womanhood and respectability. Will is particularly important in this regard, for he represents a new breed of husband — what Claudia Tate calls a "revised text of husband" — who does not require either virginity in a bride or deference in a wife. He is the kind of husband who can help make the past palatable. While *Contending Forces* works diligently to expose the horrors of white male supremacy, Will Smith is a towering example of the positive black patriarch — supportive black sons, brothers, and husbands whose loving male lustlessness both complements and enables the female passionlessness that black women writers employed in their campaign to redefine black womanhood in positive cultural terms.

Passionlessness as Plot and Politics

Many readers have argued that if white male supremacy and the sexual pathology of white patriarchy were unmasked by women writers of the late nineteenth century, black female sexuality was cloaked. In the midst of a climate that endowed black women (and men) with uncontrollable sexual appetites, these writers created passionless heroines who were pious and pure, if not always submissive and domestic. Gloria Naylor, who traces this sexual reticence to *Clotel*, notes that even into the twentieth century, when white male writers such as Stephen Crane and Theodore Dreiser were exploring what Freud called the "dark continent" of female sexuality,[26] black women in African American fiction remained "overly chaste and virtuous," heroines "whose sterling morals were instruments in the cause of racial uplift." The sexuality of the black woman was thought to reflect upon the entire race, Naylor points out, and "black female sexuality was therefore whitened and deadened to the point of invisibility."[27]

Naylor's comparison is an odd one, it seems to me. It is worth noting, at the very least, that white male writers like Crane and Dreiser had luxuries of invention and liberties of publication that black women writers did not. In addition to the privileges their status as white males accorded them, Crane and Dreiser had different intellectual imperatives, as well as different audiences. They were not, like the black women novelists to whom Naylor compares them, concerned with retrieving black womanhood from the depths of infamy into which history and literature had plunged it. They had little or nothing to lose in writing of the unseemly and the sexual, the very elements that the political agendas of early African American women writers required them to cover over.

More to the point, as I have argued, what Naylor calls the literary whitening and deadening of black female sexuality must be considered in terms of both African American history and Victorian sexual ideology, rather than through such constructs as naturalism. Viewed in historical context, the literary campaigns of black women writing in the 1890s can be interpreted as extending the project of revisioning woman that Sojourner Truth began a generation earlier. Indeed, Truth's words reverberate throughout the latter half of the nineteenth century. They resound, for example, in Harriet Jacobs's narrative of her life as a slave. Reflecting on what she feared civilized society would view as inexcusable sexual transgressions, Jacobs asked if perhaps "the slave woman ought not to be judged by the same standard as others." Jean Fagan Yellin reads Jacobs's remark as a possible call for a new definition of female morality, determined not by conformity to the "sexual behavior mandated by white patriarchy" but by the lived sexual experiences of black women in a "brutal and corrupt patriarchal racist society."[28]

Jacobs's revisionist question, like Sojourner Truth's, speaks directly to the intersection of racial and sexual ideologies. As I have argued, it is a question for which Pauline Hopkins offers an affirmative answer in *Contending Forces*, both through Mrs. Willis's response to Sappho Clark's concerns about scarred black womanhood and through the Smiths' loving acceptance of Sappho and her "illegitimate" son, Alphonse.

The passionlessness and absolute sexual purity of Frances Harper's mulatta heroine Iola Leroy, on the other hand, metaphorically extends to black women the degree of autonomy and moral authority that Nancy Cott suggests the ideology of passionlessness gave to white women of the nineteenth century. According to Cott:

> The ideology of passionlessness, conceived as self-preservation and social advancement for women, created its own contradictions: on the one hand, by exaggerating sexual propriety so far as to immobilize women and, on the other, by allowing claims of women's moral influence to obfuscate the need for other sources of power. The assertion of moral integrity within passionlessness had allowed women to retrieve their identity from a trough of sexual vulnerability and dependence. The concept could not assure women full autonomy—but what transformation in sexual ideology alone could have done so? (175)

Reduced from the heights of white bourgeois femininity to the depths of black slavery, the beautiful, desirable Iola Leroy nevertheless manages to fend off the sexual advances of her various masters to remain pure, virginal, and not only highly marriageable but empowered to *reject* the white doctor who offers her his name and protection on the condition that she forsake her black race and play white with him. Unlike William Wells Brown's characters Althesa and Mary, for whom marriage to white men is a means of rescue in which they have little say, Iola is free to choose not only whom she will marry but *if* she will marry.[29] Here claiming, rather than denying, the invisible racial mark becomes an act of empowerment and, to use Bardes and Gossett's metaphor, a declaration of independence.

The brand of literary passionlessness that Harper practices in *Iola Leroy* is as political in its purpose as Hopkins's revisionism. Harper's passionlessness is indeed rooted in a politics of self-preservation and elevation, and like its white counterpart it is not without contradiction. Even as many of these early authors sought to broaden the category of womanhood and revise standards of virtue and marriageability, their own constructions often presented linear views of a monolithic, hegemonic sexuality. Their representations frequently reflected their own intellectual and economic privilege and moral authority, as their refined fictional figures stood as beacons announcing the existence of a class of pious, pure, bourgeois black women.

However, it is not entirely accurate to claim, as Naylor does, that black female sexuality is completely erased in nineteenth-century novels. Nor should we accept without qualification Hazel Carby's assertion that in novels such as *Contending Forces* and *Iola Leroy* the authors' desire to counter claims of sexual promiscuity led to a complete repression of female sexuality. "Sexual attraction," Carby writes of *Iola Leroy*, "is displaced by a joint desire, not for each other, but to uplift the race."[30] I would argue, however, that sexual desire is not *displaced* by social purpose but *encoded* in it—regulated, submerged, and insinuated into the much safer realm of political zeal and the valorized venue of holy wedlock. In the context of my own analysis of representations of marriage, sexuality, and subjectivity at the turn of the century, the distinction between *placement* and *displacement* is critical. For if we view these writers as having completely repressed or eradicated female sexuality in their texts, we deny those texts what I consider one of their most important raison d'être: their efforts not only to counter racist imaging of black sexuality but to reclaim for black women the right to both desire and democracy.

While Iola Leroy does indeed choose as a partner a man equally committed to racial uplift, their coupling is cast in decidedly sensual, if not explicitly sexual, terms. The love scene in which Dr. Frank Latimer, a colored physician, proposes to Iola moves metaphorically from the foreplay of verbal lovemaking to the afterglow of orgasmic release:

> Seating himself near her, he poured into her ears words eloquent with love and tenderness. . . . His words were more than a tender strain wooing her to love and happiness, they were a clarion call to a life on high and holy worth. . . . Her hand lay limp in his. She did not withdraw it, but raising her lustrous eyes to his, she softly answered: "Frank, I love you."
> After he had gone, Iola sat by the window, gazing at the splendid stars, her heart quietly throbbing with a delicious sense of joy and love. . . . [A]s the waves leap up to the strand, so her soul went out to Dr. Latimer.[31]

The language and imagery of this passage—words poured into her ear, the limp hand not withdrawn, the throbbing heart, the delicious sense of joy and love, and especially the nature imagery of waves leaping up to meet the shore—are sexual signifiers. They suggest a controlled passion, about to be properly positioned within and satisfied by the institution of marriage.

Satisfaction is a word worth emphasizing, for Iola and Frank's enjoyment of their married life is obvious to friends and family. When Iola's brother good-naturedly complains to family friend Lucille Delaney that, once good company, Iola and Frank since their marriage have nothing to say except about each other, she responds: "Oh you absurd creature! . . . [T]his is their honeymoon, and they are deeply in love with each other" (277). At the risk of overreading, I will venture to suggest that it is not the newlyweds' passion for race work to which Lucille refers. Here, as in Hopkins's novel, the marital relation lends sanction to proper passions and desires. As the wise Mrs. Willis says (speaking generically) of passion in *Contending Forces*: "I do believe that in some degree passion may be beneficial, but we must guard ourselves against a sinful growth of any appetite. . . . All desires and hopes with which we are endowed are good in the sight of God, only it is left for us to discover their right uses" (155). The only right (and, at this point in the development of the black woman's novel, "safe") use of sexual passion is in the marital relation, but for nineteenth-century black women writers this positioning of passion was as much a political statement as a literary or social convention—a rewriting of the convention and an act of reclamation.

In developing conceptual frameworks through which to read the 1890s, we must be mindful of the implications of our own rhetoric when we accuse these early novelists of adopting white values and mimicking Victorian social and literary conventions. For in so saying, we inadvertently endorse the determinants of a dysfunctional society that has equated race with worth, that has constructed white as value and black as the absence of value. The near-white heroines who dominated the pages of nineteenth-century novels—no matter how distasteful their pale skin, piety, and purity may be to modern readers—served important political and literary functions.[32] They stand as signs of the racist contradictions at the heart of American society.

Along with reevaluating the rhetorical and strategic significance of these literary figures, we must also reconsider the notion that, for African American women, gender and race are divisible identities. While nineteenth-century black women writers were occupied with the welfare of their people, they were no less concerned with the political status of women. Insofar as uplifting the black race meant promoting a black patriarchy, their novels, with few exceptions, refused to go along with the prescribed program, even as they often seemed to embrace the programmed prescriptions.

In theorizing marriage on different terms—in plotting utopian unions based on gender equality, on friendship, on partnership, and on a shared commitment to uplifting the race—such novels as Frances Harper's *Iola Leroy* and Pauline Hopkins's *Contending Forces* resist in important ways the dominant discourse of deference. They also critique the dominative powers of patriarchy and begin to reclaim for black women their own female bodies. It will be a full quarter century, however, before black women writers begin to explore those bodies sexually—before social conditions and literary conventions create a space where African American women writers can dare to delve into the realm of black female desire and to explore the intimate sexual self. Getting to that point of sexual self-engagement was an evolutionary and at times a *revolutionary* process.

3

Women, Men, and Marriage
in the Ideal Estate

> Crime has no sex and yet today
> I wear the brand of shame;
> Whilst he amid the gay and proud
> Still bears an honored name.
>
> Can you blame me if I've learned to think
> Your hate of vice a sham,
> When you so coldly crush me down,
> And then excuse the man?
> — FRANCES HARPER, from "A Double Standard"

Perhaps nowhere are the contradictory impulses of the 1890s more dramatically revealed than in the variety of fiction that flowered throughout the decade. Both informed by and part of what Frances Harper called the "grandly constructive" political activism of the Woman's Era,[1] many of the novels of the period address issues much on the minds of intellectuals such as Harper, Pauline Hopkins, and Anna Julia Cooper. Of particular concern to these writers was the moral, social, and political status of African American women and, as this excerpt from "A Double Standard" suggests, the nature of male-female social relations. As I argued in chapter 2, nineteenth-century black women writers such as Hopkins and Harper employed the convention of coupling and the concept of passionlessness in advancing an often sophisticated critique of the insidious interplay of racial and sexual ideology, as they sought both to revise patriarchal standards of female respectability and to extend to black women the protection of idealized femininity.

But black women wrote another kind of novel in the 1890s — novels whose primary concern is not race or romance but religion and female moral authority. The higher spiritual ground given women in these texts and their preoccupation with female communities suggest that the ideology of passionlessness had a hand in shaping these novels as well. For passionlessness not only gave middle-class white women a way to regulate their sexual, social, and marital relations, it also fostered female friendship by privileging the spiritual over the carnal, the homosocial over the heterosexual. As Nancy Cott writes:

> [A]cceptance of the idea of passionlessness created sexual solidarity among women; it allowed them to consider their love relationships with one another

of higher character than heterosexual relationships because they excluded (male) carnal passion. "I do not believe that men can ever feel so pure an enthusiasm for women as we can feel for one another," Catharine Sedgwick recorded in her diary in 1834, upon meeting Fanny Kemble, "—ours is nearest to the love of angels."[2]

According to Cott, these notions of the ennobling angelic or spiritual aspects of female love fostered sisterhood among white women. "Women considered passionlessness an important shared trait," she argues, one "which distinguished them favorably from men" (173).

While Cott's analysis of Victorian sexual ideology focuses on white women during the first half of the nineteenth century, I hope to show in this chapter how black women writing in the 1890s were similarly affected by dominant moral and religious ideology. The chapter focuses on the work of two black literary evangelists: Emma Dunham Kelley's *Megda* (1891) and *Four Girls at Cottage City* (1898) and Amelia Johnson's *Clarence and Corinne; or, God's Way* (1890) and *The Hazeley Family* (1894). All four novels are preoccupied with Christian evangelism—what some scholars of the period call "spiritual" or "domestic feminism." They are also acutely concerned with issues of sisterhood and woman's community—a textual preoccupation which often either marginalizes both men and marriage or, as in the novels of Harper and Hopkins, reconfigures men into positive, even feminized, Christian partners. Before turning to the novels themselves, however, I want to say a few more words about some of the gender conventions and ideologies of manhood and marriage that were in operation at the end of the century and their impact on the fiction of the period.

Marriageable Men and the Discourse of Deference

If "woman" is a category nineteenth-century female intellectuals placed under revision, so, too, is "man." As Hazel Carby, Claudia Tate, and a number of other scholars have noted, the association of patriarchal power with colonialism, imperialism, racial domination, and capitalism was a shared discourse among black women thinking and writing at the turn of the century. Most scholars of the period agree as well that for these early feminist and race women, patriarchy was white. "Black men exist as brothers and betrothed who do not engage in the patriarchal exchange of women," Carby writes; rather, they function fictionally (often minimally so) within "a utopian framework that accents the possibilities of relations of equality."[3]

While this observation holds largely, though not entirely, true for the fiction of the period, patriarchy at times puts on a decidedly black face in the prose of such intellectuals as Anna Julia Cooper, who chided black men for their failure to support the social and political work of black women. "While the women of the white race can with calm assurance enter upon the work they feel by nature appointed to do, while their men give loyal support," Cooper wrote in *A Voice from the South*, "the colored woman too often finds herself hampered and shamed by a less liberal sentiment and a more conservative attitude on the part of those for whose opinion she cares most."[4]

As Cooper herself acknowledged, white men were not, of course, universally supportive of the political enterprises of their wives. Nor were black men singularly unsupportive of the reformist endeavors of black women. The latter half of the nineteenth century, however, was indeed an era in which gender conventions and racial imperatives combined in creating an ideology of deference that demanded twice over the subordination of women whose labor histories alone should have made them not-so-silent partners in their gender, marital, and familial relations. Instead, much of the prescriptive literature of the era, which addressed itself to gender conduct, not only placed these women firmly in the private sphere but also made it the black woman's duty to home, hearth, and black humanity to offer her husband unconditional support in pursuit of *his* manhood rights: suffrage in the public realm and dominion in decision making, discipline, and fiscal affairs in the private.

"All women were expected to defer to men," historian James Oliver Horton argues, "but for black women deference was a racial imperative." This imperative came complete with instructions for the care and ego-feeding of the black male. A woman should "never intimidate him with her knowledge or common sense," one delegation of black men resolved, "let him feel stable and dominant."[5] Newspapers and journals such as the *Colored American* repeatedly argued that black women owed it to the race to allow their men to feel tough and protective at all costs as part of the effort to uplift the race by uplifting its male members. Mrs. N. F. Mossell, a highly regarded race woman of the late nineteenth century, offered the following critical assessment of the sexist directives with which black women of the era were bombarded:

> For several years, every paper or magazine that has fallen into our hands gave some such teaching as this: "The wife must always meet her husband with a smile." She must continue in the present and future married life to do a host of things for his comfort and convenience. . . . She must stay at home, keep the house clean, prepare food properly and care for her children, or he will frequent the saloon, go out at night and spend his time unwisely at the least. These articles may be written by men or by women, but the moral is invariably pointed for the benefit of women; one rarely appearing by either sex for the benefit of men.[6]

For newly freed blacks, men more so than women, laying claim to America meant claiming as well the gender codes of American patriarchal society, including the acceptance of monogamous, male-dominant marriage as a symbol of civility—as a sign, ironically, of *man's* liberation from the paternal incursions of slavery. (This observation recalls Jacqueline Jones's comment, noted in chapter 1, about the pride with which freedmen paraded *their* well-dressed wives.) For women, however, the prescribed power imbalance of the evolving institution of black marriage reinscribed, as Sojourner Truth warned, the oppressions of the slave system. As Horton explains:

The ideology of gender required that black men be made to feel the "king of their castle" no matter how humble the castle and no matter the hardships extracted from women who should have been treated as fully contributing partners in the family economy. So long as black liberation meant the creation of a black patriarchy, black women could not themselves be liberated. (73)

The discourse of deference, related as it was to the betterment of the race, was not easily dismissed or displaced. Nor, however, was male dominance a gender dynamic readily accepted by black women, whose resistance to *both* sexual and racial oppression took a variety of forms. In defense of black womanhood as they defined it, African American women made speeches petitioning for full participation in the body politic, including, as early as 1832, the first public address ever given by an American woman of any race: Maria Stewart's campaign against the African Colonization Movement. While Stewart lobbied on behalf of all black people, much of her political activism was decidedly woman-centered. "How long shall the fair daughters of Africa be compelled to bury their minds and talents beneath a load of iron pots and kettles?" she asked in an essay published in 1831. "How long shall a mean set of men flatter us with their smiles, and enrich themselves with our hard earnings; their wives' fingers sparkling with rings, and they themselves laughing at our folly?"[7]

Black women organized their resistance to gender as well as racial domination through the establishment of female training schools, black suffrage societies and temperance unions, and an extensive network of women's clubs which ultimately resulted in the formation of the National Association of Colored Women (NACW) in 1896. They wrote their resistance, publishing such political texts as Ida B. Wells's antilynching manifesto *Southern Horrors: Lynch Law in All Its Phases* and Cooper's *A Voice from the South*, both published in 1892; essays and articles on the status and potential of African American women by Mary Church Terrell, first president of the NACW, and Fannie Barrier Williams, as well as by Cooper and Wells; and such highly political novels as Harper's *Iola Leroy* and Hopkins's *Contending Forces*. The resistance mounted against the discourse of deference countered advice from the black media on how to be a submissive wife with demands for the higher education and professional development of black women.

Like Maria Stewart before them, Harper and Cooper maintained that the black woman's proper place was neither the white woman's kitchen nor the black man's bedroom. Cooper, in particular, lobbied long and loud for the higher education of women, not necessarily as an alternative to marriage but most definitely as an alternative to ignorance, drudgery, and dependence. Noting that its alleged interference with the natural order of marital relations was an often-voiced complaint against the classical training of women, Cooper responded:

> I grant you that intellectual development, with the self-reliance and capacity for earning a livelihood which it gives, renders woman less dependent on the

marriage relation for physical support (which, by the way, does not always accompany it). Neither is she compelled to look to sexual love as the one sensation capable of giving tone and relish, movement and vim to the life she leads. Her horizon is extended. Her sympathies are broadened and deepened and multiplied. (68–69)

Putting her own classical training in play, Cooper took on Lord Byron, as well as black men who would be lords. To the poet's claim that love "'Tis woman's whole existence" and "Men have all these resources, [women] but one / To love again and be again undone," Cooper wrote: "This may have been true when written. *It is not true to-day.* The old, subjective, stagnant, indolent and wretched life for woman has gone. She has as many resources as men, as many activities beckon her on. As large possibilities swell and inspire her heart" (70).

The possibilities for black women and men may have been large, but their immediate resources were, for the most part, far more limited than Cooper's reckoning suggests. Most of these men and women were uneducated, over-worked or unemployed, undernourished, unhealthy, and displaced—caught between the demands of their own kitchens and the white folks' kitchens, fields, and factories in which they toiled and the squalor of the southern shanties and urban slums in which they lived. In her claims for the black woman's possibilities, Cooper's feminist vision may have roved beyond the immediate material conditions of her constituency, but in most instances her sights were firmly set on the present and the effects of racial and sexual ideology on male-female relations and the institution of marriage. She was careful to note that enhanced opportunities for black women neither destroyed nor diminished their capacity for giving and sharing love; however, she also pointed out that education and the options it afforded black women did indeed affect their status in the marriage market. Women's stock and standards went up, Cooper asserted, with their education and independence, creating a "gen-der gap" as black women advanced beyond the men of the race and found themselves largely without marriageable peers. In Cooper's view, however, the issue was not how this gap diminished the educated black woman's chances for matrimony but what black men had to do to make themselves worthy partners. "The question is not with the woman 'How shall I so cramp, stunt, simplify and nullify myself as to make me eligible to the honor of being swallowed up into some little man?'" Cooper maintained, but how the man can reach "the ideal of a generation of women who demand the noblest, grandest and best achievements of which he is capable" (70–71).

Cooper's response to the discourse of deference, which dominated an in-creasingly patriarchal black community, was forceful and direct. Like much of her work, however, it was not without contradiction. Even as she argued for the political, social, educational, and financial independence of women, she demanded for them as well the patriarchal protection of black men, whom she called upon to defend black female virtue, particularly, as Louise Newman has noted so well, within the middle-class Christian home. Newman argues, in fact, that Cooper's essays "were tinged with Christian ethnocentrism" and a sense of social Darwinism that led her to marginalize Asian and non-Christian women, even as she insisted that black women be recognized as the social, moral, and intellectual equals of white women.[8] While she had a finely honed sense of the imperialist impulse and its power to colonize the female mind and body, she never quite managed to fully extricate her own mind from the tenets of true womanhood, as she proclaimed the purity and chastity—but most emphatically not the submission and domesticity—of black women.

At the same time, however, Cooper, like many of her sister activists, including Mary Church Terrell and Ida B. Wells, was the daughter of a former slave and knew well the particular legacies for black women of that peculiar institution. She *was* such a legacy. Her father was her mother's master, a relation about which Cooper knew few details since her mother was "too shamed-faced" to speak of it. Cooper and her contemporary black clubwomen gave voice to the unspoken: the continued sexual exploitation of black women left vulnerable and unprotected by law and by custom. As Paula Giddings has argued, one of the main missions of the club movement was to defend the moral integrity of *all* black women. "Significantly," Giddings writes, "this was done not by separating themselves along class lines from other women, but by defending the history of all Black women and redefining the criteria of true womanhood" (85). It was the *protection* of "true womanhood" that Cooper and other middle-class intellectuals sought for the masses of black women, who, even while the American judicial system deemed them "no more than chattel," nevertheless "maintained ideals of womanhood." These women, Cooper argued, had defended—and continued to defend—often to the death, not only their own bodies but those of their daughters. "The painful, patient, and silent toil of mothers to gain title to the bodies of their daughters," Cooper said at the World Columbian Exposition, "the despairing fight . . . to keep hallow their own persons, would furnish material for epics."[9] And so it has.

Although Cooper did not write such fictive epics, her concerns are also the concerns of those who did. The contradictory impulses in Cooper's corpus are the contradictions of the epoch—contradictions which seem to me the inevitable consequences of the complex and complicated process of self-invention and reconstruction.

Epics of Evangelism and Empowerment

According to Deborah McDowell, the mission of spiritual uplift was as urgent in the late nineteenth century as was "organizing against lynching, rape, Jim Crow, and black disenfranchisement."[10] Evangelical fiction, scholars contend, contributed to the crusade to uplift the black race by bringing souls and spirits to Christianity rather than by directly confronting racism and sexism. For, as McDowell points out, in the minds of many nineteenth-century intellectuals, "only the elevation of the spirit would obliterate racism and other 'earthly' injustice" (xxix).

While I feel a tremendous temptation to claim the novels of writers like Kelley and Johnson as narratives of black female resistance and racial empowerment, for purposes of this study my energy is perhaps better spent in attempting to situate these works within the wider discourse of nineteenth-century literary evangelism as practiced by such white women writers as Harriet Beecher Stowe and Elizabeth Stuart Phelps. The texts of Kelley and Johnson rely heavily on the conventions of the sentimental genre, building their story lines around the classic, formulaic themes of domestic management, temperance, and Christian evangelism. As such, these novels seem to me more a part of the dominant literary discourse Harper and Hopkins wrote outside of than of the textual revisionist activism in which they participated.

In the "evangelical allegories" of Emma Dunham Kelley and the "scripture lessons" of Amelia Johnson, the characters are drawn without clear racial markings, perhaps in an effort to make them and their subject matter—spiritual salvation and home protection—transcendent topics, larger than race. In *Megda*, for example, the characters are unmarked by race, except for repeated references to white skin, especially white hands and pale faces. Kelley's *Cottage City* characters are fair-skinned and blued-eyed as well, but the girls' complaints about having to sit in "nigger heaven"—the segregated, "colored only" balcony section of the theater—identify them as "black." In *Megda*, *Clarence and Corinne*, and *The Hazeley Family*, there are no such easily read clues or color codes, leading some to conclude, perhaps incorrectly, that the characters are Caucasian.

Molly Hite asserts that the "most immediate question confronting the reader of *Megda* is also the most important: what color are the characters?"[11] To query too intensely the characters' racial identity, however, may be to place undue emphasis on the very subjectivity Kelley has chosen to place under erasure. Taking as the most important question the color of the characters in any of these texts racializes precisely what the authors have endeavored to couch in religious rather than racial terms. "Whiteness," as Kelley uses it awkwardly but conventionally, is not so much a racial mark as an extended metaphor for spiritual purity in keeping with the text's and the genre's explicit concerns with religious salvation and the implied message that redemption transcends race.[12] Since these texts are evangelical allegories and not romance or realism, the color of the characters may be less important than what their racelessness signifies. In fact, as allegorical figures, these characters might be most effectively read as *raceless*—"transparent," as Kelley describes her most pious, most pure, most "white" heroine. If, as Henry Louis Gates has argued, race is "a trope of ultimate, irreducible difference,"[13] perhaps in Kelley's texts "whiteness" (however unfortunately chosen) or "transparency" is a trope of irreducible racelessness.

Yet both our critical need to know the race of these characters and the authors' textual need to use whiteness as the signifier of piety and purity point to the impossibility of the racelessness that Kelley and some of her contemporaries theorized. For them spiritual worth seems not to have been possible in color or conceivable as nonwhite. Ultimately, however, I am far more concerned about our racial coding than about their color schemes. Kelley and Johnson may simply have called the Christian's bluff, as it were, textually disembodying characters whose spiritual salvation was their primary concern. Or they may merely have invoked the dominant metaphors of their day. But what does it suggest about our interpretive needs as critics and our interpellation as subjects of racial ideology if we assume that figures not clearly identified as black or white are necessarily the latter? In any case, all metaphors aside, it is important to note as well that if these characters are presented without clear racial coding it is likely at least in part because such "ethnic neutrality," to use Hortense Spillers's term, was the price of publication in the repressive racial and political climate of the 1890s.[14]

The courtship that occurs in these evangelical texts is, for the most part, the wooing of souls into Christianity rather than men and women into marriage. In fact, in Johnson's work in particular, marriage is oddly marginalized, reported upon rather than represented in the final moments of the text as a kind of inevitable afterthought. First comes God, then comes marriage (we rarely get as far as the baby carriage). And they lived happily ever after—in church. Matrimony, then, in these texts, is at once a ubiquitous subject and a marginal one, as the marriage *ideal* is championed without attention to the inner workings of the marriage *relation*. In keeping with convention, in novel after the novel the "loose ends" of social, racial, and spiritual conflict are neatly tied up with the binding knot of wedlock, creating what might be called an "ideal estate." Yet many of these texts which end in the heroine's marriage are not without their own critiques of this other peculiar institution or, more specifically, of patriarchal versions of the institution.

Four Girls at Cottage City

In Emma Dunham Kelley's *Four Girls at Cottage City* (1898), for example, women's culture—what Carroll Smith-Rosenberg has called "the female world of love and ritual"—is privileged, rather than courtship or marriage.[15] A vacation cottage room becomes a summer sanctuary for four apparently working-class and lower-middle-class city girls: sisters Jessie and Garnet Dare and their friends, Vera Earle and Allie Hunt. Their three-week vacation becomes a rite of passage from the "happy, light-hearted, careless, gay" days of callow youth into the maturity, selflessness, and charity of womanhood and Christianity.

Although males are by no means absent from *Cottage City*, the few present are, for the most part, harmless, hovering boys or grandfatherly older men. Mr. Atherton, for example, the kind, old "Grandpa" who, with his wife, operates the Martha's Vineyard cottage at which Kelley's heroines spend their vacation, is not permitted to get too close to his female guests. "Mother," his wife, is clearly the "ruling spirit" of Hotel d' Atherton; she gently but "determinedly" keeps Grandpa in his proper place—in the shadows, perpetually behind her. When he tries to step around Mother's protective shield, her "slender, aged hand quickly force[s] him back again, and he retire[s] obediently" (37). Mother, then, functions as a protective screen between the girls and Grandpa, using her body to shield the girls' from his "peering" male gaze and to physically prohibit him from entering what the text presents as a female sanctum or, as Deborah McDowell suggests, "a woman's room" (xxxv).

The girls' two gentlemen callers are also depicted as intruders, but, unlike Mr. Atherton, they are allowed momentary, if not entirely welcomed, entry into the female realm, perhaps foreshadowing the roles these two young men will ultimately play in the girls' daily lives. For the moment, anyway, the boys are nuisances, interlopers who have no place in the female realm—in the intimate spaces of these young girls' lives. Jessie Dare conveys this sentiment directly when she announces at one point that she is not going to the theater with her girlfriends and the two ubiquitous boys, whom the girls have not been able to get rid of since meeting them on the ferry to the Vineyard:

> I'm not going because I'm tired to death of having those two fellows tied to our apron strings everywhere we go. We can't move but what "the *gen-tle-men* will *call* for us at such and *such* a time." . . . When we came down here I thought we four girls were going around together and have a good time. There's no fun when there's a parcel of men around. (129)

This petulant outburst of resistance to male society is followed immediately by peals of laughter, first from Vera Earle and then from the other girls, as Vera and Jessie tumble onto the bed together, laughing in what becomes a hilarious melee of rolling, hugging female bodies. (The juxtaposition of these two scenes is ripe for psychosexual analysis: the rejection of the male at one moment and the grasping and rolling on the bed with the female at the next.) Vera's infectious laughing spell was brought on, she explains, by the fervor of Jessie's scornful, antimale sentiments. Vera, closer to womanhood than her younger companion, suspects that Jessie's girlish distaste for male society is likely to change as she matures. "I hope when you are twenty-seven," she chuckles, "you will be as indignant at having a 'parcel of men' around as you are at seventeen" (130–31). Vera's voice in this passage is the knowing voice of reason, which acknowledges, as the text itself does, the *necessity*, but not the *centrality*, of men in the lives of women.[16]

The marginal status of both men and marriage in *Cottage City* is part of a utopian vision not unlike that of Stowe and other white nineteenth-century women evangelicals, for whom the grandly constructive work of saving the world is indeed the work of *Christian* women. Truly Christian men, however—especially men whose Christianity is rooted in kindness and charity (coded in the text as feminine) rather than dogma and didacticism (coded as masculine)—can be part of this work as well, it seems. Both Fred Travers and Erfort Richards prove themselves not only worthy, respectful friends of womanhood but loyal champions of humanity and Christian charity when they join the girls in helping an impoverished laundrywoman named Charlotte Hood and her crippled son, Robin. Mrs. Hood, who Vera says wears a sermon of suffering and redemption on her "luminous" face, functions in the text as the spiritual minister who, by both word and example, brings the young people to Christ. The coupling with which this novel is primarily concerned, then, is not between man and woman but between the unredeemed and Christ.

Once this all-important evangelical union has been achieved through the ministry of Charlotte Hood, Kelley can turn her attention to the spirits of the flesh.

In what is structurally an appendix set five years after the Cottage City vacation, we rejoin the girls and boys, now women and men, as Jessie Dare, once determined to be an "old maid," marries none other than the same Erfort Richards whose attention she earlier scorned. Vera, we learn in this same scene, has married "Cousin Fred" Travers, and it is in their home in Pawtucket, Rhode Island, that Jessie and Erfort are about to exchange vows. The good couple say "I do," and the novel concludes, it seems, quite conventionally with a simple nuptial ceremony, uniting Christian friends. It is important to note, however, that even married, Vera and Jessie have scarcely left the female world of love and ritual; they have merely opened a door in a corner of that world to admit their feminized, lustless mates, men with whom the narrator assures us "we can safely trust our little girl[s]" (374). Kelley, then, extends the matrifocality that has dominated the novel into her heroines' utopian marital relations. Humanized through their close contact with a community of women, feminized men are adopted into a female subculture, where best friends and their husbands live next door to each other and all parties are committed to lifetimes of Christian service.

Megda

In *Megda*, as in *Cottage City*, Kelley foregrounds female community, locating much of the novel's action in and around the girls' school in which the central characters live out their adolescence. Largely from the perspective of Megda Randal, Kelley traces the woman-centered development and male-centered spiritual conversion of several female friends as they move from callow, carefree schoolgirls to responsible, Christian women, spiritually fit to take on the traditional roles of wives and mothers within decidedly Christian marriages. The novel revolves around funny, feisty, independent Megda, who preaches gender equality and despises what she views as the deceit and hypocrisy of Christianity and the weakness of women, who she believes should claim equal footing with men. She is openly critical of her girlfriends, who she feels lack "firmness of mind, independence of thought and action," and contemptuous of their conversions to Christianity (64). Despite her lack of faith in just about anyone or anything except herself, Megda is beloved of all — family, friends, teachers — except the devious, deceitful, and of course doomed Maude, who is as openly jealous of Megda as Megda is contemptuous of her.

The opening pages of the text find Megda and her friends and schoolmates on the cusp of both womanhood and Christianity, just moments away from the rituals and rites of baptism, graduation, and marriage. Megda experiences a triple sense of loss and resentment as she loses first the shelter of the safe, familiar girls' school environment and then the intimate society of her girlfriends as, one by one, they are claimed by God, by men, and by marriage. The refrain from family, friends, and pastor — "Oh, what a Christian she will make"—suggests that it is only a matter of time before Megda, too, is claimed by the Lord. Indeed, she does eventually "find the peace that passeth understanding" by giving herself to God, and in so doing becomes a candidate not only for baptism but for the sacrament of holy wedlock.

The leading candidate for husband is the Reverend Arthur Stanley, who is presented as an uncompromisingly good man, perhaps the finest specimen of "true manhood"—piety, purity, benevolent paternity, and domesticity—who ever walked the pages of women's fiction. Even the unsanctified Megda is impressed with and attracted to the young Baptist minister, who clearly looks upon her with considerable affection. Their first encounter provides the reader with some of the best fun among the serious subject matter of the period. Walking home in a blustering rainstorm, Megda meets Mr. Stanley, who gallantly offers her the strength of his arm and the protection of his umbrella. The wind promptly dances with and totally demolishes the umbrella and then sends Stanley's hat flying as well. In "hot pursuit after the whirling hat," Megda and Stanley crash into each other and knock each other down, "Megda having the added humiliation of knowing that she was sitting squarely on the hat" (281, 21). The scene is funny enough, but the good laugh the two have over it and the extended joke they make of it render it even more so. Stanley asks for a ribbon from Megda with which to secure the hat on his head long enough to walk her home. He keeps the ribbon and sends her the deformed hat by special messenger the next day.

The encounter has all the warmth and innocent charm of courtship ritual and suggests that these two will be wed by novel's end. Friends and family both note the reverend's interest in Megda and, like the reader, expect a romance. Megda's brother Hal, for example, notices Mr. Stanley staring at his sister in church and mischievously kicks Megda's foot under the pew and calls her attention to the minister's "dark-blue eyes gazing earnestly at her" (111). However, the promised romance is forestalled, it seems permanently, by what the text presents as Megda's unworthiness. Her obstinateness, her lack of both Christian faith and human charity, stand in the way of her marrying the holy Arthur Stanley. At one point the good Reverend Stanley takes it upon himself to apprise Megda of her shortcomings:

> You are a girl of noble impulses, although you do not always follow them. Your character is made up of contradictory points. . . . You are liable to scoff at the wisdom of superior minds. . . . You have little patience with your weaker sisters. . . . You have a keen perception; you are quick to see the faults of others, but are most unnaturally blind to your own. (181)

Stanley is particularly well positioned to offer this last criticism, since he is depicted without fault. The reckoning goes on for three pages, finally concluding with the advice that all Megda really needs to do is make herself worthy of herself (and, by implication, worthy of Stanley). "You can do this in only one way," the reverend informs his pupil. "Give yourself, just as you are, to the Saviour. Do not try to make yourself better by your own strength—you cannot do it," he continues. "Take the accomplishments He has given you and consecrate them and yourself all to His glory, and your life will be one of God's most perfect creations" (183). The text's mission is, of course, evangelical, and Stanley's advice is meant to extend beyond Megda to all the unredeemed among us who have not yet entrusted ourselves and our souls to God and his anointed shepherds such as Reverend Stanley.

As her punishment for not accepting Jesus Christ as her personal savior soon enough, Megda has to stand faithfully and cheerfully by as maid of honor as her childhood friend, the very good, very devout, very rich, very perfect, and very "white" Ethel Lawton prepares to marry the equally perfect Arthur Stanley, to whom, unlike feisty, proud, irreverent Megda, she is "the very pearl of womanhood" (265). Now a Christian, baptized in the river like Jesus, Megda has been divested of her judgmental tendencies and suddenly feels only the deepest love and admiration for all of her girlhood friends. Formerly fiercely competitive, she experiences no sense of rivalry with the saintly Ethel, even though she has won the affection of the man for whom Megda, too, has romantic feelings. The three—Arthur Stanley, the ominously (and conveniently) sickly Ethel, and Megda—share and delight in a special friendship, a holy trinity.

The day before Ethel and Arthur's wedding, all the girls gather at the bride's home for a series of scenes much like those described by Smith-Rosenberg as rituals of female bonding: laughing, trying on dresses, hugging and teasing each other. But, contrary to both tradition and superstition, Stanley is present for the last of these rituals, as Ethel and Megda put on their gowns and present themselves for his approval. Both women are wearing white, but Stanley, who has made his choice, has no problem claiming his rightful bride; "oblivious to Meg's presence," he takes Ethel into his arms and calls her "wife." It is a title the frail Ethel will enjoy only metaphorically. Too good for life on earth, like the heroines of so many nineteenth-century sentimental novels, she is claimed by a male power even stronger than Stanley's and dies on the morning of her wedding day. In a tearful ceremony, she is buried in her wedding dress.

While hardly a scene original with Kelley, this wedding-day death and wedding-gown burial reflect an ambivalence about marriage that is threaded throughout the novel. Marriage, we are told more than once, is the thing that breaks the "golden chain" of female friendship. It is also, as Megda thinks at one point, "almost as solemn a thing as death" (318). Ethel's death reproduces the classic sentimental plot in which the sainted, virginal heroine—too good for life on evil earth and, by implication, too pure for sex in marriage—is spared the taint of both by the gift of death. Ethel is the kind of angelic female figure who exists solely to serve as what Nina Baym calls "living lessons for others." Baym suggests that these perfect heroines are representations not of womanhood but of sainthood. "[T]hese characters are not models of what every woman should try to achieve or become," Baym writes. "They exist on another plane, in humanity but not of it, and their Christlike function is not limited or directed to gender."[17] If Ethel, as the patron saint of *Megda*, is an icon to be worshiped, Megda is a model to be emulated. Exorcised of excessive pride and a host of other sinful passions, she becomes a true Christian. And she gets, if not her man, Ethel's.

However solemn and deathlike the institution of marriage, its reproductive function is also essential to the evangelical mission. Marry each other and be fruitful and multiply is what good Christians do. In the four years following Ethel's wedding-day demise, most of Megda's friends marry or become engaged to good, Christian men from the girls' inner circle of friends. May, Maude, and Megda are each, in quite different ways, exceptions to the series of couplings that Megda complains breaks the links in the golden chain of friendship. Lest the reader think her undesirable, Megda, too, is given her chance at matrimony: she receives and rejects a sudden, completely unexpected, and entirely unwelcome proposal from Professor Weir, one of the teachers at her alma mater, where she has been hired to teach elocution. Her friend May gives away "her chance" at marriage. Realizing that her girlfriend Ruth and her boyfriend, Melvin, love each other—"all unconsciously," of course—May, "like a heroine in a romance . . . nobly sacrificed [her] own love and happiness to theirs," vowing to live her life as an "old maid" (361–63). Maude, who was actually the first of the group to marry, is spoken of as being "literally lost" to her friends (301). Deceitful and calculating, Maude is a marginal figure in the community of young women, who after her marriage to a man from outside the circle of friends disappears from the text until the end.[18]

The nostalgia Megda experiences at losing even the troublesome Maude becomes active resistance to the idea of her best friend Laurie's marrying. As Megda asserts at one point, she loves Laurie too dearly to surrender any part of her friend's affection, even to her own beloved brother, Hal, Laurie's intended. (Laurie, by the way, is the same best friend described by the unsaved Megda as weak, mindless, and easily led.) Both for Megda and for the author, this marriage resistance seems to mark the transition from the homosocial world of adolescent love and ritual to the heterosexual world of mature womanhood—a transition rooted in ambivalence and nostalgia. Yet Megda, who loves teaching and "could never be satisfied with leading an idle life," promptly forgets her career ambitions and her resistance to marriage when Stanley finally proposes (314).

As in *Cottage City*, the last chapter of *Megda* leaps five years into the future, where the reader is given a glimpse of the ideal estate of the Reverend and Mrs. Arthur Stanley. The Stanley home, like its patriarch, is "a perfect little nest of beauty and comfort . . . planned by Arthur himself and built for *him* as a wedding present by Judge Lawton [Ethel's father] and furnished according to Meg's tastes by Judge Lawton's wife" (376; emphasis added). An acquiescent Megda who would willingly allow others to design and decorate her home may not be easy for the modern reader to conceptualize. Indeed, the traditional Christian wife and mother Megda becomes in the last chapter seems plotted in contradistinction to the independent, proud, even feminist spirit exhibited by the young schoolgirl who preached gender equality and female independence. But there is more to tickle the feminist consciousness:

"Even after five years of constant companionship with such a man as Mr. Stanley," we are told, "Meg is yet far from being perfect." Stanley's perfection, on the other hand, is confirmed by Kelley's comment that Megda's husband "loves every little fault in her." It seems that the old Megda, who loved herself and her female friends fiercely, has been humbled by Christianity: the saved, married Megda sees herself as unworthy of either her husband or "her Father's love and mercy" in blessing her with such a man and such a marriage. Self-love and sister love have been replaced by love of God and love of *a* man, which seem oddly conflated in the person of Arthur Stanley.

So pure of heart is the new, saved, married Megda that, like many fictional nineteenth-century second wives, she is apparently untroubled by the lingering shadow of her Stanley's perfect first love, even giving the name Ethel to the daughter born to her and Arthur:

> Meg knew how much Ethel had been to Mr. Stanley, and Mr. Stanley knew that Meg knew it, and although he loved Meg deeply and tenderly now, he knew and she knew, that there was a corner of his heart where even she could never enter. And Meg was glad that it was so. Had he forgotten thus early and easily, he would not—to Meg—have seemed worthy of either her love or Ethel's. (373)

These, too, are popular sentiments of the nineteenth century, when wives (and children) often died young and were promptly replaced. Children were named in honor of deceased wives, siblings, and other lost loved ones. (Stowe, for example, named her twin daughters Harriet after herself and Eliza after her husband's first wife.) Nevertheless, Megda's assent in all marital matters seems far removed from the spirit of the young woman who refused to cast herself (or her similarly independent friend) as the acquiescent Ophelia in a school play because she could not imagine either of them meekly accepting being jilted by Hamlet. "No, girls," Megda explained to her friends, "I cannot imagine Dell speaking like that to any man any more than I can imagine myself doing it" (44–45).

Neither can the reader. But, then, Stanley is no Hamlet. Though we are told that Stanley has learned how to control Megda with a look, the text presents the reverend not as an overbearing patriarch but as a "tender, loving husband"—a spiritual guide and protector—in keeping with its positive portrayal of *Christian* men (376). This construction is quite a thing apart from the feminist vision of *Cottage City*, in which a woman serves as spiritual guide and minister in a decidedly maternal ecclesiastical order. I cannot help wondering if the seven years between the publication of *Megda* and *Cottage City* and perhaps the author's own maturity and marriage account in some measure for the differences in vision. *Megda* is a schoolgirl's romantic fantasy; *Cottage City* is a woman's. But the contradictions of *Megda*, on the other hand, may be nothing more elaborate than signs of the lingering tension between the unreconciled impulses of woman's culture in transition: between "true woman" as phallocentric wife and mother and "new woman" as gynocentric feminist.

Clarence and Corinne and The Hazeley Family

Amelia Johnson's two novels *Clarence and Corinne; or, God's Way* (1890) and *The Hazeley Family* (1894) are also conventional moral polemics concerned with women's spiritual and domestic development and with home protection, linking them to the "angel of the home" strain of nineteenth-century women's fiction. Despite the "racelessness" of these texts, the concern with the sanctity of the home places them at the center of African American sociopolitical discourse. Children were the wealth and the future of the black nation. As the birthplace and nursery of future generations, the home was the focal point of social reform for activists like Mary Church Terrell, who believed in uplifting the race by uplifting its youth. As black clubwoman Josephine Bruce, wife of Reconstruction-era Mississippi senator Blanche Bruce, explained:

> The Negro home is rapidly assuming the position designated for it. It is distinctly becoming the center of social and intellectual life; it is building up strength and righteousness in its sons and daughters, and equipping them for the inevitable battles of life which grow out of the struggle for existence.[19]

Both of Johnson's novels present young characters whose lives are torn asunder and set on the wrong path by wayward parents who fail to equip their children for life's inevitable battles. For Clarence and Corinne Burton, the failed parent is a "heartless" father and for Flora Hazeley, a "careless" mother. Children in both novels, for a time anyway, are displaced from their rightful homes or, through the effects of poverty, death, and "demon alcohol," are denied the protection of parental guidance and, by Western standards, "normal," nuclear family and home life. Clarence and Corinne's earliest years are spent in abject poverty; they are too poor even to go to school because they have nothing to wear but rags. Their father is an alcoholic who drinks and gambles away his meager earnings. Numb from poverty and from emotional and physical battering, their "poor broken-spirited, abused" mother is benignly rather than maliciously neglectful like her husband. When their mother dies of a heart condition (meant to be read as a broken heart) and their father abandons them, the two children are separated, sent off in separate directions and down different paths. Despite the obstacles placed in "their way," the central characters of both novels ultimately find "God's Way" and manage to become responsible, professional men—doctors and ministers are particular favorites—and domestic-minded women, most of whom marry by novel's end and establish "good Christian homes." But while both novels end with weddings, they feature quite different couplings.

In *Clarence and Corinne*, brother and sister siblings marry brother and sister siblings—Charlie and Bebe Reade—who were all best friends at one point in their youth. The four set up housekeeping together under the same roof, thus reuniting families and friends torn from each other by poverty and social pathology. Here, too, it seems, familiarity breeds content; or, as Hortense Spillers suggests: in marrying their gender doubles, Clarence and Corinne get to "have their cake and eat it too" (xxxv). They find the brother and sister they never had, as well as husband and wife. Clarence and Corinne also "parent" each other in a way their mother and father did not. Clarence, who becomes a doctor, provides a home first for his dearly loved, long-lost sister, who keeps house for him, and then for his extended family, which also includes his father-in-law and spiritual minister, Reverend Reade.

It may shed some light on the text's structural and stylistic shortcomings and its relationship to other nineteenth-century evangelical fictions to say that these unions and reunions all occur in the closing moments of the novel. In yet another appendix that leaps an unspecified number of years ahead, the story's loose ends are swiftly tied with a pair of wedding knots. "[T]here was a marriage speedily," Johnson writes, "and the bride was Bebe Reade, while the groom was Dr. Burton. There was another, also, soon after. This time Corinne Burton and Charley Reade took the principal parts" (186–87). This hastily delivered, "all's well that ends well" conclusion suggests once again the extent to which marriage is ancillary to the proselytizing and moralizing that are Johnson's major concerns. The multiple marriages also draw all of the wanderers into the social fold after the fashion of the classical comedy.

Both of Johnson's novels were published by the American Baptist Publication Society and were apparently well received in their day in both white and black religious communities, which appreciated the texts as the Christian exemplars they were intended to be. Quoting from Baltimore's *Baptist Messenger*, Hortense Spillers notes, for example, that for black religious publications like the *Messenger* Johnson's work "'is one of the silent, yet powerful agents at work to break down unreasonable prejudice, which is a hindrance to both races.' From this angle," Spillers argues, "it is unimportant exactly *what* and *how* Mrs. Johnson wrote, but altogether significant *that* she did" (xxviii). I would argue that while the fact that Johnson wrote at all was certainly important to the black community looking for models and representatives, *what* she wrote was extremely important to her contemporary religious and reform-minded audiences.

In Johnson's second novel, *The Hazeley Family*, it is not the heroine Flora Hazeley who marries in the final chapter, entitled "A Homely Wedding," but the younger brother she has nurtured. Flora functions as a surrogate mother for much of the novel, transforming her disorderly home into a happy, healthy, warm environment and, in effect, teaching her good but "careless" mother how to parent. In presenting Flora as a *single* homemaker who finds joy and fulfillment in serving others, Kelley implies an important social function for women independent of marriage, but a function still decidedly domestic. Flora Hazeley is one of few leading female characters still unmarried or unengaged by novel's end. She, too, however, stands firmly within her own time as an important social figure—a cultural custodian and keeper of the sacred realm of the home.

An Unmarried True Woman

The importance and political potential of the independent unmarried woman outside of the home is well illustrated in a short story by the multitalented Frances Harper. In "The Two Offers" (1859), believed to be the first published short story by an African American, Harper presents a heroine generally (and perhaps incorrectly) presumed white—though nothing marks her racially except perhaps her class—named Janette Alston, who chooses a career as a writer and a vocation as an antislavery activist, not necessarily *instead* of loving a man but *because* of loving herself, her genius, her potential. Her story of social action, civic success, and personal and professional fulfillment is juxtaposed to that of her cousin Laura Lagrange, who suffers through an unfortunate union with a man who "look[s] upon marriage not as divine sacrament for the soul's development and human progression, but as the title deed that gave him possession of the woman he thought he loved."[20] Laura dies alone, calling in vain for the wayward husband who fails her in death as in life. Janette, on the other hand, without husband or child of her own, is loved by all those whose lives she brightens through her social-welfare activism and her literary offerings.

Like Flora Hazeley, Janette Alston achieves true woman status through the alternative means identified by Barbara Welter in her study of nineteenth-century gender ideology. According to Welter, marriage was the best but by no means the only entrée into the realm of true womanhood in the nineteenth century. Much of the prescriptive literature of the period advocated remaining single above entering into the kind of bad marriages that Laura Lagrange and *Megda*'s Maude Leonard make. "Maiden ladies," Welter writes, were depicted in women's magazines as "unselfish ministers to the sick, teachers of the young, or moral preceptors with their pens, beloved of the entire village."[21] It is such unmarried, unselfish social ministers that both Amelia Johnson's novel and Frances Harper's story present.

Harper's fiction presents something else as well, however, rewriting, if not completely debunking, the notion and limitations of the ideology of true womanhood. "The Two Offers" is a parable of sorts whose title is a double entendre, referring to both the two marriage proposals Laura Lagrange is contemplating at the opening of the tale and to the two cousins' ultimately quite different offerings to society. And here, too, the larger messages the author wants to convey transcend race. Harper argues that because of the way females are socialized, because of ideologies of womanhood *and* manliness, the "all-consuming love" women are trained to want is likely to be just that—all-consuming, the only thing they have. Expressing sentiments that seem a hundred years ahead of their time, Harper writes:

> Talk as you will of woman's deep capacity for loving—of the strength of her affectional nature. I do not deny it. But will the mere possession of any human love fully satisfy all the demands of her whole being? You may paint her in poetry or fiction as a frail vine, clinging to her brother man for support and

dying when deprived of it, and all this may sound well enough to please the imaginations of schoolgirls, or lovelorn maidens. But woman—the true woman—if you would render her happy, it needs more than the mere development of her affectional nature. Her conscience should be enlightened, her faith in the true and right established, and scope given to her heaven-endowed and God-given faculties. (64, 65)

Ultimately arguing for the higher education and training of women and not just for their benefit but for the greater good of society at large, Harper continues:

> The true aim of female education should be, not a development of one or two, but all the faculties of the human soul, because no perfect womanhood is developed by imperfect culture. Intense love is often akin to intense suffering, and to trust the whole wealth of a woman's nature on the frail bark of human love may often be like trusting a cargo of gold and precious gems to a bark that has never battled with the storm or buffeted the waves. (65)

Harper's (I think) self-consciously subversive critique of ideology and gender conventions anticipated by a hundred years *The Feminine Mystique* and the rise of radical feminism. While Kelley and Johnson toyed with the "ideal" of holy wedlock, Harper, in her poetry, prose, and politics, addressed herself to the "real" of the marital relation, identifying marriage as an institution externally beneficial to society but internally fraught with misery and self-denial for women. Writers of the twenties, thirties, and forties will extend Harper's analysis of the other peculiar institution in increasingly intimate detail, using the coupling convention as the launching pad for a wide-ranging critique of patriarchal ideology and social values.

4

Blues Notes on Black Sexuality:
Sex and the Texts of the
Twenties and Thirties

> Because there was a man somewhere in a candystripe silk shirt,
> gracile and dangerous as a jaguar and because a woman moaned
> for him in sixty-watt gloom and mourned him Faithless Love
> Twotiming Love Oh Love Oh Careless Aggravating Love,
>
> > She came out on the stage in yards of pearls, emerging like
> > a favorite scenic view, flashed her golden smile and sang.
>
> —ROBERT HAYDEN, from "Homage to the Empress of the Blues"

Jazz. Blues. Boogie-woogie, black bottom, shimmy, shake, and mess around. Black bodies moving by the millions from southern shacks to northern slums, moving to the beat of the New Negro in a new world. Freud. Sex. Speakeasies and bootlegged gin. Marcus Garvey. Victory in Europe. Breadlines. Unemployment. Race riots and mob violence. Rent parties and literary salons. Detroit. Chicago. *Home to Harlem*. *Nigger Heaven*. The "authentic," "real colored thing." Josephine Baker. Ma Rainey. Bessie Smith. "Love Oh Love Oh Careless Aggravating Love."

For many students of the 1920s and 1930s, few icons represent the "truth" of a moment at once the best of times and the worst of times as dramatically as the image of the black women blues artists who sang of sex and love, loss and longing. For black poet Robert Hayden, who grew up in the slums of Detroit in the twenties and thirties, the blues were black truth, and blues artists like Bessie Smith, whom he memorialized in the poem excerpted above, were lifelines reaching back through northern ghettos into the rural reaches of the Deep South. Bessie, as Hayden heard her, sang "about the uncertainties and sorrows of life as poor Negro people knew them—especially those who had not been out of the South very long."[1] While blues women such as Bessie Smith and Ma Rainey perhaps sang most often of erotic encounters, their songs captured as well the material conditions of a society in flux.

For Hayden and for millions of his contemporaries, the blues—"folk" blues, "classic" blues, "race-record" blues—are signifying art forms that grew out of and speak to the emotional, social, and cultural dimensions of both southern rural and northern urban black American historical experiences. Driven from the South by poverty, lynch law and Jim Crow rule, mechanization, and the myriad hardships of sharecropping, hundreds of thousands of southern blacks (more than 2 million in the first three decades of the century alone) migrated north in successive waves that swelled and blackened urban centers such as Chicago, Detroit, Philadelphia, and New York between the last decades of the nineteenth century and the Great Depression. Installed in these modern environs, newly arrived blacks often found that while the North might hold certain advantages in terms of employment and education, the urban metropolis was by no means the promised land they had left the South in search of. They often found that they had traded country shacks for city tenements, cotton fields for urban factories (when indeed they could find factory work). But while the fields had at least been familiar territory, the modern city was a foreign realm with a wealth of new experiences that challenged their values, their faith, their endurance, and sometimes their sanity. Some members of the new black urban proletariat were swept into the whirlwind of the clubs and cabarets. Others turned more deeply into their religions, finding comfort and shelter in the storefront churches that lined the streets of almost every black neighborhood. Still others were drawn into the thriving literary and cultural life of bohemian Harlem, propelled into the explosion of artistic activity that for a time made Harlem reportedly the most important black cultural center in the world.

This chapter, however, is not primarily a study of the Great Migration, the Great Depression, the Great War, or even the "great sex" sung by such blues artists as Bessie Smith, Ma Rainey, and Ida Cox. This section of the study focuses on a slightly different cultural form, what I call the "bourgeois blues"—the cultural commentaries of black women writers, most of whom have traditionally been positioned outside of and separate from the blues modality. This chapter and the two that follow explore the different ways in which three black women writers of the twenties and thirties—Jessie Fauset, Nella Larsen, and Zora Neale Hurston—use coupling as a metaphor through which to examine and critique the color consciousness, class stratification, social conventions, and gender relations of their burgeoning black middle- and working-class communities. I argue that while these writers sang their own brand of "somebody done somebody wrong" songs about shifting gender and social relations, with the exception of Zora Neale Hurston, their contributions to the Jazz Age, the Harlem Renaissance, the Roaring Twenties have often been covered over by the stellar performances of blues artists such as Bessie Smith and Ma Rainey, whose songs have become synonymous with the moment.

For cultural critic Hazel Carby, reading the period more than half a century later, blues singers of bygone days are an "empowered presence," pioneers who claimed their sexual subjectivity through their songs and produced a black women's discourse on black sexuality.[2] For literary theorist Houston Baker, the blues constitute "a vibrant network"—the "'always already' of Afro-American culture," the "multiplex, enabling *script* in which Afro-American cultural discourse is inscribed."[3]

Carby's observation reflects the efforts of contemporary feminist criticism to establish black women as active agents within history rather than as helpless victims of history. Her words also demonstrate the leadership role she has played in moving African American cultural studies out of the realm of the intellectual, where the written words of the literati have been privileged, into the world of the material, where other cultural forms such as the blues await analysis. Baker's assertion, on the other hand, reflects the extent to which contemporary literary and cultural theory has already made the blues—and the kind and quality of black life the form depicts—the metonym for authentic blackness. As Carby has argued elsewhere, contemporary African American cultural criticism is actively engaged in "recreating a romantic discourse of a rural black folk in which to situate the source of an Afro-American culture."[4] The quintessential signifers of the folk are the blues, on the one hand, and Zora Neale Hurston, on the other.

In *Blues, Ideology and Afro-American Literature: A Vernacular Theory*, Baker not only situates the southern rural folk experience as the source of African American culture, he makes such sitings an intellectual imperative, arguing that the blues should be privileged in the study of American culture as a way of remapping "expressive geographies" in the United States. "My own ludic uses of the blues are various," he maintains, "and each refiguration implies the valorization of vernacular facets of American culture" (11). Demonstrating just how broad and varied his claims for the blues are, Baker goes on to suggest that "blues energy" may be found in "unlikely expressive spaces in Afro-America." Of these spaces and those who would map them, he writes that

> a properly trained critic—one versed in the vernacular and unconstrained by traditional historical determinants—may well be able to discover blues inscriptions and liberating rhythms even in some familiarly neglected works of Afro-American expressive culture. Who, after all, has dismissed such works? Normally, they have been written off by commentators (black and white alike) constrained by a single standard of criticism. Who is to decipher such neglected expressive instances? Surely, the blues critic is the most likely agent. (115)

Ironically, Baker's vernacular theory of a blues matrix and a germinal black folk culture is itself in danger of becoming a constraining "single standard of criticism"—a contemporary convention that too often dismisses rather then deciphers, excludes rather than explores. Claiming the blues and the folk as the grand signifiers of *the* black experience leaves the blues critic little room to decipher other inscriptions and liberating rhythms. Too often writers whose expressive geographies are perceived as lying outside the blues space are not remapped but *de*mapped. While Hurston and her southern rural settings are privileged in such a construction, other black women novelists, whose settings are the urban North and whose subjects are middle-class black women, are not only dismissed in the name of the vernacular, they are condemned (along with the critics who read them) for historical conservatism. They are marginalized within or excluded from the construction of an African American literary canon for, as Baker asserts in his recent study of black female expressivity, "willfully refus[ing] to conceptualize a southern, vernacular ancestry as a site of both consuming violence and discrete value."[5] In this critical construction, no other site has black cultural currency.

Moreover, the complex and often uniquely female psychic and physical violence that propels many "familiarly neglected" women's novels remains undeciphered: the devastating consequences of John Langley's attempt to blackmail Sappho Clark into becoming his mistress in *Contending Forces*, for example, or the numerous and perhaps ultimately killing pregnancies of Helga Crane Green in Nella Larsen's *Quicksand* (1928), or the rabid racial self-hatred and class pretensions of white-skinned Olivia Blanchard Cary, whose heartless rejection of her brown-skinned son drives him to suicide in Jessie Fauset's *Comedy: American Style* (1933).

However attractive and culturally affirming, the valorization of the vernacular has yielded what I would argue is an inherently exclusionary literary practice that filters a wide range of complex and often contradictory impulses and energies into a single modality consisting of the blues and the folk. In this chapter I call into question the utopian trend in contemporary cultural criticism that readily reads resistance in such privileged, so-called authentically black discourses as the classic blues of the 1920s and the folkloric fiction of Zora Neale Hurston, while denigrating other cultural forms for their perceived adherence to and promotion of traditional (white) values. Raising questions about the "primitivism" and "racialism" of the early twentieth century and what I call the "Hurstonism" of contemporary cultural criticism, I argue that much of the discourse that champions the sexual "self-invention" and "authenticity" of blues queens such as Bessie Smith and signifying sisters such as Zora Neale Hurston does so without examining the reflexive nature of the invention, without interrogating the role of ideology in shaping the period, its artists, and its attention both to the folk and to black female sexuality.

To set the stage for the textual readings of Fauset's, Larsen's, and Hurston's work that follow in chapters 5 and 6, I want to position these authors within the ethos of the Harlem era. This includes assessing the impact of "Hurstonism"—the conspicuous consumption of Zora Neale Hurston as the initiator of the African American (woman's) literary tradition—on the critical construction of Fauset and Larsen. Within and against the backdrop of racialism and primitivism, these writers launched their critiques and sang their particular versions of the blues. Thanks in large measure to reconsiderations by a number of black feminist critics, more positive attention has been directed toward the passion and politics of Fauset's and Larsen's work, as well as that of the better-known Hurston—to their concerns with female sexuality, for example, and with gender, power, and social relations.

While much of my own work argues against merely replacing traditional determinants of intellectual and literary history with vernacular theories of cultural production built primarily on the blues, I attempt in this second part of the study to take up Baker's challenge, to identify what might be called "blues inscriptions" in the works of Fauset and Larsen, as well as Hurston. Though by no means as risqué and ripe with sexual innuendo as the lyrics sung by Bessie Smith, the often parodic prose of Fauset's, Larsen's, and Hurston's "bourgeois blues" also takes as its principal subject the concern with black female desire and erotic relationships that occupies the classic blues. And here, too, the theme is not only men and women in love, lust, and longing, but societies in transition and power relations in flux.

Yet if it is possible to decipher blues inscriptions in the prose of Fauset and Larsen, as well as Hurston, it is also possible to trace *anti*blues inscriptions in their novels. As I read them, their texts are unique in their attention to the extremes of their historical moment and the powers of competing ideologies and colliding material conditions. While Hazel Carby argues, quite convincingly, that "different cultural forms negotiate and resolve different sets of social contradictions,"[6] I would argue that Fauset and Larsen were acutely aware of and fully engaged with a wider range of social conditions and ideological apparatuses than many critics have acknowledged. They both wrote within and defined themselves against what Carby calls the romanticization and elevation of the discursive category of the folk. Far from merely denigrating the folk and championing the black middle class, however, Fauset and Larsen actually critiqued both the pretensions of the petite (or petty) bourgeoisie and the primitivism assigned the transplanted urban masses. Because of its double vision, their fiction offers a potentially more complex critique of a changing society and the ideological aspects of the epoch than the classic blues of their contemporaries.

Ideology as the Mother of Invention

While black blues queens such as Bessie Smith and Ma Rainey sang of sex and sexuality—heterosexuality, homosexuality, bisexuality—with startling explicitness, black women writers of the 1920s and 1930s such as Jessie Fauset and Nella Larsen were in most instances considerably more reticent in their attentions to the black female body. Literary history and feminist criticism have often judged these writers harshly for what black scholar Gloria Hull calls "their restrained treatment of sex," which she says "helped to place them outside the sensational mainstream" of their era.[7] Black feminist critics such as Cheryl Wall and Barbara Christian reflect a widely held critical opinion when they argue that (like their nineteenth-century counterparts) Larsen and Fauset, along with most black women poets of the period, tried to rebut racist imaging of black women as morally loose by presenting a class of black women as prim, proper, and bourgeois as middle-class white ladies. In inventing sophisticated, light-skinned, middle-class heroines, the argument goes, these writers adhered to traditional notions of womanhood and made themselves and their characters slaves to the conventions of an "alien tradition." The "genuine," "more honest" poetry of the period, these critics insist, was the lyrics of blues singers such as Bessie Smith and Ma Rainey, whose artistic integrity and racial authenticity are confirmed by their displays of what Hull calls a "raunchy, woman-proud sexuality that echoed the explicitness of this licentious era."[8]

While these readings of Fauset's and Larsen's work seem to me to miss the finer points of their social critiques, what I want to challenge here is the implicit definition of what "genuine," "authentic" African American art is. I want to point out some of the problems that arise when African American expressive culture is viewed through the lens of vernacular theories of cultural production and the master narrative of the blues as sexual signifier.

First, such evaluations often erase the contexts and complexities of a wide range of African American historical experiences and replace them with a single, monolithic, if valorized, construction: "authentic" blacks are southern, rural, and sexually uninhibited. "Middle-class," when applied to black artists and their subjects, becomes pejorative, a sign of having mortgaged one's black aesthetic to the alien conventions of the dominant culture. An era marked by the divergent value systems and colliding imperatives of such internally stratified constituencies as the black bourgeoisie, black bohemia, the working masses, black nationalists, the Harlem-centered literati, and the so-called Talented Tenth is narrowly characterized as "licentious" and sexually "sensational."

A second irony lies in the implication that Fauset's and Larsen's novels are somehow less than authentically black, where *black* is taken to mean sensational, licentious, raunchy. It is, as I argued in chapter 2, an internally dysfunctional reading of the racial subject and the semiotics of the black body that categorizes moral value by color and by class and defines "authentic blackness" as the absence thereof. Such evaluations, in effect, make class, culture, and morality linear concepts in which the genuine, honest, authentic black experience is that of a unilaterally permissive rural peasantry or a homogeneously uninhibited urban proletariat.

Third, such folk-rooted, hierarchical readings of Bessie's blues and Jessie's fiction ironically privilege what is ultimately a narrow representation of women's experiences. As a black feminist discourse or as a narrative theory of the black female subject, the fiction of Fauset and Larsen might actually be said to attend to a much wider array of "genuine" women's issues than the woman-proud lyrics of their blues-singing sisters. Cultural critic Sandra Lieb notes, for example, that such feminized subjects as motherhood, reproduction, children, and family relations are missing thematically from the repertoires of blues artists like Ma Rainey.[9] The omission of this "typically female" subject matter can, and I think should, be read as part of the particular, counterconventional politics of the classic blues, which necessarily transcends the image of archetypal earth mother. What is of interest to me here, however, is not the thematic silences of the classic blues but the fact that these silences have gone largely unnoted by the same feminist critics who chide Fauset and Larsen for *their* sins of omission—for their alleged inattention to the actual human conditions of the masses of black women of their era.

Addressing the limited view of women's lives offered by what she calls the "daughters of the Black middle class," Cheryl Wall argues that to "discover the broader dimensions of Black women's reality, one must turn to an art born from folk culture and perfected by women who had liberated their creative powers": the blues. This "folk art equals real life" equation is as problematic for the blues as expressive realism is for the novel. There is little evidence to support the assumption that the majority of or even many black women—even poor, southern, rural black women—lived the kind of sexually liberated lives or held the kind of freewheeling values refracted in the blues. Like other expressive media, the blues invoke the fantastic. They, too, create an unreal estate, a surreal realm, which even theorists who argue against expressive realism still claim as the authentic. Such readings of literary and social history place blues women outside ideology and bourgeois women in the midst of it. Fauset and Larsen are identified as daughters of the black middle class, manipulated by the moral and aesthetic dictates of white patriarchal order and governed by white standards of womanhood, beauty, femininity, and the like. Bessie Smith, Ma Rainey, and Zora Neale Hurston, on the other hand, are invented by their audiences as signifying sisters, sexually and artistically liberated and unapologetically black, beyond the pale of white social influences. What does it mean, then, that Ma Rainey reportedly used lightening creams and heavy greasepaint to whiten her dark skin? One of her biographers suggests it means that Rainey, too, was not unaffected by ideology and "conform[ed] to the prejudice against dark skin (shared at the time by many blacks as well as whites)" (Lieb, 8). Perhaps it merely means, however, that Rainey had a fondness for the smell of the greasepaint as well as for the roar of the crowd. That is to say, whether written by Hurston or sung by Rainey, what Wall calls black women's reality is still *representation*, textual invention that the audience generates as *real*. Realism, in other words, is as much a code as romance, as much artifice as lightening creams and greasepaint.

The final irony I want to address lies in the choice of the classic blues of Bessie Smith as the privileged signifier of the genuine, authentic, pure black experience. This particular manifestation of the blues is, arguably, an appropriative art form that blends the material and techniques of traditional African American music with the presentational modes of popular *white* American musical theater, most specifically minstrelsy and vaudeville.[10] Some cultural historians maintain, in fact, that the music popularly called classic blues would be more appropriately labeled vaudeville blues, to reflect the degree to which the form was influenced by the American music hall and the vaudeville stage.[11]

As Ralph Ellison has argued, classic blues were both public entertainment and private ritual,[12] but the fact that what was once local lore could be packaged and distributed, I would argue, altered and institutionalized the form irrevocably, as video technology and mass production have altered reggae and rap. The classic blues, the variety of blues sung and recorded by professional performers such as Bessie Smith and Ma Rainey, are so called both because they standardized and universalized particular, recurrent lyrics, themes, and techniques, and because they re-formed the ritualistic elements of a once private or communal African American folk modality into public entertainment available for mass consumption. Although blues originally were recorded only by white women performers such as Sophie Tucker, black women stage and recording artists became the principal instruments through which the sexually explicit lyrics of the classic blues began to reach the ears of white America as well as black in the early 1920s.[13] But the "whys" of the commercialization and the feminization of the blues—that is to say, how mass production mass-produced the black female as sexual subject—is a complex question that is often eclipsed by the stellar proportions of the phenomenon's "whos."

At least part of the "why" of the popularization and feminization of the blues must be located in the primitivist proclivities of the historical moment. Primitivism, as a prevalent ideology of the early twentieth century, is characterized by an exuberance for the simple, the at-once innocent and sexually uninhibited—qualities the primitivist ascribes to the racially othered, whose alterity is fetishized. Almost by definition, primitivism thrives on icons. In the early twentieth century, no single icon combined the erotic, the exotic, and the innocent to the extent that the new Negro seemed to; for the newly discovered African American was not new at all but ancient, primal, and primitive—a panacea for an overindustrialized society dying from an acute case of modernity. Such notions were fostered by the work of Sigmund Freud, who endowed "races at a low level of civilization" with an untrammeled sexuality, which he claimed both shielded them from neuroses and inhibited their cultural development. Civilization, Freud argued, advances at the expense of human sexuality. His "dark continent" metaphor for female sexuality was, as Mary Ann Doane has argued brilliantly, a deliberate attempt to link the unknowable female sexual self with the unknown, dark-skinned, "infantile" inhabitants of the African continent.[14]

Such linkages were not new with Freud, however. For centuries the black body had functioned as a sign of both the assumed excessive sexuality and the racial primitivism of the African. According to Sander Gilman, by the eighteenth century the sexuality of the black male and female had become an icon for deviant sexuality in general.[15] In the nineteenth century the fascination with the black female body, in particular, and the primitive sexual anatomy and appetite attributed to the African woman increased the degree to which the black female functioned as an erotic icon in the racial and sexual ideology of Western civilization. It is this iconography that Nella Larsen critiques in *Quicksand* (1928), for example, where a white Danish painter named Axel Olsen propositions the novel's mulatta heroine, Helga Crane, assuming that "the warm impulsive nature of the women of Africa" will make her eager to become his mistress.[16] It is this iconography that helped make a bare-breasted Josephine Baker the rage in Paris in the twenties. And it is this same iconography that accounts, at least in part, for the hegemony of black women in the record industry throughout the decade.[17]

Under what might be called the cult of true primitivism, sex—the quintessential subject matter of the blues—was precisely what hot-blooded African women were assumed to have always in mind and body. Blues such as Mary Dixon's "All Around Mama" complemented that already established image:

I've had men of all sizes, had 'em tall and lean
Had 'em short, had 'em flabby, had 'em in between,
I'm an all around mama, I'm an all around mama,
I'm an all around mama, with an all around mind.[18]

Out of the mouths of black women such lyrics spoke boldly to sexual freedom and personal choice, but they also spoke to the racial and sexual iconography that cast the African woman as a hypersexual primitive. In singing the "Copulating Blues," the "Courting Blues," the "Empty Bed Blues," black women artists seemed to claim that image as their own, chew it up, and spit it out in the faces of their accusers. Whether self-affirming or self-deprecating (and many in the black community argued that it was the latter), the move fit the primitivism and exoticism of the thoroughly modern moment.

With such songs as "I'm a Mighty Tight Woman" and "Put a Little Sugar in My Bowl," red-hot mamas punned, parodied, and played with black female desire.[19] They in effect plumbed and inverted their positions as long-exploited, fetishized commodities. But identifying women blues artists as the site of a struggle for black female subjectivity necessarily raises complex questions about agency and interpellation, self and subject, person and persona. Problematizing Hazel Carby's observation that these blues women invented themselves as sexual subjects, I want to suggest that the many colliding ideologies, colluding imperatives, and conflicting agendas of the era make it difficult to determine definitively who constructed whom in the cultural kaleidoscope of the 1920s and 1930s. If black women blues singers claimed their sexual subjectivity through their songs, did they also on some level objectify, exoticize, and eroticize the female body in the process? Did these infinitely inventive blues women create the moment through their songs and exploit that moment? Or did the moment create and exploit them? It was, after all, their ability to sell records that made black women so essential to the race record industry in the 1920s. They were abandoned by the industry as quickly as they had been taken up when the increasing popularity of dance bands in the late twenties and early thirties created a new market and a new source of profit (Harrison, 8). Perhaps the answer to the question of agency and interpellation lies somewhere between the two possibilities—in exploring the reflexive nature of ideology and invention, in examining critically the ideological aspects of the epoch that made possible the invention of both the explicitly sexual black female subjects sung in the songs of blues women like Bessie Smith and Ma Rainey and the often more covertly sexual subjects written in the fiction of Jessie Fauset, Nella Larsen, and Zora Neale Hurston.

Interestingly, despite their dismissal as "vapidly genteel lace-curtain romances,"[20] several of Fauset's and Larsen's novels, in particular, seem to me to lay the groundwork for such an ideologically charged analysis. Their fiction tackles some of the most significant social contradictions of the emerging modern era, including the questions of black female agency, cultural authenticity, and racial and sexual iconography.

Joanna Marshall, for example, the colored heroine of Fauset's first novel,

There Is Confusion (1924), is fiercely determined to have a career as a classical dancer at a time when both her race and her gender limit her personal and professional options to marriage, on the one hand, and exotic dancing, on the other. Her childhood sweetheart self-servingly advises her to "found [her] life on love" and marry a man who understands her (him), and he will make sure that she has the time for herself and her career.[21] Determined not to be like the women she has read about in romance novels, who have "'counted the world well lost for love' until it was too late," Joanna, for a time anyway, resists both love and marriage. Fully focused on her career, she understands that "for a woman love usually means a household of children, the getting of a thousand meals, picking up laundry, no time for herself for meditation, or reading" (95). Her professional plans, however, are undermined by racial discrimination as well as by gender conventions. Even training is hard to come by because, as a French dance instructor tells her, "the white Americans like not to study with the brown Americans," and as a poor man, he is bound by the prejudices of his white clientele. After Joanna solves this problem by convincing the Frenchman to hold a separate dance class for a group of black students she rounds up, she finds that the door to the classical stage is still closed to her, despite her talent and training. "Couldn't make any money out of you," a white agent tells her as he refuses to represent her. "America doesn't want to see a colored dancer in the role of a *première danseuse*. . . . She wants you to be absurd, grotesque" (148). He suggests that she cork herself up and look for work doing the real colored thing, blackface burlesque.

Joanna's big break comes when the white board of directors of a Greenwich Village theater gives her a chance at "dancing like colored people" in a production called "The Dance of the Nations." In auditioning for the role, Joanna draws not on her classical training but on the folk rhythms and wild, whirling motions she learned long before from colored children playing games in the streets of west Philadelphia. The spirit and abandon with which she dances at her audition land her the role of black America, a part formerly played by a white performer who, the board has decided, has no notion of how to dance like colored people. Though her part is originally a small one, Joanna's "authentic" colored dancing promptly makes her the show's main attraction, so much so that she ultimately dons a wig and a white mask and assumes the roles of red and white America, as well as black. She becomes such a "sensation" (Fauset's word) in her multiple roles that the show moves to Broadway with her as its star.

Acknowledging that the folk dance, which makes Joanna Marshall a Broadway star, is in effect borrowed from the black masses of which she herself is not a part, Carolyn Sylvander suggests that Fauset appears to be saying that "real" (Sylvander's word) black artistic excellence is achieved by combining the stuff of the masses with the skill of the traditionally trained artist. "One must be open to and recognize both ingredients," Sylvander concludes. This may indeed by a part of Fauset's message, but the critique implicit in "The Dance of the Nations" episode cuts much deeper than a transparent commentary on folk material as the basis for "real" black art. In her representation of the racism and racialism that affect her heroine's career, Fauset implicitly challenges the very notion of the real and the authentic; she questions the possibility of the production of a "real" black art in a white-controlled cultural market. For not only do white culture keepers determine what authentic black art is, they control the who, how, where, and when of public cultural production and consumption as well.

While the Harlem-centered cultural production of the 1920s certainly had a powerful, inventive black presence, the period and its art were shaped as well by the interest and patronage of white intellectuals and culture keepers for whom Harlem was Africa, conveniently relocated around the corner. Nightly safaris into its jungles were a must for large numbers of white Americans who flocked to the speakeasies, gin joints, cabarets, and music halls for a taste of "primitive" black culture, often displacing the local black patrons. Nella Larsen takes note of this displacement in *Passing*, where a black character remarks that so many white people come to black affairs in Harlem that "[p]retty soon the coloured people won't be allowed in at all, or will have to sit in Jim Crowed sections" (198).

Chief among the white devotees of the Negro who converged on Harlem in the twenties were cultural barons Carl and Fania Van Vechten. A music and drama critic cum successful novelist and photographer, Carl Van Vechten was a bit of a Renaissance man who, together with his actress wife, Fania Marinoff, took up the Negro, as it were, in the early twenties. "Jazz, the blues, Negro Spirituals, all stimulate me," Van Vechten reportedly remarked to H. L. Mencken in the summer of 1924. "Doubtless, I shall discard them too in time."[22] Monied, connected, and—to use the writer's own description of himself—"violently interested in Negroes . . . almost an addiction,"[23] the Van Vechtens and their pace-setting parties, patronage, and publishing contacts did much to bring black writers along throughout the twenties.

In addition, the 1926 publication of Van Vechten's controversial but extremely popular and commercially successful novel *Nigger Heaven* directed increased attention to things black, including black literature. Grounded, many of its critics—from Marcus Garvey to W. E. B. Du Bois—argued, in the gutter of Harlem nightlife, Van Vechten's sensational novel was a stunning commercial success that, perhaps more than any other single factor, created a market for literary renderings of the seamy, "primitive" side of black life. As Cardy Wintz writes of the novel, "Its popularity fueled the rapidly growing white fascination with black art and literature and further stimulated the white influx into Harlem's bars and cabarets."[24] Since its depiction of the Harlem cabaret scene attracted far more attention than its portrait of black intellectual life, Van Vechten's novel also valorized stereotypes about blacks that pleasure-seeking white audiences expected to see realized in their forays into the "nigger heaven" of Harlem.

But while the hunger pangs of white intellectuals, sick of their own society and beguiled by difference, undoubtedly helped shape the Harlem of the 1920s, the moment's cultural engineering had a black face as well. Decidedly nationalistic, one school of black artists and intellectuals looked to Africa and to the folk traditions of the rural South for definition, sustenance, and artistic inspiration. From black nationalists like Marcus Garvey to Afrocentric, folk-oriented writers like Claude McKay and Langston Hughes, the affirmation of a racial past meant the rejection of a Western present and the celebration of the material and cultural condition of the black masses. Other members of the black intelligentsia and literati, such as Jessie Fauset and Nella Larsen, chose both to affirm and scrutinize not the distant, unknown land of Africa but America—not as it was but as it could be—and themselves as African Americans. Far from simply embracing the bourgeois materialism that their more radical contemporaries rejected, these artists and intellectuals often critiqued and even mocked the very conservatism and bourgeois pretensions attributed to them.

Fauset's alleged conservatism and elitism have been perennially at issue.[25] Like Hurston, she evidently shaved a good nine years off her age; when Harlem was "in vogue," Jessie Fauset was actually already well into her forties, part of an older and, indeed, in many ways more conservative order. At the same time, however, she was not only at the center of the times that were the twenties, she helped create them. Despite the fact that Langston Hughes credited her (along with Charles S. Johnson and Alain Locke) with having "mid-wifed" the Harlem Renaissance into being,[26] Fauset has most often been critically positioned within the so-called rear guard of renaissance writing. This anterior positioning is meant to indicate the degree to which her conservative ideology and middle-class themes fall outside the "blues matrix," to use Baker's term, and lag behind the sexually explicit, earthy material of such male trend-setters as McKay, Hughes, and Countee Cullen.

More than midwife and far more than rear guard, Jessie Fauset was herself both an initiator of and a central figure in the cultural explosion of the 1920s. Under her stewardship, numerous young, black writers—including Jean Toomer, Langston Hughes, Nella Larsen, and Gloria Douglas Johnson—passed into the world of the Harlem literati. In her role as literary editor of the NAACP's influential journal *Crisis* from 1919 to 1926, Fauset was a source of encouragement, support, and exposure for both burgeoning black talents and more established writers. *Crisis*, along with *Opportunity*, the Urban League's powerful monthly journal, helped shape the literary climate of the era.

Fauset's role in helping to "invent" the Harlem Renaissance, as it were, has been largely overshadowed by the gigantic proportions of her mentor and boss, W. E. B. Du Bois, whose luminary presence as editor and major policy-maker dominated *Crisis*. While Du Bois is rightly credited with building *Crisis* into one of the black community's most powerful political organs, the magazine's preeminent position in the realm of African American letters was due in large measure to the efforts of Jessie Fauset, who was wholly involved with and instrumental in setting the Harlem literary scene. One of the most prolific writers of the period, she was herself, by virtue of her successful publication record, a source of inspiration and encouragement for aspiring authors. In addition to numerous articles, short stories, and poems, she published four relatively well-received novels in less than ten years: *There Is Confusion* (1924), *Plum Bun* (1929), *The Chinaberry Tree* (1931), and *Comedy: American Style* (1933).[27]

Following on the heels of Jean Toomer's innovative modernist text *Cane* (1923), the publication of *There Is Confusion* marked an important moment in African American literature, the significance of which was not lost on the black intelligentsia or literati. Charles Johnson, editor of *Opportunity*, used the event as an occasion to bring together what turned out to be more than a hundred writers, critics, editors, and publishers, including such white luminaries as Eugene O'Neill and H. L. Mencken. This "small dinner party" became what historian David Levering Lewis has called the "dress rehearsal" for the furious cultural activity that Alain Locke would dub the Harlem Renaissance. Reviewing *There Is Confusion* for the *Messenger*, black writer, editor, and intellectual George Schuyler urged his readers to purchase the novel and to help make it the commercial success that *Cane* had not been, for he realized that only profit-making texts would keep white publishers like Boni and Liveright interested in the work of black writers. "If the novel is a financial success," he wrote, "there will be a widening field of opportunity for our rising group of young writers, struggling to express the yearnings, hopes, and aspirations of the race" (Lewis, 124).

Among the young writers who may have benefited from Fauset's success was Nella Larsen, who worked as both a nurse and a librarian before she began writing in the mid-1920s. Plunged into the midst of the Harlem elite by both her marriage to a socially prominent black physics professor and her job as a librarian at the Harlem branch of the New York Public Library, Larsen was inspired and encouraged by her contacts among the black literati. Fauset and other black novelists and intellectuals such as Walter White encouraged her to write, and Carl Van Vechten brought her first novel, *Quicksand* (1928), to the attention of his publisher, Alfred A. Knopf, who accepted it immediately and asked to see additional manuscripts.

While Claude McKay's sensational novel *Home to Harlem*, also published in 1928, was the "black book" that became that year's best-seller, *Quicksand* won Larsen the prestigious William E. Harmon Foundation Prize (a medal awarded annually to blacks who had made significant contributions in a variety of fields), and *Passing*, published just thirteen months after *Quicksand*, helped bring Larsen a Guggenheim Fellowship in 1930.[28] Both novels were well reviewed, receiving positive notices from both the white and the black press. In an oft-quoted review published in *Crisis*, Du Bois, for example, hailed *Quicksand* as a "courageous piece of work" at the same time that he condemned McKay's *Home to Harlem* as a novel so "nauseating" in its preoccupation with the sexual and the seamy that it left him as a reader in desperate need of a bath.

Du Bois's review suggests the extent to which the primitivist proclivities of the so-called "Harlem school" of renaissance-era writing were a point of contention between champions of the folk, such as Claude McKay and Langston Hughes, and old-school New Negro intellectuals, such as Benjamin Brawley, Walter White, and Du Bois. The spirit of this ideological conflict is captured as well in Gwendolyn Bennett's review of *Quicksand* for *Opportunity*. Noting with relief that Larsen's book "does not set as its tempo that of the Harlem cabaret," Bennett, herself an up-and-coming black poet, went on to describe the novel as the "psychological struggle of an interesting cultured Negro woman against her environment."[29] While Bennett's review of *Quicksand* identifies the subject of the novel as a woman's psychological struggle, few readers were as gynocentrically focused, and the gender-specific psychosexual intricacies of *Quicksand* would receive little attention until the rediscovery and reclamation of the novel as a feminist text in the 1970s and 1980s. Missing, for the most part, Larsen's innovative examination of the combined effects of racial and sexual ideology on women's lives and psyches, many critics have merely echoed Robert Bone's dismissive characterization of the novel's protagonist as "a neurotic young woman of mixed parentage, who is unable to make a satisfactory adjustment in either race" (Bone, 102). Thadious Davis offers what I would argue is a more accurate assessment of the author's work and her legacy to later writers:

> [Larsen's] two published novels . . . have at their center the same issues that feminists today explore: gender identity, racial oppression, sexuality and desire, work and aspiration, marriage and ambition, reproduction and motherhood, family and autonomy, class and social mobility. Her intricate explorations of the personal consciousness and psychology of women transcend the limits of a single fictive character because on a subsurface level they address the conditions of, and ambivalence toward, women in an emergent modern society.[30]

Though it often has not been recognized as such, Larsen's work, as Davis suggests, represents a thoroughly modernist effort to invent a black female ego and to define a black female subject narrativistically. Indeed, her explorations of the female psychosexual self link her work both thematically and stylistically to that of contemporary black feminist writers, even as her treatment of the crises and conflicts of her day places her squarely within the Harlem Renaissance era.

By the early 1930s the Harlem moment had largely passed. The economy had failed, and the Van Vechtens, it seemed, had indeed discarded the Negro.[31] Fania Marinoff complained publicly that she never had liked the house parties, the honky-tonks, and the general hollowness of the Harlem scene. Her remarks were quoted by Floyd Calvin in a newspaper article in which he issued a warning to "Negroes who bow and scrape to patronizing whites. . . . Nine times out of ten," he wrote, "the whites are looking for something, and when they get it, then they go off and make fun of you."[32] From record company, to Broadway theater, to Harlem speakeasy (the overwhelming majority of which were owned by white racketeers), the "Negro craze" had made white men and women wealthy, while most of the impoverished black masses who were the putative subjects of the period's so-called authentic black art did not even know they had passed through a renaissance. Instead, they knew riots, unemployment, overcrowding, and in the depression years ahead, they would know hunger and breadlines.

"Hurstonism" and the Blues-Folk Moment

Zora Neale Hurston, who came of age as a novelist a decade after Fauset and Larsen, was at once in step and at odds with the conflicting rhythms of her times. As historian Paula Giddings writes, "Hurston's work was controversial because she neither romanticized Black folk life nor condemned it, thus falling between two schools of cultural thought."[33] Hurston's use of folklore and folk English seemed to respond to the primitivist impulses of the era, but it placed her fiction outside the realm of what the black intelligentsia considered positive representations of the Negro. At the same time, however, her particular depiction of class, caste, and gender struggles among black folk, rather than against whites, positioned her fiction outside the seamy, sensational literary niche carved out by Claude McKay, Langston Hughes, and Carl Van Vechten (whom Hurston called a "negrotarian") or the racial-protest realm of Richard Wright. Wright, in fact, accused Hurston of pandering to white tastes and perpetuating a minstrel image of blacks. "Her characters eat and laugh and cry and work and kill," he wrote; "they swing like a pendulum eternally in that safe and narrow orbit in which America likes to see the Negro live: between laughter and tears."[34] Criticism from other male contemporaries such as Alain Locke and Sterling Brown echoed Wright's judgment that Hurston had exploited the "quaint" side of her people and robbed black fiction of its protest purpose. Still others complained, however, that Hurston had actually internalized primitivist ideology and abandoned the project of revisioning black womanhood that had been the cause célèbre of so many of her sister writers.

Ever a controversial figure, Hurston is perhaps better characterized as a writer who, like Fauset and Larsen but on very different terms, challenged the dominant image of the rural racial primitive, even as she embraced the folk and the rich vernacular culture of the rural South. The world she represented on paper was a world similar to that sung in the blues, and as with the blues, her work has been privileged for its depiction of the authentic African American historical experience.

Rediscovered in the 1970s and reclaimed by contemporary black feminist writers such as Alice Walker, Hurston is widely recognized today as the essential black literary foremother, and *Their Eyes Were Watching God* is pointed to as the enabling text of a canon of African American women writers. According to Cheryl Wall, for example, "The developing tradition of black women's writing nurtured now in the poetry and prose of such writers as Toni Morrison and Alice Walker began with the work of Zora Neale Hurston."[35] Wall goes on to note that while Hurston was not the first African American woman to publish a novel, "she was the first to create a language and imagery that reflected the reality of black women's lives." Rooted in the cultural traditions of the black rural South, Hurston, Wall suggests, "became the first authentic black female voice in American literature" (371).

What, then, of Harriet Wilson and Frances Harper, Pauline Hopkins and Emma Dunham Kelley, Jessie Fauset and Nella Larsen, and all the other black female literary voices who spoke before Hurston or in a language different from hers? Are they false? And by what meter are we to measure "reality" and "authenticity"? Such extended claims for Hurston's voice, like Baker's claims for the blues, reflect a bias in current critical practice for vernacular theories of African American cultural production. They also reflect contemporary critical concerns with intertextuality and tradition: concerns that have united theorists and practitioners in searching for models—what black scholar Michael Awkward calls "inspiriting influences." Whether the approach is intertextual and linguistic or contextual and thematic, both the concern with grammatical models and the assumption of an identifiable tradition have led a great many theorists and critics of African American women's fiction in search of a black female precursor, in search of Zora Neale Hurston. As Deborah McDowell has argued, in a great many contemporary studies of black women's literature, "everything looks back to Zora Neale Hurston, who is the precursor of Toni Morrison, Paule Marshall, and Alice Walker." McDowell goes on to point out that this problematic notion of intertextuality "gives *Their Eyes Were Watching God* too great a weight to carry, however pivotal and salient a text it is in the Afro-American literary tradition."[36] These theories of intertextuality and "unanxious" literary influence are problematic in part because of the extent to which they embrace Hurston, Walker, and Morrison even as they elide Fauset, Larsen, Dorothy West, Ann Petry, Marita Bonner, Paule Marshall, Toni Cade Bambara, and a host of other black women writers whose urban settings disrupt a seamless folk narrative.

For Michael Awkward, as for Cheryl Wall, Zora Neale Hurston is the "initiator of an Afro-American women's tradition in novels," the primary literary or "inspiriting influence." Drawing on the work of Michel Foucault, Awkward describes Hurston as an "initiator of discursive practices." *Their Eyes Were Watching God*, he maintains, "not only refigures the dual consciousness code defined by Du Bois, but also delineates strategies that lead to a unity between the 'selves' of its protagonist."[37] In this claim and others like it, Hurston is taken out of context—out of her text milieu—and placed on high in much the same fashion as her heroine Janie. There are, after all, several works by other black women novelists which refigure—even *prefigure*—from a female perspective Du Bois's double consciousness concept. Such a double or, rather, triple consciousness is evident in Wilson's *Our Nig*, Harper's *Iola Leroy*, Hopkins's *Contending Forces*, Fauset's *Plum Bun*, and Larsen's *Quicksand* and *Passing*, all of which predate *Their Eyes Were Watching God*. In addition, as I have argued throughout this study, most of these works can be read as overtly or covertly advancing a project similar to Hurston's: subverting patriarchal authority, problematizing female identity and sexuality, and critiquing both gender conventions and power relations. Hurston's work is unmistakably pivotal in that process, but it does not exist in isolation; nor, as

Dianne Sadoff has ably demonstrated, are the lines of literary matrilineage between Hurston and such contemporary writers as Walker and Morrison as seamless and anxiety-free as Awkward and others attempt to draw them.[38]

Awkward suggests that Hurston provides for Walker what Sandra Gilbert and Susan Gubar call "unique bonds that link women in . . . that secret sisterhood of their literary subculture" (7). If this sisterhood indeed "inspirits" works of art that configure into a tradition, what are the origins of that sisterhood? Who are Hurston's inspiriting sisters? Who are Hurston's literary precursors? Claimed as the "initiator"—to use Awkward's word—of a black women's tradition in the novel, Hurston is most often presented as if without precursor, model, example, or inspiriting influence. Such a construction seems to me inherently ahistorical and runs the risk of turning literary history into a compendium of artistic anomalies and ossified individual talents.

An example of the possible consequences of what I call the "precursor perplex" is the argument advanced by Elliott Butler-Evans in *Race, Gender, and Desire*. Like Michael Awkward and a number of contemporary scholars, Butler-Evans draws on Gilbert and Gubar's revision of Bloom's theory of literary influence. In *The Madwoman in the Attic* Gilbert and Gubar argue that the woman writer's struggle to define herself as an artist frequently begins with her "actively seeking a *female* precursor who . . . proves by example that a revolt against patriarchal literary authority is possible."[39] Acknowledging Hazel Carby's influence, Butler-Evans stops short of naming Hurston as the source from which contemporary African American feminist fiction flows, but he nevertheless feminizes and reifies Hurston's narrative strategies based on a number of troubling assumptions.

> Hurston wrote during the Harlem Renaissance and the Great Depression, two moments in history when Black letters were dominated by male voices, and a politicized Black male discourse focused on racial oppression. Introducing a female subject and protofeminist discourse, Hurston focused on the deconstruction of privileged and valorized epistemologies and the substitution of alternative feminine perceptions.[40]

Like many scholars who look back to but not before or around Hurston, Butler-Evans accepts the conventional notion of the late nineteenth and early twentieth centuries and the so-called Harlem Renaissance as eras of exceptional black male intellectual and creative genius.[41] Accordingly, he presents Hurston's work as an anomalous, "feminine," "domestic" voice interjected into a politically charged *male* space rather than as part of a continuum of black women's writing both acutely aware and consistently critical of racial and sexual ideology and the patriarchal socialization of women.

Butler-Evans makes a similarly troubling distinction between the political writing of the period and Hurston's work, which he says "stressed the private and the domestic" (42). "While novels by Black males focused on racial struggles between Blacks and whites," Butler-Evans writes, "Hurston's novel explored the personal, internal struggles between men and women in the Black community" (44–45). Dichotomies such as the ones Butler-Evans establishes here rest precariously on a highly problematic concept of separate spheres and distinctly feminine and masculine epistemologies and subject matter. Not only does this kind of analysis fail to acknowledge both the range of Hurston's grasp of multiple discursive fields and the depth of her critique of interlocking ideologies, but it also obscures the fact that even novels by black men focusing on racial struggles, including those by male writers of the Harlem Renaissance era, frequently revolve around gender, familial, social, and sexual relations. Claude McKay, for example, may have been the enfant terrible of the Harlem Renaissance, but all three of his novels—*Home to Harlem* (1928), *Banjo* (1929), and *Banana Bottom* (1933)—depend, in varying degrees, on the intimate interactions of men and women.[42]

Elizabeth Ammons asks, "What happens when women rather than men are taken as the starting point for literary history at the turn of the century?" In answering this question Ammons argues that there emerges a rich context for and connections between women writers like Edith Wharton and Jessie Fauset. A writer like Zora Neale Hurston ceases to be the rare exceptional genius or, as Ammons says of Wharton, "the incredible lone achiever who somehow slips through into masculine terrain, where she stands immeasurably superior to and different from all but one or two of her less extraordinary, less spectacular sisters."[43]

Despite the way she has been constructed by many contemporary literary scholars, Zora Neale Hurston did not give birth to herself, unread and unassisted by literary models and inspiriting influences. Hurston, too, passed through a birth canal that reaches back not only through the all-black town of Eatonville, Florida, in which she was raised, through folklore and slave narratives and blues rhythms, but through the fiction of such precursors as Frances Harper and Pauline Hopkins, as well as that of her contemporaries Jessie Fauset, Nella Larsen, Alice Dunbar-Nelson, and Marita Bonner.

Hurston's last novel, *Seraph on the Suwanee* (1948), for example, bears a striking resemblance to Dunbar-Nelson's unpublished novella "A Modern Undine" (ca. 1901–3), including startling similarities in plot, theme, characterization, and even dialogue.[44] Both texts are studies in female psychology that explore the effects of personality, paranoia, jealousy, and misunderstandings on the marital relation. In both stories an aloof, disdainful, introverted, twenty-one- or twenty-five-year old white woman—considered an "old maid" by her southern society—marries an adoring, devoted, though chauvinistic, stranger whose affections are resisted rather than embraced. Both heroines give birth to deformed sons, of whom they become obsessively protective and who, despite their mothers' constant care, die untimely deaths, for which the wives unjustly hold their husbands partially responsible. The climax of each text is a dramatic scene in which the husband confronts his wife with the constancy of his love and his sense of its failure and futility before leaving her. In "A Modern Undine" we are told at this moment of crisis: "All the pent-up, unrealized misery of the past six years had suddenly flooded to his lips, and poured forth in a torrent of almost inarticulate words. His nerves were raw, sore to the touch, like a thing flayed alive." Hurston uses similar terms in describing the "raw-red abraded flesh" that symbolizes the love pains of *Seraph*'s similarly spurned and tormented husband.

Hurston's novella is far more developed than Dunbar-Nelson's seventy-page, unfinished manuscript. Nevertheless, the two texts have so much in common that their similarities raise questions about the relationship between Hurston and Dunbar-Nelson—about the influence of the latter on the former. Dunbar-Nelson had been dead for fourteen years when *Seraph on the Suwanee* was published in 1948, but both women operated in and around Harlem in the twenties, and Dunbar-Nelson apparently circulated a draft of her novella for critique. Did Hurston have access to Dunbar-Nelson's unpublished manuscript? Was the widow of Paul Laurence Dunbar an inspiriting influence for Zora Neale Hurston? Or do their respective stories share a common source?

In any case, how Hurston constructed her voice, how she enlarged upon and reshaped inherited traditions, how she entered into and redirected an already established discourse, are all questions we need to ask of her work. When we take a "great books," "great men," or even a "great women" approach to the study of African American literary history; when we extract from its historical and cultural contexts and privilege a particular text, making it the "signpost of tradition," to use Gates's term, we run the risk of merely replicating the exclusive, essentialist, canon-constructing Western methodologies we claim to repudiate.

Jessie Fauset, Nella Larsen, and Zora Neale Hurston are only three of the many female voices and visions, politics and poetics which helped shape the literary life and cultural climate of the 1920s and 1930s. As with other blues literature, the tenuous nature of male-female relationships lies at the core of their respective fictive inventions. But Jessie's blues and Nella's blues and Zora's blues confront, as well, the roles that social values, patriarchal ideology, and racial oppression play in making erotic relationships tenuous. I read their "bourgeois blues" as subtle, frequently subversive responses to the oppressive, materialist rhythms of their evolving black communities. Equally important, however, is the degree to which Fauset's and Larsen's texts, in particular, comment on and critique the bohemian, as well as the bourgeois, and implicitly challenge the hegemony of primitivism and exoticism that critics and historians have long read as the real stuff of the Harlem Renaissance. To the extent that they critique both the conservative middle class and the primal peasantry (and, in Hurston's case, class stratification among the folk), the pretentious and the primitive, the works of Fauset, Larsen, and Hurston reflect the essential tensions of their historical moment.

What I have tried to do in this chapter is to unhinge the fixity with which the blues and the folk have come to be claimed as the master narratives of *the* black experience, narrowly defined. While I do not want to deny or diminish the importance of either of these discursive fields as a cultural index, I do want to argue for other indices—for wider analytical angles that allow us to plot African American expressive geographies in inclusive rather than exclusive terms. I have argued as well for the importance of historical specificity and attention to ideology and iconography in decoding and remapping African American cultural cartography—in retheorizing such expansive, explosive, ideologically charged spaces as "the folk," "the bourgeois," "the authentic," and "the real." The novels of Jessie Fauset and Nella Larsen are only two examples of familiarly neglected works whose representations of the 1920s and 1930s can serve to remind contemporary cultural critics and theorists that the era known as the Harlem Renaissance was not a monolithic, one-dimensional blues moment.

As I hope the readings in chapter 5 will demonstrate, Fauset's and Larsen's fictions are important to literary and cultural theory not just because of what they tell us about the sexual, social, aesthetic, and intellectual codes of their time but because of what our responses to them can tell us about our own. Our moment echoes theirs in its romanticization of the folk and its preoccupation with cultural authenticity. That Fauset and Larsen are often left out or pushed to the margins—the "rear guard"—in contemporary mappings of African American expressive geographies suggests that we have learned little about the elusive (if not the illusive) nature of "the real colored thing" from the battles fought over the bodies of black female sexual icons such as Bessie Smith and Josephine Baker in the 1920s.

While I do not mean to diminish the significance of these artists or their accomplishments, I am left wondering what it is about *our* moment that has made us turn to theirs. What, for example, accounts for the current resurgence of interest in Josephine Baker's life and art, which has once again made of her a spectacle?[45] Are we, in our attempts at cultural criticism, modern-day primitivists? Are our Afrocentric interests and our vernacular theories and our feminist concerns for female agency colluding with primitivist proclivities like those that helped to bring the black "other" into vogue in the 1920s? Are we, like the moments in which they lived and worked, inventing these artists as icons? Insisting on this question—debating who (or what) invented whom—invokes an argument as eternally reflexive as which came first, chicken or egg, acorn or oak, flower or fruit? Perhaps what is most important is our own awareness of just how complex and ideologically charged are both the question and our attempts at answers.

5

The Bourgeois, Wedding Bell Blues of Jessie Fauset and Nella Larsen

> The twenties marked the heyday of classic blues singers, all of whom were female. Free of the burdens of an alien tradition, a Bessie Smith could establish the standard of her art: in the process she would compose a more honest poetry than any of her literary sisters. They lacked the connection to the cultural traditions which shaped Smith's art: nonetheless, some produced work which "signified." The work of the greatest signifier, Zora Neale Hurston, was born, like Bessie's, from folk tradition and on occasion even from performance.
>
> — CHERYL A. WALL, "Poets and Versifiers, Singers and Signifiers: Women of the Harlem Renaissance"

It is only through a disturbing twist of literary fate and intellectual history that Jessie Fauset and Nella Larsen have been criticized for not measuring up to the sexual and textual liberation of their blues-singing sisters. At another time, in another context, these two women authors might have been praised for their roles in advancing literary discourse toward a moment where black female desire could be boldly sung on the printed page as well as on the nightclub stage. Perpetually measured against Bessie Smith, on the one hand, and Zora Neale Hurston, on the other, however, Fauset and Larsen have rarely been read in terms of their own particular contributions to modernism, to American and African American literature, and to the development of the woman's novel. In contrast to the raunchy lyrics of the blues and the graphic portraits of "low-class Negro life"[1] painted by such male writers as Claude McKay, the fiction of Fauset and Larsen seems to some readers sexually stultified and anachronistically reticent. In the wider continuum of a woman-centered literary history, however, Fauset's and Larsen's forays into the forbidden realm of female sexual desire appear progressive, counterconventional, perhaps the most courageous, if tentative, literary efforts to explore sexual politics from a female perspective since Kate Chopin published *The Awakening* in 1899.

Banned from libraries, critically censured across the country, and panned even by sister novelist Willa Cather, *The Awakening* was not quite the beacon it might have been, beckoning other women writers—black and white—boldly into the realm of the erotic imagination. Indeed, the novel's critical rejection virtually silenced Chopin herself. Nevertheless, *The Awakening* stands as a pivotal text in the development of American women's literature. As Elaine Showalter has pointed out, in its solitary defiance, *The Awakening* speaks for a transitional phase in American women's writing. It looks back to the woman's culturists and local colorists of the ante- and postbellum periods and around at the burgeoning modernists of the 1890s.[2] But *The Awakening*, I would add, also looks several generations ahead of its own New Woman era to the feminist writers of the 1970s and 1980s.

Much the same claim can be made for the fiction of Fauset and Larsen, as well as Hurston. Largely unacknowledged benchmarks in the continuum of American women's writing, novels like Fauset's *Plum Bum* and Larsen's *Passing*, both published in 1929, echo the racial and gender politics and the passionlessness of their nineteenth-century predecessors. At the same time, however, these texts anticipate the frank explorations of passion, power, desire, and danger that would characterize black women's novels of the 1970s and 1980s. As social and cultural critiques, the novels of Fauset, Larsen, and Hurston rewrite the revisionist, political projects of their predecessors in a number of ways: (1) Black women begin to become actively sexual beings, implicitly questioning their positioning as objects of male desire and contemplating, if not fully exploring, their sexual selves; (2) marriage ceases to be celebrated on paper as the quintessential signifier of civil liberty and becomes instead the symbol of material achievement; as such, it serves as the focal point of at times biting critiques of bourgeois black society and so-called middle-class values; (3) patriarchy, once primarily the private property of white male privilege, is recast as a pervasive institution whose ideological apparatuses affect black men as well as white, resulting ultimately in the oppression of black women within their own communities, households, and erotic and marital relations; (4) heroines cease to be singularly and uniformly heroic, good, pure, blameless—victims of patriarchal privilege and racial oppression who persevere against all odds; they become instead multidimensional figures, full of human (and, in some cases, monstrous) faults and foibles.

In this chapter I explore the ways in which Jessie Fauset and Nella Larsen use the metaphor of coupling to critique the social practices and gender conventions that limit women's choices and narrowly define, prescribe, and proscribe women's roles in a changing world order. Like Kate Chopin, these two writers helped pave the way toward fuller explorations of the inner reaches of the erotic imagination.[3] Far from silent on the topic of sexuality, Fauset and Larsen are more rightly claimed, I believe, as the first black women novelists to depict openly sensual black female subjects, as the first black writers to explore the dialectics of female desire and to address what having children can mean to a woman's physical and mental health, as well as to her independence. They were the first black women artists to depict successful, independent, single black professional and working-class women, not all of whom ultimately surrender their careers to male-dominated, bourgeois marriages, as many critics have charged.

The Working Body

Marise Davies, one of several significant women characters in Fauset's fourth novel, *Comedy: American Style*, achieves a stunning success on the Broadway stage despite her brown skin. Not only does she not surrender her career or her independence when she marries an equally dark-skinned doctor, but she is also the one who rules the marriage—dressing her husband and setting him up in practice, at least somewhat against his will. "Do you remember all my talk about not being willing for my wife to help me?" Marise's husband complains to a friend. "God! *Help* me! My wife does everything for me. I wanted an office in a side street, but Marise bought me a three story house on Seventh Avenue because she wants me to have a sanitarium some day."[4] Marise, it seems, is in charge of not only her own life but her husband's as well. Maggie Ellersley in Fauset's first novel, *There Is Confusion*, learns hair care from a Madame Harkness, who has perfected products for treating black hair. Maggie learns the trade well and goes on to develop her own highly successful hair care business. Her business success gives her a financial base from which to support the man she marries, a colored soldier who was gassed fighting for his country during the First World War. Laurentine Strange, in *The Chinaberry Tree*, is similarly successful as a dress designer, with her own business in which she employs two assistants.

Some critics, however, read these treatments of women professionals as less than positive representations of women's labor. Barbara Christian, who views Fauset's depictions of working women as even less progressive than Frances Harper's, writes:

> Fauset's heroines tend to be less independent than Iola Leroy, closer to the image of the contemporary pampered young woman, the darling of her daddy, and the jewel of her lover's eye. . . . Laurentine is a seamstress and a very good dress designer—feminine skills that along with her light complexion recommend her to the upper class. No teacher of Sunday School or composer of papers on the education of black mothers, the heroine of *The Chinaberry Tree* is touted as the first Negro to introduce fashionable pajamas to her small New Jersey town.[5]

In her criticism of Fauset, Christian seems to echo the conventional, chauvinistic judgment of Robert Bone, whose only comment about *The Chinaberry Tree* in his study of the Negro novel is the quip that it "seems to be a novel about the first colored woman in New Jersey to wear lounging pajamas."[6] Placing Fauset in a woman-centered historical context may give a different kind of import to labor such as dress design, hat making, and hair culture. Dressmaking, for example, is an age-old art for black women traceable to Africa, to the weaving and wrapping of cloth. Before their profit potential as breeders was discovered, their skill at weaving and sewing helped make African women valuable slaves. The fact that Laurentine Strange is a dress designer and seamstress—lounging pajamas and all—speaks with historical specificity to the limited professional options for African American women in the

1920s. Laurentine's art, by the way, is the same craft that Celie practices in *The Color Purple* when she goes into business making Alice Walker's version of lounging pajamas: unique one-size-fits-all pants.[7]

Additionally, while today major corporations such as Revlon and Clairol make fortunes selling hair care products and cosmetics especially for black hair and skin, in the early twentieth century no such line of products existed. Madame C. J. Walker, a onetime washerwoman, pulled herself and her daughter out of abject poverty by developing and successfully marketing internationally a line of products specifically for black hair, scalp, and skin. Not only did Madame Walker's business acumen make her the first black woman millionaire, it also aided thousands of black women whom she employed as sales agents and hair care consultants and as technicians in her factories and laboratories. When Walker died in 1919, she donated two-thirds of her considerable fortune to charity and stipulated in her will that her business always be controlled by women.[8] Fauset's imaging of dress designers and hair care specialists, then, has a historical significance critics have often missed.

Phebe Grant, a key player in *Comedy: American Style*, is another woman character who does not surrender her career to husband, home, and family. Instead, she sacrifices the leisure critics generally attribute to Fauset's heroines in service to her extended family. In the final act of *Comedy*, poor, lower-class, light-complexioned Phebe Grant marries a proper Philadelphia Negro, Christopher Cary, who, like his father, is a physician. Chris is the second of three children born to the Carys. Teresa, the oldest, by the time of her brother's marriage is herself a long-suffering wife, in effect living in exile in Paris with the white Frenchman her mother bartered her off to a few chapters earlier. Teresa cannot return to America, at least not with her white husband, because he might discover what his mother-in-law, Mrs. Olivia Cary, has worked so hard to hide: that Teresa, that all the Carys, are colored.

The white-skinned Carys have never been quite as well-to-do as Mrs. Olivia Blanchard Cary would wish, but they have been nearly as white. (Fauset consistently indulges in a kind of exponential criticism, assigning her characters names that speak, often paradoxically, to some defining aspect of their personalities. The name Olivia Blanchard Cary conveys the essential tensions of the text. *Blanchard* suggests Mrs. Cary's preoccupation with whitening or "blanching" herself and her family, while the name *Olivia* implies the concern with complexion—olive and otherwise—that assumes tragic proportions in this comedy.) For much of the novel the Carys live a seemingly perfect but internally dysfunctional bourgeois life, which includes passing for white whenever possible, in keeping with the dictates of the color-obsessed Olivia Cary. For Mrs. Cary, passing for white means marrying her daughter off to a white man, almost any white man, even a ne'er-do-well opportunist like Aristide Pailleron, the Frenchman she "buys" for Teresa. (Here, too, the character's name seems carefully chosen and evocative, with the first name perhaps suggesting the aristocracy to which Aristide pretends and the surname Pailleron [from *paille*, meaning straw or flaw, or *pailler*, to cover with straw] linguistically establishing Mrs. Cary's chosen son-in-law as a kind of straw man or fake.) The sole purpose of matrimony, as far as Olivia Blanchard is concerned, is social advancement and skin lightening. Such was the motivation behind her own marriage to young, light-skinned Dr. Christopher Cary, with whom she was sure she would have perfect white children, whose pale skin and proper breeding would be an entrée *for her* into the upper echelons of Caucasian society. As Fauset writes:

> Olivia with very little love for her husband, Dr. Cary, with no enthusiasm, as such, for the institution of matrimony and with absolutely no urge for the maternal life, had none the less gone cheerfully and willingly into both marriage and motherhood because she believed that through her children she might obtain her heart's desire. She could, she was sure, imbue her offspring with precept and example to such an extent that it would never enter their minds to acknowledge the strain of black blood which in considerable dilution would flow through their veins. (37)

Olivia's heart's desire—what her mother refers to at one point as her "one consuming ambition"—is to be "white." Although she would have preferred marriage to a white man, Olivia's plan for personal racial uplift has definite class as well as color requirements. Acknowledging that it was "highly unlikely that she would meet with and marry a white man of Cary's education, standing and popularity," she settled for the ambitious young Harvard medical student (28). During their courtship Christopher Cary, the object of Olivia's social rather than romantic desire, was not unaware of his "lady's" cold aloofness, but having been trained by his mother that "you can always tell a good woman because she is so cold," Cary mistook that aloofness for genteel virginity and sexual innocence. "'A good woman,' his mother had told him since Sex and Girls first obtruded themselves on his far from unwilling consciousness, 'comes to her husband entirely ignorant.'" As a physician in training, however, the more he studied biology, the more he "questioned the wisdom of such ignorance, but he supposed that was just the hard luck of being a woman" (27). It did not take long for Cary to learn bitterly that his wife's "much prized aloofness" was not the "*insigne* of a wealth of feeling" but "merely the result of an absolute vacuum of passion" (38).

In what might be read as a critique of passionlessness, Fauset takes a number of swipes at the values and facades surrounding courtship and coupling among her middle-class subjects. A good woman pretends aloofness; the greater the aloofness, the greater prize the woman. The joke, in this instance, however, is on Christopher Cary, for beneath his bride's cold exterior is an equally icy interior. The punch line is one he will have to live with for a very long time. The Carys' passionless, but by no means sexless, marriage produces three children. The eldest, Teresa, bursts from the womb as white-skinned and straight-haired as Olivia hoped she would be. "Every time [Olivia] appeared in public with the little girl," we are told, "she was presenting incontestable proof of her white womanhood. . . ." (37). The second child, Chris, Jr., is as perfectly white as his sister, and both offspring advance their mother's plan to pass blithely into the white world.

Ultimately, however, for Olivia Cary, passing for white comes to mean denying her third child, for Oliver, as he is named in her honor before she sees the color of his skin, has the great misfortune to be born brown. As he grows up his mother explains away the presence of this little brown boy in her white household by dressing him in butler garb and passing him off to her white friends and fellow clubwomen as the Mexican valet.

Oliver's older brother and sister, Chris and Teresa, are kind and loving, but their caring is ultimately little shield against their mother's obsessive cruelty. When Chris comes home from boarding school unexpectedly and finds his brother playing butler (Oliver thinks it's a game) to his mother and her white friends, he manages to get himself expelled from school so he can live at home and run interference between his mother's colorism and his brother's color. Teresa is similarly protective. Secretly engaged to an "identifiably colored" man, she promises Oliver that she will take him to live with her after she marries. An outcast in his own home, Oliver delights in Teresa's promise, which literally represents a lifeline to him. Tragically, however, Mrs. Cary learns of her daughter's plans just as Teresa and her black fiancé are about to elope. With characteristic cruelty (and not entirely without assistance from the weak-willed Teresa), she successfully sabotages her daughter's wedding plans and then manipulates her husband into sending her and Teresa to Paris, where she marries her daughter off as a white woman to a white Frenchman.

Mrs. Cary intercedes, as well, in her son's courtship of Broadway star Marise Davies. Marise's skin color is too dark for her to join the Cary family, as Olivia makes clear in a visit to Marise's apartment. "I want you to know," she tells Marise, "that it would not be at all in keeping with the plans which his father and I have long since cherished . . ." Marise interrupts Mrs. Cary and finishes the thought for her: "To see him married to a woman as dark as I. . . . You needn't warn me, Mrs. Cary," Marise continues. "I have no desire to break into your sacred ranks. . . . There's not a colored person in Philadelphia who doesn't know in what regard the Carys hold people who show color" (268).

When Marise, motivated at least in part by Mrs. Cary's hostility, later rejects Chris Cary's marriage proposal, the young doctor then turns to Phebe Grant, whom he suddenly realizes he has loved all along, not failing to note that her light skin, if not her social background, will please his mother. As light in complexion as her mother-in-law, Phebe Grant, by contrast, is fiercely proud of her Negro heritage and unashamed of either her working-class background or her illegitimate birth. She has pulled herself out of the depths of poverty through hard work and perseverance and supports herself and her mother by operating a dress and millinery shop. Not only does Phebe continue to work in the shop after her marriage to Chris Cary, Jr., she is the one who, through her commercial and common sense, saves her husband's family from financial ruin when the senior Dr. Cary's mental and physical health begins to fail following Oliver's tragic death.

Miserable in his role as family outcast, a distraught Oliver writes to his sister in France, reminding her of her promise to take him in. Her response is crushing. "Oliver, my husband doesn't know I'm colored," her letter reads in part. "Perhaps I might have gotten around that. But just the other day he talked to me very bitterly about people of mixed blood, especially Americans. So, darling, you see with your tell-tale color . . ." (224–25). Finally comprehending the racial reasons behind both his mother's disdain and his beloved sister's failure to keep her promise of a home, Oliver commits suicide. His father, Doctor Cary, Sr., is particularly devastated and lets his medical practice and business affairs deteriorate to the point that the Carys end up in near-bankruptcy.

It is daughter-in-law Phebe who reestablishes order in the midst of the Cary family tragedy and chaos. She reorders her own household to accommodate her in-laws, converting part of her house into quarters for them and part into offices for the two doctors Cary. Her reward is constant complaints from her mother-in-law, who treats Phebe's brown-skinned mother the same way she treated her own brown-skinned son: as a hired servant.

The stress of juggling the demands of both work and family — of shouldering the lion's share of the financial burden for two households and running interference between the two warring mothers-in-law — takes its toll on Phebe, ultimately leading her to look for escape in the arms of another man. In her frustration and disappointment, she comes dangerously close to having an affair with the brown-skinned childhood sweetheart who years before rejected her — ostensibly because of her too-light skin — to marry her much darker friend, the same successful actress Marise Davies mentioned earlier. Realizing at the last minute, however, that her own needs and desires (sexual and otherwise) have brought her to the brink of betraying both husband and friend for a man incapable of loving her, Phebe walks away from what the text makes clear was to have been a sexual assignation. She returns to her home and husband, glad to have escaped a life full of deception and "the cloying sweetness of furtive joys" (314). Her reward for coming home is the welcome news that the evil mother-in-law has been shipped off permanently to Europe, news delivered in the younger Carys' bedroom by an attentive husband who evidently has in mind a sexual assignation and some not-so-furtive joys of his own.

Despite having what is for Phebe and Chris Cary a happy ending, *Comedy: American Style* is not the simple, "ding-dong, the wicked matriarch is dead," lace-curtain portrait of idealized romance — of easy female independence, sexual purity, and marital harmony — that Fauset's critics have claimed her work to be. Schematically complex, the novel is constructed as a play in three acts, with additional chapters entitled "The Plot," "The Characters," and, finally, "Curtain." "Phebe's Act," the fifth chapter, indeed ends comically, but Phebe's story is only one small part of a larger drama that is by no means a romantic comedy. Olivia Blanchard Cary's cruelty intrudes on every chapter of the text, causing literal and figurative death: her younger son's suicide, her husband's emotional and financial collapse, and her daughter's dead-alive marriage to a man almost as self-obsessed and cruel as his mother-in-law. The final curtain falls on Olivia, living an impoverished existence in Paris, grotesque, pathetic, and alone—rejected even by her daughter or, rather, by her white son-in-law with whom she hoped to make her home.

Comedy: American Style is a complex picture of the mixed blessings, burdens, temptations, and conflicting desires with which middle- and working-class black women and men must contend in a racist, patriarchal society. The comic ending of its final act, like its title, is ironic: it is a play on forms as its title is a play on words. For comedy "American style" is of the Greek kind: Fauset's novel is not a comedy of manners but a tragedy of them. Only in America, the text tells us more than once, can skin color breed such comic tragedy—such "artificial dilemma."

In *Comedy: American Style*, as in *Plum Bun*, Fauset draws on the romantic form and traditional social and literary conventions to explore racial and class ideology and to critique the ways in which the sentimental romance idealizes love, marriage, and family. Expanding Deborah McDowell's incisive reassessment of *Plum Bun* as a bildungsroman, one could argue that each of Fauset's novels transcends both its passing theme and its traditional form to become a novel of female and social development. More than simple insignia of a new black bourgeoisie, Fauset's texts can be read as cultural critiques that inscribe, expose, and in some instances even ridicule the romantic illusions and class pretensions of their heroines.

Interestingly, for all her alleged privileging of the bourgeois, Fauset draws her most positive portraits from the working class. Her most consistently positively presented women characters are, arguably, Maggie Ellersley of *There Is Confusion* and Phebe Grant of *Comedy: American Style*, both of whom come from impoverished, lower-class backgrounds. Fauset's Maggie, like Stephen Crane's, is a child of the tenderloin, and Phebe Grant is the offspring of a colored mother and a white father. Through her positive portrayals of working-class characters like Phebe and Maggie, Fauset accomplishes something in her fiction for which she has been given little credit. As Thadious Davis argues:

> [I]n portraying the Ellersley family as neither defeated by urban poverty, dehumanized by unhealthful tenements, nor isolated from supportive networks, [Fauset] resists confusing the lower class's moral values with environmental or situational contexts and renders one truth about the lives of working-class, urban dwellers often ignored by commentators seeking the exotic and primitive.[9]

Part of the truth to which Davis refers is the fact that moral values are neither class-specific nor culture-bound; that is to say, morality cuts across class lines and cultural spaces.

Fauset, Larsen, and the Sexual Subject

Hazel Carby maintains that, as a discourse, women's blues of the 1920s and early 1930s "articulates a cultural and political struggle over sexual relations: a struggle that is directed against the objectification of female sexuality within a patriarchal order."[10] Jessie Fauset and Nella Larsen, as I have argued, also participate in this battle over the black female body, locating that struggle within both marital relations and wider social, political, and professional engagements. Fauset and Larsen, however, are concerned with the colonized *mind*—with female sexual subjectivity—as well as with the objectified body. Accordingly, their texts implicitly explore the ways in which social forces and patriarchal ideology inspire, if not demand, the participation of black women in their own objectification and domination. Characters such as Joanna Marshall in *There Is Confusion* and Helga Crane in *Quicksand* ultimately discover that acceptance as a woman and as an artist means defining themselves by someone else's terms and objectifying themselves for someone else's gaze.

Ostrich feathers, beaded satin, yards of pearls, hats, headdresses, and furs are among the accoutrements black women blues singers donned in constructing their performance personas and staking out their sexual ground. In the novels of Jessie Fauset and Nella Larsen, such accessories not only construct the woman character but also help to tell her story. Silks and satins, capes and coats, dresses and lounging pajamas are as central to the bourgeois brand of "somebody done somebody wrong" songs that these texts sing as were paints and powders to the classic blues performance. Not only is tremendous attention paid in these novels to what women put on their bodies, but the characters are finely aware of how their bodies look in what they put on them as well. It is important to understand, however, that all this dressing and draping, primping and preening is not merely the frivolous fluff of which novels of manners are made—the affectations and petty preoccupations of bourgeois domesticity, as many critics have suggested. Rather, clothes function semiotically as sexual and racial signifiers. As part of the texts' signifying systems, the dressed or, in Harlem slang, the "draped-down" body is the literary equivalent of the woman-proud blues lyric—one of the not-always-so-subtle instruments through which both Fauset and Larsen sing and sign female sexuality.

Helga Crane, for example, the heroine of Larsen's first novel, *Quicksand* (1928), is a studied and deliberate dresser whose relationship to her wardrobe is a recurrent theme in the text. Throughout the novel Helga, the daughter of a white Danish mother and a black father, struggles to define and declare her sexual self in the face of iconographies that objectify, exoticize, "ladify," and otherwise oppress her. Clothes (putting them on the body rather than taking them off) are part of the stuff of Helga's bourgeois blues. They signal both her sexuality and her tenuous relationship to the moral and behavioral codes of the two disparate societies she stands among but not of. As a teacher at Naxos, a southern school for upwardly mobile Negroes, Helga is immediately established as a person apart from the white-worshiping "great [black] community" around her. "A slight girl of twenty-two," with "skin like yellow satin," Helga, we learn in the early pages of the novel, is too fond of vivid green and gold negligees and glistening brocaded mules to be a proper Naxos Negro. Rather, her taste in colorful clothes links her to that other life whose bodacious blues rhythms will not be entirely repressed, no matter how bourgeois her surroundings. A Naxos Negro's knowledge of place is confirmed by conservatism, good taste, and moderation in all things, including proper attire. Helga's distinctive dark purples, deep reds, clinging silks, and luxurious woolens signify the pride, vanity, and "uppity" otherness that bring her into disfavor at Naxos. "Clothes," as Larsen writes, "had been one of [Helga's] difficulties at Naxos," with its "intolerant dislike of difference." Larsen continues:

> Helga Crane loved clothes, elaborate ones. Nevertheless she had tried not to offend. But with small success, for, although she had affected the deceptively simple variety, the hawk eyes of dean and matrons had detected the subtle difference from their own irreproachably conventional garments. (18)

Perhaps even more than her yellow skin, Helga Crane's clothes mark her racial and sexual alterity. At one point in the novel Helga seeks refuge from American racism with her aunt and uncle in Copenhagen, where she immediately becomes a sensation, a curiosity. Herr and Fru Dahl, Helga's wealthy white relatives, dress, decorate, and display their newly acquired niece like a doll (or "dahl"). A kind of fantastic attention is lavished upon her: an attention that first perturbs, then excites, and eventually *incites* Helga. As Larsen writes:

> Incited. That was it, the guiding principle of her life in Copenhagen. She was incited to make an impression. She was incited to inflame attention and admiration. She was dressed for it, subtly schooled for it. And after a little while she gave herself wholly to the fascinating business of being seen, gaped at, desired. Against the solid background of Herr Dahl's wealth and generosity she submitted to her aunt's arrangement of her life to one end, the amusing one of being noticed and flattered.[11]

However initially amused and flattered Helga may be by all the attention lavished upon her, she eventually becomes dissatisfied with what she comes to view as her "peacock life": with being a black objet d'art, perpetually displayed for white consumption. She comes face-to-face with the consequences of having participated in her own objectification when her most ardent "collector," the white painter Axel Olsen, follows up an indecent sexual proposition with an equally insulting marriage proposal. "You know, Helga," Olsen says in what Larsen describes as his "assured, despotic way," "[y]ou have the warm impulsive nature of the women of Africa, but, my love, you have, I fear, the soul of a prostitute. You sell yourself to the highest bidder" (86).

The price that the highest bidder must pay is, of course, marriage. The preferred liaison would be concubinage, fit enough for a hot-blooded daughter of Africa, but the corruption of Helga's white lineage and Western breeding, Olsen implies, has made her hold out for marriage. Having failed in his attempt to make her his mistress, he has deigned to propose matrimony. Full of himself and a generous dose of racialism and primitivism, he is oblivious to his own offensiveness and taken aback at Helga's rebuff. Ironically, while Helga is articulate in rejecting Olsen, in a way that she does not quite understand he has the last word. For he has painted her portrait, a picture that he tells her in parting is "the true Helga Crane" after all. It is a portrait Helga insists is not of her at all, but of "some disgusting sensual creature with her features" (89). But if the picture is not of the *real* Helga Crane, it is of the image she has, for a time, surrendered herself to. For Olsen, as for her aunt and uncle, Helga has functioned as the fetishized commodity. Through Helga's Copenhagen excursion, Larsen critiques the moment's fascination with and specularization of the black female body.

At the end of the novel, clothes again become the great *un*equalizer that distinguishes the now married and perpetually pregnant Helga from the folk— from the tiny, rural Alabama community around which she has draped her life and to which she is trying desperately to belong. Fatally (as opposed to fatefully) married to a grandiloquent Baptist preacher, Mrs. Reverend Pleasant Green immediately makes herself unpopular with the women of her husband's "prim- itive flock" by trying to "help them with their clothes," tactfully pointing out that aprons and sunbonnets are not proper Sunday church attire (118–19).

The final pages of the novel not only return Helga Crane Green to the South (as a site of psychic and physical violence) but also place her in the ill-fitting and doubly ironic role of matron, helpmate, race woman. Like the deans and matrons at Naxos who judged her wardrobe harshly, Helga sets herself up as the standard-bearer of proper dress, "gentler deportment," and home beautifi- cation. In other words, here in the backwoods of Alabama, it is Helga who comes to represent the convention, prescription, smug self-satisfaction, and perhaps even the white ladyhood she so despised in her Naxos colleagues. Her sense of style and propriety makes her even more a misfit among her husband's poor parishioners than her fondness for the unconventional had made her at Naxos. To the black women she tries to instruct, she is an "uppity, meddlin' No'the'nah." Even as she is devoured and diminished by too many children too quickly come, even as the body she once thought of only as "something on which to hang lovely fabrics" becomes constantly swollen with child and racked with pain, the women around her pity not Helga but her husband.

We hear no more talk of satin gowns and brocaded mules. But as the story closes, like a lid on a casket, we are left wondering if the next garment to drape the perhaps terminally pregnant Helga will be a shroud. Yet it is not childbirth or motherhood, or even patriarchy, that overcomes Helga as much as it is the irreconcilable social, psychosexual, and racial contradictions that become her quicksand. Helga is unable to *fashion* an individual identity against the competing ideological and iconographic forces that ultimately ren- der her invisible. Unlike her blues-singing contemporaries, she does not have the luxury of donning a woman-proud persona and acting out the days of her life as a performer on a stage. Helga, however, also has sung the blues; it is just that no one has listened. Ultimately, then, the unreal estate that Larsen constructs for her heroine is not a bourgeois materialism but a subalterity in which her blues cannot be heard.

If beads and boas and brocades helped to empower black women blues per- formers, a decided deliberateness in dressing is one of the ways in which the women characters of Fauset's and Larsen's novels are sexually empowered to attract and seduce—to do business in and around the marriage market. But the empowerment, as both authors explore, is for the most part illusory. In their novels, lace and satin are as constricting and confining as gender roles and colored skin, as the "draped-down" would-be seducer becomes not only the seduced but the fetishized commodity as well. Two of Fauset's novels, *The Chinaberry Tree* and *Plum Bun*, provide a fitting forum for exploring both the issue of dressing for social success and the relationship between racial iconography and sexual commodification.

Metaphorically reminiscent of Charles Chesnutt's *House Behind the Cedars* (1900), *The Chinaberry Tree* is concerned with the consequences of miscegenation, adultery, and confining social and sexual values—the "Thou shalt nots," as Fauset calls them in her foreword—of a people who, by virtue of their history as "victims of many phases of immorality," can ill afford to judge others of their race but who do so nevertheless.[12] Like Chesnutt's white-skinned heroine Rena Walden, Laurentine Strange, *Chinaberry*'s central female figure, is the illegitimate daughter of a white gentleman and his longtime colored mistress.[13] Unlike Rena, however, Laurentine does not attempt to escape the burdens of her mixed heritage by passing for white. She plots instead to *pass* into the welcoming arms of bourgeois black society through marriage to a colored man of means and property.

Because of her family history, Laurentine is a social outcast, believed by the colored people of her hometown (Red Brook, New Jersey) to possess bad blood. To a certain extent, however, Laurentine's "quarantine" is self-imposed, for she has internalized the value system that blames the victim and holds the child responsible for the sins of the father—and the mother. She has bought the myth of her own bad mixed blood. Scandalized by her illegitimate birth, she is obsessed with being, acting, appearing decent. Her exemplary life, her successful, white-clients-only dressmaking business, and her financial independence are not enough decency, however. Her personal prayer is for "peace and security, a home life like other women, a name, protection" (21). As she assesses her own particular human condition, her only hope for legitimacy, respectability, acceptance, and safety is a single colored man in want of a wife. Dressing the parts of woman/wife/mother is an essential aspect of the coupling process. With one eye on the mirror and the other on marriage, Laurentine chooses her attire like a blues queen preparing for performance: "She would wear the red dress . . . a shallow, round neck, not too low . . . not too elaborate either as though one were deliberately dressing up, as it were" (52). Fauset's irony is clear, for, of course, Laurentine *is* very deliberately dressing up.

On the off chance that her well-to-do colored suitor, Phil Hackett, might pop in to see her unexpectedly, Laurentine armors herself in a red housedress, "trim and snug and perfect, a little dressier than usual" for the time of day (52). Later, as she prepares for an evening date she expects to end in a marriage proposal, she dresses "feverishly" in a "ravishing" red gown and thin smoky stockings. She lets down her long straight hair because, as Fauset tells us, "she who knew so little of men knew that colored men liked their wives to have straight hair, 'good' hair." Yet, even as Laurentine reckons her womanly wiles, even as she primps and plots and powders, even as she dresses for subtle seduction, "her face hot and flushed" with excitement, she contemplates her own purity: her family life might not be blameless, but she herself has been "as pure as snow, as chaste as a nun" (58–59)—in a ravishing red, figure-hugging habit.

Taken inside Laurentine's consciousness as well as her bedroom, the reader sees the character doubly exposed. In Fauset's work, such dressing scenes (and her novels are full of them) often unfold in the form of double-edged, revealing details that cut through to the underside of the garments, leaving the characters exposed, vulnerable—almost as if the very act of dressing the body is an undressing of the soul. Consider Laurentine again, dressing for Phil Hackett's gaze:

> But she was beautiful, she knew it . . . and if she married Phil she would exercise the spell of her beauty on him to its fullest extent.
>
> Still pleased with the vision, she studied herself. Her slender, well-moulded figure showed to every advantage in a dress of green developed in silk and wool. . . .
>
> She picked up her rouge but excited anticipation had already given her a beautiful flush, so she put it down again, applying her lipstick ever so slightly. (35)

The doorbell rings, signaling Phil's arrival, and Laurentine hurriedly completes gift wrapping her personal package by draping herself in a green cloth coat, with a high mink collar, that fits "so beautifully, so snugly." If her business continues to prosper, she muses, she will be able to afford a fur coat, but how much better still to receive such a gift from Phil Hackett. "With her taste, with her skilful fingers and his money she would be able to show Red Brook what dressing really meant. . . . Oh God," she says, "you know all I want is a chance to show them how decent I am" (35–36). Marriage to Phil Hackett is the vehicle through which Laurentine hopes to ride into the realm of decency, into the high society of Red Brook's black elite. And she misses no opportunity to flaunt her wares—decently, of course. Phil's "admiring gaze," the text tells us, made her grow "surer of herself, even provocative" (38).

Such scenes reveal both the psychosexual contradictions with which Fauset is concerned and her critique of the historical conditions that produce what might be called a trauma of pretense and hypocrisy. Critics, however, have often missed Fauset's irony, mistaking parody for praise. Historically, black women like Laurentine Strange are as "always already sexual" as the blues women against whom they define themselves. What we see exposed, if we read between the lines of Fauset's fiction, is the hypocrisy of the historical moment. What we hear if we listen closely to her prose is Fauset's critical, mocking tone, suggesting not sympathy for or accord with the value systems of her class- and clothes-conscious heroines, as many critics have insisted, but a kind of aloof derision, perhaps at moments even disdain, for their self-deception and self-hatred. Elizabeth Ammons, who has also taken note of the often disdainful timbre in Fauset's voice, characterizes her tone as a "subtle assertion of authorial superiority, even to women characters with whom [Fauset] supposedly sympathize[s]."[14] Ammons suggests that this authorial superiority may derive from Fauset's class consciousness and particular standards of propriety. I would argue, however, that it is the *characters'*, not Fauset's, class pretensions and standards of propriety and decency that are at issue here.

While it is abundantly clear that Emma Dunham Kelley loves Megda and her four Cottage City girls,[15] Fauset frequently seems neither to love nor even like many of the women and men she creates. There is little, if any, liking shown *Plum Bun*'s light-skinned Angela Murray, for example, when she denies knowing her brown-skinned sister, Jinny, to avoid revealing her own colored heritage to the white man she hopes will marry her. Fauset's novels do, however, create a climate of understanding for such less-than-likeable heroines as Angela. The degree of understanding varies directly with the extent to which these characters are presented as products of ideology, as victims of their socialization in a materialist, racist, sexist society. In keeping with the sociopolitical energies of Fauset's novels, the degree of sympathy increases as the characters divest themselves of moral blindness, selfishness, naïveté, materialism, cruelty, racialism, and excessive pride and propriety and learn the "truth" about themselves and their historical situations.

The particular "truth" Fauset seems to want to tell about values and the human condition is presented through Asshur Lane, one of two black male rescuers and protectors in *The Chinaberry Tree*. Unaware of the less-than-respectable circumstances of her own birth, Laurentine's cousin, Melissa Paul, at one point remarks with sympathetic indignation that Laurentine's chances for a good marriage are limited by the fact that her parents were not married to each other.[16] Asshur replies with considerable fervor:

> Well, what of it? And let me tell you my dear girl there're worse things in this world than not being married. And any man who lets the facts of Laurentine's parentage stand in his way, any colored man especially, doesn't deserve the name of man. How many of us can trace his ancestry back more than three generations? Perhaps a few thousand of all the millions of colored people in this country. (73)

If not the text's *raisonneur,* Asshur is its historian or, more correctly, its sociologist. (In fact, we are told immediately, "But Melissa was not interested in sociology.") His words echo Fauset's prefatory comment about African Americans as the "victims of many phases of immorality" who still insist on a certain set of "Thou shalt nots." Both Asshur's remarks and Fauset's seem to point toward the same "propriety gap" with which nineteenth-century women novelists were concerned: the difference between the *ideal* standards prescribed by white America and the *real* conditions under which black Americans work, live, and love. Like her sister nineteenth-century novelists, Fauset seems—at least at moments—to call for revised standards of womanhood, decency, propriety, given the historical realities with which all African Americans are confronted. Life in America has left none of its black inhabitants pure or perfect, has placed no one in a position to throw stones.

But Fauset's message seems ultimately a mixed one, for Laurentine and her cousin Melissa, who only at the end of the novel learns of her own illegitimate birth, are both "rescued" from social marginality by the promise of protection and respectability through marriage to "splendid" men—men unconcerned with their beloveds' family histories. Asshur Lane will marry Melissa, and while Phil Hackett was ultimately too politically ambitious to risk his future on Laurentine's past, Stephen Denleigh, yet another colored physician, is proud to have her as his future wife. This is the kind of ending that has left Fauset's readers complaining of her novels' sudden collapse into convention and sentimentality. I would argue, however, that Fauset's ending is problematically conventional only if *The Chinaberry Tree* is mistakenly read as realism. Fauset's creation of an "ideal estate," in which Laurentine and Melissa retreat into thoughts of their respective rescues from the social abyss of illegitimacy and near-incest—even as "their men" contemplate marriage, home, children, and domesticity—seems to me a final swipe at the very form she has employed to critique both itself and the social values that elevate, idealize, and romanticize love and marriage.

Comparing Fauset's *Plum Bun* to Larsen's *Quicksand*, white feminist critic Missy Dehn Kubitschek asserts that "*Plum Bun* is in most ways a lesser novel because it displays a fundamental confusion of genre, being neither romance nor realism."[17] *The Chinaberry Tree*, like most of Fauset's fiction, displays the same fundamental confusion of form, and this, I would argue, may be its greatest strength. For Fauset is indeed writing neither realism nor naturalism; nor is she falling back on pure romanticism. She is interrogating old forms and inventing something new. This rewriting, re-creation, this confusion of genre, is indeed fundamental; it is precisely what African American writers have done historically, from William Wells Brown to Alice Walker. In this instance this "confusion" is Fauset's particular, though unacknowledged, gift to modernism.

While hardly as overtly erotic as blues like "Put a Little Sugar in My Bowl," *Plum Bun*, Fauset's second novel, is nevertheless profoundly concerned with sex and sexuality—a bourgeois version of the copulating blues. In fact, the entire novel can be read as an extended sexual metaphor that raises critical questions about the relationship between power and passion, dollars and desire, and offers an implicit critique of the would-be blues moment and folk modality. The text takes its title and central metaphor from a nursery rhyme: "To market, to market, to buy a plum bun. Home again, home again, market is done." (In the version I grew up on, the item to be purchased at market was a "fat hen.") A plum bun, in the blues idiom with which Fauset plays brilliantly, is, as one of her male characters remarks, "a particularly attractive piece." The title, in its metaphorical connection to both the nursery rhyme and the sexual vernacular, announces the text's concern with the mature, blues themes of sex as a consumable commodity and the female body as a bargaining chip in a high-stakes game of strip poker, which lays the characters bare without the textual removal of a single piece of clothing. *Plum Bun* has no nudity, no sexually explicit love scenes. No groping, petting, or fondling. Yet, as Deborah McDowell points out in her introduction to the Pandora edition, the novel "brims with sexual winks and innuendos,"[18] from its lewdly suggestive title to the tightly conceived formal structures that track the heroine's growth and development through rites of passage: sections of the novel significantly named "Home," "Market," "Plum Bun," "Home Again," and "Market Is Done."

Angela Murray, the not-always-sympathetic mulatta heroine of *Plum Bun*, is another of Fauset's sexually embodied beings. Angela's aim is to beg, borrow, or steal for herself the "happily ever after" fantasy marriage of which fairy tales are made. As models of such marriages, she holds before her the tales of perfect love read to her at bedtime by her light-skinned mother, whose own marriage to a much darker man would seem to Angela blissfully happy were it not for the difference in her parents' skin colors—a difference of far greater concern to her than to them. Light like her mother but color-struck to a degree her mother is not, Angela believes that "being coloured in America . . . [is] nothing short of a curse" (53).

While Angela has a painfully well-honed understanding of race relations in the United States, she does not seem to understand that fairy tales, as any aficionado of the blues knows, are not the stuff of which real erotic relations are made. After her parents' deaths, she leaves both her Philadelphia "Home" and her dark-skinned sister behind and goes to "Market," to New York City, where she intends to rid herself of the burdens of racial prejudice once and for all by passing for white and marrying herself off to a wealthy, influential white man. Finding such a man and making such a marriage become her goals. Ironically, she is detoured from the one by finding the other. She is, in effect, diverted from matrimony by her own desires—material and sexual—even as she thinks she is closing in on the diamond ring. She finds a plum-bun prince easily enough: wealthy, white Roger Fielding. But Fielding doesn't quite play the marriage market by the rules of Angela's fairy tales. As Deborah McDowell explains:

> Angela's and Roger's trips to the market are for two different plum buns. For her the plum bun is power and influence attainable only through marriage to a wealthy white man. For him, the plum bun is sex, a consumable to be bought, used up, and expended. Put still another way, Angela's game play for marriage is Roger's foreplay for sex. (xiv)

Their "his and her" shopping lists make the market an at-once passionate and perilous place for Angela, as her relationship with Roger becomes a contest of wills and won'ts. In over her head (or some other part of her anatomy), Angela seeks advice from a friend, Martha Burden, who schools her in the conventions of coupling and the ABCs of trading in the flesh:

It is a game, and the hardest game in the world for a woman, but the most fascinating; the hardest in which to strike a happy medium. You see, you have to be careful not to withhold too much and yet to give very little. If we don't give enough we lose them. If we give too much we lose ourselves. (145)

Martha Burden's voice, it seems, is the voice of experience; her advice is a lesson in sexual politics and the "burdens" of gender. "Oh, Angele," she tells her pupil, "God doesn't like women." Curiously enough, to Angela (known to her white friends as Angele) Roger Fielding is a "blonde, glorious god," overwhelming and persistent. What Angela does not see is that like the God Martha cites, her glorious blonde god Roger doesn't like women either, except for that one thing mothers warn their daughters about.

Angela attempts to play the love game on Martha's terms rather than Roger's, but Roger's trump card turns out to be Angela's own sexual desire, as his constant proximity leaves her "appalled by her thoughts and longings" (200). On the proverbial terrible night, too cold and rainy for Angela to drive him from the "leaping, golden flames" of *her fire*, Roger presses his advantage, and, with a kiss, "her very bones turned to water" (201). Her panting, "Oh, Roger, must it be like this? Can't it be any other way?" is no match for the arms around her and the voice she hears only from a great distance "breaking, pleading, promising": "Everything will be all right, darling, darling. I swear it. Only trust me, trust me!" (202–3).

Thus, even in the guise of a white woman, Angela gets caught in the trap Alex Olsen attempted to spring on Helga Crane in *Quicksand*. Hoist on the petard of her own passion, she becomes not the willing wife of Roger Fielding but his reluctant mistress. The man she hoped to maneuver into marriage maneuvers her into bed. Completing her risqué play with nursery rhyme and adult blues themes, Fauset sends Angela "to market" to buy a "plum bun" and brings her "Home Again" with an empty basket (or perhaps, in the spirit of "Put a Little Sugar in My Bowl," with a hot dog for her roll). Angela gambles her most valuable stock—her virginity—in what the novel, in splendid signification, constructs as a commodities exchange, and she loses, quite literally, her pants. But market is not done . . . yet. And Angela, who, like any good blues woman, has a backdoor man waiting in the wings, will have her turn to send Roger packing and to find a "happily ever after" ending in the arms of another man, who like her has learned the lesson of passing.

While *Plum Bun*, like much of Fauset's work, has been rejected by many critics as just another novel of manners, its structurally complex and sexually sophisticated mannerisms, as feminist scholars such as Deborah McDowell have demonstrated, defy such easy dismissals. If Bessie Smith and Ma Rainey made being woman-proud and sexually active seem easy, Fauset showed how complex and complicated womanhood and virginity could be in the Roaring Twenties. Long before critics talked in terms of dialectics, Fauset explored the disparities of desire and danger and the complications of identity and ideology in the lives of women across class and racial lines.

Passing Fancies

However concerned with authenticity, ideology, sexuality, and the social contradictions of the day *There Is Confusion*, *Quicksand*, *The Chinaberry Tree*,
and *Plum Bun* may be, perhaps no novel of the era attends to the iconography
of the black female body and the dialectics of desire more dramatically than
Nella Larsen's second novel, *Passing* (1929). In fact, in *Passing* the degree of
notice Irene Redfield takes of her friend Clare Kendry's draped-down body
has led Deborah McDowell to argue that Larsen establishes (if only by implication) the possibility of a sexual attraction between the two women characters.
To support her claim, McDowell reads carefully the body language of the
text. Steeped as it is in double entendres, red dresses, bare shoulders, and fire
imagery, the novel indeed presents a plethora of erotic figures to be read.
Irene is ever aware of Clare's "tempting mouth," her "seductive caressing
smile," her "arresting eyes," her "incredibly beautiful face," which sends a
"slight shiver" over the spectator. As seen through Irene's eyes, Clare is "a
lovely creature," "really almost too good-looking," whose gaze leaves her
feeling "petted and caressed."

McDowell takes as additional evidence of an erotic attraction between the
two women the text's opening image: an envelope containing a letter from the
long-lost Clare, who has been passing for white. McDowell views this envelope as a metaphorical vagina and argues that Irene, to whom the envelope is
addressed, is justified in her reluctance to open it, given the sexual overtones
of the letter it contains:

> For I am lonely . . . cannot help longing to be with you again, as I have never
> longed for anything before; and I have wanted many things in my life. . . .
> It's like an ache, a pain that never ceases . . . and it's your fault, 'Rene dear.
> At least partly. For I wouldn't now, perhaps, have this terrible, this wild
> desire if I hadn't seen you that time in Chicago.[19]

The letter leaves Irene with flaming cheeks and a rush of feeling for which she
can find no name. The eroticism of this and other sexually loaded passages is
textually confirmed, according to McDowell, by Larsen's use of fire imagery,
"the conventional representation of sexual desire" (xxvii).

McDowell's reading is an enabling one. It redirects our long-diverted critical
attention to the treatment of female sexuality not only in Larsen's work but in
that of her contemporaries as well, and it raises important questions about the
homoerotic undertones and overtones of this and other texts. Who owns the
gaze? Is the gaze inherently masculine or essentially sexual? What happens
when women gaze upon each other? Is the very act of gazing upon the female
body an appropriation of the masculine and an invocation of the erotic? Is
there a grammar of the female gaze? These are among the questions occa-
sioned by McDowell's reading of a lesbian subtext in *Passing*. I am not certain,
however, that this provocative interpretation, despite its attention to the figurative language of the text, ultimately supports its own thesis or answers its

own questions about what McDowell describes tentatively as Larsen's flirtation with the suggestion of the idea of a lesbian relationship between Irene and Clare (xxiii).

To express my skepticism more directly: I am not convinced that the metaphors in *Passing* always hold the erotic meanings McDowell assigns to them. I am not convinced, for example, that the envelope containing Clare's letter is the metaphorical vagina McDowell constructs it to be. With its "extraordinary size," "thin Italian paper," and purple ink, the mysterious missive, and Irene's reaction to it, might as readily be taken to symbolize the enveloped self afraid to confront its absent (repressed, denied, buried) other—a calling card from the grave of buried feelings, as it were.

What happens if we historicize Larsen's grammar, placing it within the blues/bohemian/bourgeois moment? Does such a placement give the text's linguistic figures a different face value altogether? Viewed in historical perspective, the looking, touching, and caressing that McDowell reads as signs of lesbian attraction may have more to do with homosociability than with either homo- or heterosexuality, with the nature of both women's culture and social and linguistic conventions at the time. That is to say, the interaction between Clare and Irene may reflect the moment's preoccupation with the "always already sexual" black female body, or it may suggest a not necessarily sexual way of being women together, which the spread of Freudian thought recoded and perhaps destroyed. It may also reflect a woman's way of talking through the body—of expressing material or experiential desire in bodily terms. As Lauren Berlant has argued, "there may be a difference between wanting someone sexually and wanting someone's body." What Irene wants, Berlant suggests, is not to make love to Clare, but "to occupy, to experience the privileges of Clare's body . . . to wear [Clare's] way of wearing her body, like a prosthesis, or a fetish."[20] "Fetish" seems to me very much the right trope: a figuring of the black female body as fetishized commodity that Larsen earlier critiqued in *Quicksand*. But if Irene wants to wear the experiences of Clare's fetishized body, Clare wants to don Irene's as well, including, perhaps, Irene's husband, Dr. Brian Redfield.

Here I think we come to the crux of Larsen's complex social and psychosexual critique. Clare and Irene—the exotic and the elite—may represent the dialectics of the Harlem Renaissance moment itself. Written as part vamp, part flapper, and part femme fatale, Clare reflects the bohemian fascination with sexuality, the Greenwich Village high life, the glamorous, the risqué, the foreign, and the forbidden. Irene, on the other hand, with her race work, literary salons, and house parties, signifies the propriety, the manners, the social and racial uplift, and especially the security with which the black bourgeoisie of the 1920s was preoccupied. For Irene, after all, "security was the most important and desired thing in life." Not for "happiness, love, or some wild ecstacy that she had never known would she exchange her security" (235). Viewed in this light, the text's actual sexual preference may be for the autoerotic: Clare and Irene may be read as body doubles or, perhaps more precisely, as halved selves through whom Larsen explores a host of dialectics, not the least of which are desire and danger, woman-proud promiscuity and repression, freedom and confinement.

At the risk of mixing my own bourgeois blues metaphor, I might even suggest that Larsen has rescored "The Love Song of J. Alfred Prufrock," creating a "you and I" who represent opposing sides of a divided self. But "The Love Song of Irene Redfield" is sung without the touch of levity or the conscious self-consciousness of Eliot's poem. Irene issues no wake-up call to "you and I"; she invites no engagement with her alter ego. She is bent instead on denying the other, on preserving the status quo of her comfortable, secure middle-class existence.

Larsen has given us something more than just another simple doubling or dividing, however, for Clare is less Irene's alter ego than her alter libido, the buried, long-denied sexual self whose absence in his wife has led Irene's husband, Brian, to conclude, with some bitterness, that sex (with Irene?) is a joke. To Irene's concerns that their older son is picking up "some queer ideas about things—some things—from older boys," Brian responds scornfully: "D'you mean ideas about sex, Irene? . . . Well, what of it? . . . The sooner and the more he learns about sex, the better for him. And most certainly if he learns that it's a grand joke, the greatest in the world. It'll keep him from lots of disappointments later on" (188–89). The fact that Irene cannot bring herself to say the word *sex*, even to her husband, suggests that she may be the source of Brian's own sexual disappointments. The Redfields' marriage, we know, is largely passionless. The couple sleep in separate bedrooms, and there is a general chill in the air between them, which warms up only in the presence of the decidedly sensual Clare, who Irene suspects is "capable of heights and depths of feeling that she, Irene Redfield, had never known. Indeed, never cared to know" (195). This "suspicion" (Larsen's word) will later be linked to another: that Brian and Clare are having an affair, that Brian has found in Clare Kendry the heights and depths of feeling missing in his wife.

But if Clare is Irene's alter libido, Irene is Clare's as well, a connection to the "primitive" Negro past, gone but too instinctual to be forgotten. This instinctive need to rejoin—the need of the exotic sexual other (Clare) to reconnect with its equally (but differently) exotic racial self (Irene, though perhaps more what Irene represents than with what she is)—may be the source of the longing, the ache, the unceasing pain, and the wild desire Clare writes of in her letter to Irene. A closer look at the letter, with the phrases McDowell omits, lends support to this possible interpretation. (Italics indicate the omitted phrases; except for the closing set, the ellipses are Larsen's.)

> ". . . For I am lonely, so lonely . . . cannot help longing to be with you again, as I have never longed for anything before; and I have wanted many things in my life. . . . *You can't know how in this pale life of mine I am all the time seeing the bright pictures of that other that I once thought I was glad to be free of.* . . . It's like an ache, a pain that never ceases. . . ." *Sheets upon thin sheets of it. And ending with,* "and it's your fault. . . ." (145)

While McDowell's edited version of the letter situates Irene as the absolute object of Clare's desire, the actual letter directs the bulk of that "wild desire" to the *other* Negro life Irene represents: the black life Clare shed like a dead skin some time ago and now wants to reclaim, it seems, by appropriating the experiences of Irene's skin, a bit like any other primitivist. Clare, in fact, can be read as a comment on primitivists who enjoy the privileges of white skin by day but flock to Harlem by night to enjoy the pleasures they associate with black flesh. Irene suggests as much herself when she tells Clare at one point that white people come to Harlem for the same reason Clare has started coming: "[T]o see Negroes . . . to get material to turn into shekels . . . to gaze on the great and near great while they gaze on the Negroes" (198). The threat to Irene in this configuration is the threat of the displaced other attempting to reclaim its racial self through the absorption of its alternate subjectivity. Put another way, the object of desire for both Irene and Clare is a total subjectivity, a whole self—coded in both racial and sexual terms, repressed in Irene and expressed in Clare. The problem is that two halves make only one whole; therefore, the completeness Clare is so intent on pursuing can be attained only at the expense of Irene's subjectivity. In such a reading, the danger Irene senses but cannot name is a fear of a loss of self, and the attraction—the "inexplicable onrush of affectionate feeling"—is love for lost self.

This reading of possible autoerotic signification in *Passing* is by no means a denial of McDowell's homoerotic theory, however, but a possible expansion of it. For there is no essential sexual self; homosexuality is often encoded textually as self-love or narcissism. Through her "unseeing eyes," Irene comes to view Clare as the intruding, insinuating other she loves to hate, but Clare may actually be the threatening, disruptive, daring, sexual self—with "a having way"—that Irene hates to love. Hates enough and fears enough perhaps to kill.

But this interplay of self and other can be read on a variety of levels: the failure, even betrayal, of female friendship, for example, a failure with tragic consequences. "Unseeing" as her eyes may be, Irene recognizes a kind of duplicity in Clare's sudden friendship. She has the sense at times that Clare is acting, and views her friend's "catlike" ways as a threat to her own stability. "The trouble with Clare," she concludes, "was, not only that she wanted to have her cake and eat it too, but that she wanted to nibble at the cake of other folk as well" (182). Irene begins to suspect that the particular cake Clare has been nibbling at is the "devil's food" of Dr. Brian Redfield.

For McDowell, an affair between friend and husband exists only in Irene's imagination, as a projection "of her own developing passion for Clare onto Brian" (xxviii). The novel itself, however, leaves wonderfully ambiguous the question of an affair between Brian and Clare, even as it drops a number of clues that would seem to confirm Irene's suspicions. If we read Clare as a departed daughter desperate to return to the racial fold, an affair between her and Brian becomes almost a narrative necessity. For just as marriage to a white man confirmed Clare as white, coupling with a black man is an alchemy that may turn her black again.

Even in a more conservative reading, however, Irene is not irrationally out of line to be suspicious of a friend who warns: "I haven't any proper morals or sense of duty, as you have, that makes me act as I do. . . . Can't you realize that I'm not like you a bit? Why, to get the things I want badly enough, I'd do anything, hurt anybody, throw anything away. Really, 'Rene, I'm not safe" (210). This revelation of self is followed by a fit of uncontrollable and inconsolable crying. Irene will later remember this tearful warning and link it directly to what she reads as Clare's willingness to sacrifice the respectability and security of marriage (what Irene holds most dear about her own marriage), to hurt friends and break up families, even to give up her child, if Brian and the black world he is a part of are what she wants. The text turns in part, however, on the fact that Irene is as determined to keep what she has as Clare is to get what she wants.

While it is again a detail that can be read on a variety of levels, it is interesting to note that Irene's eyes cease to be described as "unseeing" at the precise moment she becomes aware of the affair between Clare and Brian—real or imagined. "She closed her unseeing eyes and clenched her fists," we are told, in what I believe is the last reference to Irene's myopia. After a generous flow of "hot tears of rage and shame," she says to her face in the mirror: "I do think . . . that you've been something—oh, very much—of a damned fool" (218). While critics have generally read the repeated reference to Irene's "unseeing eyes" as an indication of the distorted vision that makes her an untrustworthy narrator, the description may also mean that Irene is the proverbial "last one to know" wife who has been blind to a friend's play for her husband.

As her own internally stagnant but externally proper marriage withers even more, Irene becomes increasingly convinced that Brian is having an affair with Clare. Her fears for her own marriage or, rather, the outward appearance of her marriage, mount when she meets Clare's husband, John Bellew, on the street as she is walking arm in arm with an "unmistakably colored" woman friend. She knows that it is a short step from Bellew's realizing that his wife's white-skinned childhood friend, Irene, is colored to his realizing that his white-skinned wife is colored, too. Irene is afraid that nigger-hating Bellew will divorce Clare, leaving her free for Brian. She keeps her fears and her suspicions to herself, however, and begins to think: "If Clare should die! Then—Oh, it was vile! To think, yes, to wish that!" But while they make her feel faint and sick, thoughts of Clare's death continue to dance in her head.

With the stage thus set and the key players thus primed, the curtain opens on a Harlem apartment party, where an outraged John Bellew suddenly bursts in and confronts his wife with the truth of her racial identity: "So you're a nigger, a damned dirty nigger!" Clare, standing serene by an open window, is unperturbed, smiling that famous faint smile that so maddens Irene. With a "terror tinged with ferocity," the text tells us, Irene rushes across the room and lays her hand on Clare's bare arm. "She couldn't have Clare Kendry cast aside by Bellew. She couldn't have her free" (239). In the confusion that follows and with Irene by her side, Clare falls, throws herself, or is pushed out the window and plummets six stories to her death.

Many critics read Clare's death at the end of the novel as yet another unfortunate "concession to convention." Once again, a high-spirited, defiant heroine is confined to either the deathbed of marriage or the graveyard. For Cheryl Wall, Clare's death is merely the typical fate of the mulatta heroine.[21] For Robert Bone, however, Clare's "passing" is the text's tragic flaw—"a false and shoddy denouement [that] prevents the novel from rising above mediocrity."[22] For Deborah McDowell, Larsen's ending seems to "punish the very values the novel implicitly affirms, to honor the very value system the text implicitly satirizes" (xxx–xxxi). And while Margaret Perry acknowledges that Larsen may have wanted the ending to leave the reader perpetually perplexed, she maintains that the ambiguity of the circumstances of Clare's death "does not give the book any artistic complexity that might intrigue the imagination."[23]

I would argue, however, that in its purposeful ambiguity, *Passing* ultimately affirms neither Irene's values nor Clare's; rather, it holds both up to scrutiny, if not ridicule, as signs of the times. But as Thadious Davis, Claudia Tate, and others have pointed out, how one views the ending of *Passing* may depend on who one holds to be the novel's central figure. As my own reading no doubt reveals, *Passing* seems to me to be very much Irene's story. Clare, however central to the unraveling of the plot, is a foil against whom Irene's middle-class consciousness develops or, more correctly, deteriorates in demonic degrees. When Irene instead of Clare is taken to be the central figure and when murder rather than suicide or accident is viewed as the cause of Clare's death, the text's heroine ceases to be a typical, passive, conventional tragic mulatta who pales beside the powerful image of woman-proud blues performers. She becomes instead a protector of the precious domestic realm— defender of middle-class marriage, bourgeois home, family, fidelity, and, above all, security. She gives new meaning to the term "home protection." As a wife, betrayed by friend and husband alike, fighting for her marriage, Irene gains what Houston Baker might call "blues force" as a heroine. She becomes, in such a reading, at once an active agent in the ordering of her own life and a grotesque, which may be precisely the point.

The infinite possibilities of Larsen's fictive invention, in my view, make *Passing* artistically complex beyond the limits of any particular reading or any single rhythm. Perhaps this is why I want not to discredit Deborah McDowell's inspired and empowering interpretation but to disrupt the fixity of the reading—to wrest it from the assumption that Larsen's sexual signifying *necessarily* suggests lesbian attraction, particularly where no "definition" is offered for "lesbian." Ironically, while she has elsewhere chided Barbara Smith for her "vague and imprecise" definition of lesbianism,[24] McDowell offers no clarification of her own usage of the term. She appears to take "lesbian relationship" to mean a necessarily *physical* attraction of female body to female body for seizure of erotic pleasure and sexual satisfaction. *Passing* seems to me, however, to transcend such limited definitions. What is most engaging about the text is the multiplicity of meanings inspired by Larsen's brilliant use of the body and her clever manipulation of both metaphor and materiality. Larsen accomplishes in *Passing* that "surplus of signifiers"—the superabundance of interpretability—which, according to Frank Kermode, makes a work a classic.[25] In both *Quicksand* and *Passing*, Larsen creates that unreal estate I spoke of earlier, a fantastic realm we as critics seem to need to ground in a particular objective reality. McDowell's reading opens windows into the text, to be sure, but it also seems to me to hinge precisely what Larsen, in splendid ambiguity, has so cleverly unhinged.

The heroines of Jessie Fauset and Nella Larsen are by no means spayed, passionless decorations, adorning the pristine pages of immaculately conceived lace-curtain romances. They are, on the contrary, implicitly sexual beings, finely tuned to both the power and the vulnerability of their own female bodies. At a moment when black female sexuality was either completely unwritten to avoid endorsing sexual stereotypes or sensationally overwritten to both defy and exploit those stereotypes, Fauset and Larsen edged the discourse into another realm: a realm precariously balanced on the cusp of the respectable and the risqué; a realm that is at times *neutral*, perhaps, but never *neuter*; a realm in which they, too, participate in reclaiming the black body and in defining African American expressive culture.

6

Stoning the Romance: Passion, Patriarchy, and the Modern Marriage Plot

> The thought of her husband roused in her a deep and contemptuous hatred. At his every approach she had forcibly to subdue a furious inclination to scream out in protest. Shame, too, swept over her at every thought of her marriage. Marriage. This sacred thing of which parsons and other Christian folk ranted so sanctimoniously, how immoral—according to their own standards—it could be! But Helga felt also a modicum of pity for him, as for one already abandoned. She meant to leave him. . . .
>
> Of the children Helga tried not to think. She wanted not to leave them—if possible. . . . How, then, was she to escape from the oppression, the degradation, that her life had become? . . . It was almost hopeless. . . .
>
> And hardly had she left her bed and become able to walk again without pain, hardly had the children returned from the homes of the neighbors, when she began to have her fifth child.
>
> —NELLA LARSEN, *Quicksand*

If Jessie Fauset and Nella Larsen are transitional figures whose novels form a bridge between the literary passionlessness of the 1890s and the sexual openness of the modern era, Zora Neale Hurston is a pivotal point whose texts traverse the terrain between concern with the politics of sexuality, often covertly expressed in the fiction of black women writers of the nineteenth and early twentieth centuries, and the openly scathing critiques of erotic relations as the root of female oppression which characterize the contemporary black feminist text. But while critics have privileged Hurston's *Their Eyes Were Watching God* as the premier black feminist novel, in part because of its critique of the institution of marriage, few texts in the entire history of African American women's fiction depict matrimony and childbearing as woman's ruination more dramatically than Larsen's *Quicksand*. Helga Crane, the novel's troubled, sensual heroine, ultimately surrenders herself to and satisfies her sexual hunger through what seems the only legitimate outlet for that "nameless, shameful impulse": marriage.

The morning after a textually ambiguous but presumably sexual encounter with the minister who walked her to her hotel from the sanctified church in which they met, Helga decides to sanction spiritually the physical intimacy of the previous evening by marrying the preacher. While she is concerned about surrendering her independence, she takes comfort in the thought that she has found both sexual outlet and spiritual salvation, for she is convinced that marriage to a minister must bring with it a double blessing. Sure of herself and, if not quite the man, her ability to manipulate him into marriage, Helga sets off in pursuit of Rev. Pleasant Green. "How could he," she thinks, as she dresses for seduction, "a naive creature like that, hold out against her?" She will "pretend" distress, fear, remorse, if she has to, but she will be married before the day is over.[1]

"And so in the confusion of seductive repentance," the text announces, "Helga Crane was married to the grandiloquent Reverend Mr. Pleasant Green, that rattish yellow man, who had so kindly, so unctuously, proffered his escort to her hotel on the memorable night of her conversion" (118). *Conversion* is an interesting word, used satirically by Larsen to refer to and to link Helga's religious and sexual initiations. Indeed, Larsen seems in this text to indict marriage, family, and religion as institutions which conspire to constrict and confine female sexual and spiritual independence. Within the confines of her marriage, Helga finds considerable sexual, if not total spiritual, fulfillment. Sexual intercourse, it appears, is freely enjoyed and frequently engaged in. Though filled with a general "gladness in living," Helga becomes particularly fond of the bodily comforts of the Alabama country nights. "And night came at the end of every day," we are told. "Emotional, palpitating, amorous, all that was living in her sprang like rank weeds[2] at the tingling thought of night, with a vitality so strong that it devoured all shoots of reason" (122). Larsen implies, however, that it is not her husband who makes Helga's nights so enrapturing, but *sex* with her husband, whose corpulence, stale sweat, and dirty fingernails, Helga manages, in the heat of passion, to pretend away.

The price of Helga's evening delights, however, is three babies, including twin boys, born within the short space of twenty months. The pregnancies and the babies they yield sap Helga's physical and emotional strength. Faint, fatigued, and friendless, she tries not to notice that even Reverend Green has lost interest in her, except for those rare moments when she is not either "preparing for or recovering from childbirth." When she turns to her soul-saving husband for help with her physical salvation, the reverend tells her that her help cometh from the Lord. But ultimately it is Reverend Green who is forthcoming, as he impregnates her yet again. Even as she plots her escape, Helga, barely recovered from the near-fatal delivery of her fourth child, finds herself pregnant with the fifth. In a move that would seem to link her vision to that of radical feminists writing today, Larsen leaves her heroine sinking in a quicksand of endless childbearing, nearly dead of marriage and maternity.

Decades before *The Feminine Mystique* declared to the world the discontent, dissatisfaction, and nameless yearning of the modern white housewife, black female artists and intellectuals such as Larsen and Hurston recognized that monogamous marriage was perhaps the greatest site of woman's oppression. Like such white women writers of the 1920s as Ellen Glasgow, Agnes Smedley, and Edith Summers Kelley,[3] black women novelists began to treat holy wedlock as an institution that kept women not only from the grandly constructive work Frances Harper and Anna Julia Cooper envisioned for them but also from themselves. It is no accident, then, that so many modern novels hatch marriage plots that unhinge notions of matrimonial bliss, ultimately treating romantic relationships as hotly contested terrain.

In black women's novels of the 1930s and 1940s, marriage is no longer the relation of rescue and protection it was in the nineteenth century; holy wedlock is no longer a site of utopian partnership, but a seat of emotional confinement, sexual commodification, and male domination, as well as infidelity, brutality, and betrayal. This emphasis on the cataclysmic quality of eros and the devastating consequences of female desire reverberates throughout the body of modern African American women's fiction, as author after author explores on paper the burdens and mixed blessings of love, marriage, and maternity in the lives of women. These explorations frequently center around critiques of and challenges to patriarchal authority, as black women novelists attempt to claim both female subjectivity and poetic authority. But this body of fiction also presents some exceptions to these rules or, at least, some different ways of addressing the issue of male-female power relations. One such exception is Dorothy West's *The Living Is Easy*, published in 1948, the same year as *Seraph on the Suwanee*.

In *The Living Is Easy*, it is not man who stands alone as the very principle of patriarchy, as in much of Hurston's work, but woman who stands beside or, rather, in front of him. Cold, calculating, class-conscious Cleo Jericho Judson, who might be described as the Scarlett O'Hara of black fiction, rules the Judson family and its rented manor like a patriarch, constantly maneuvering her husband, Bart Judson, Boston's leading black capitalist, out of as many of his "Almighty Dollars" as she can beg, borrow, or—quite frequently—steal. In fact, Cleo's "despotic nature," we are told, "found Mr. Judson a rival."[4] He rules a fruit market; she rules the house as if it were a kingdom and its inhabitants her serfs. Cleo is so bent on being in charge that she spent her wedding night laying down not her body but the terms of her marriage: spelling out what she would and would not do.

Chief among the "would nots" is sexual intercourse, for, as Cleo announced on her wedding night, "she had no intention of renouncing her maidenhead for one man if she had married to preserve it from another" (the sexual advances of her former employer). Her husband at first meets her declaration with patience, throwing his energy into buying and selling the fruit he loves almost as much as his wife. "There was rich satisfaction in seeing it ripen," West writes, speaking ostensibly of the fruit but with obvious sexual overtones, "seeing the downiness on it, the blush on it, feeling the firmness of its flesh." Bart could fondle the produce in a way he could not fondle his untouchable wife. But Cleo does not ripen, and the Judson marriage eventually evolves into what West describes as a "sex battle" in which Cleo surrenders to Bart's superior physical strength but wins the war nevertheless with "a weapon that would cut [her husband] down quickly and cleanly. She was ice." As West writes of the couple's lovemaking:

> Neither her mouth nor body moved to meet his. The open eyes were wide with mocking at the busyness below. There was no moment when everything in her was wrenched and she was one with the man who could submerge her in himself.
>
> Five years later, she conceived a child on a night when her body's hunger broke down her controlled resistance. For there was no real abhorrence of sex in her. Her need of love was as urgent as her aliveness indicated. But her perversity would not permit her to weaken. She would not face the knowledge that she was incomplete in herself. (35–36)

If controlled resistance is what Bart receives from Cleo in bed, active aggression is what he gets from her in other aspects of their marriage. Cleo's goal is to "bend a houseful of human souls to her will." To her the idea of being a helpmate is "the same thing as being a man's slave," and she has no intention of bowing for a moment to male power of any kind (71). She is presented as a master manipulator, whose cruelty and deceit wreak havoc on the family she tries to control. Bart Judson, on the other hand, is depicted as a caring, gentle man who, while he indeed loves the "Almighty Dollar," loves his wife and daughter far too much to be nearly as stingy with his money as Cleo constantly tells him he is, even as she picks his pockets bare and burdens him with more mouths to feed.

Bart thinks he is Mr. Big Business, the banana king of Boston, but however adept he is in the marketplace, Cleo is always several steps ahead of him in every other realm of their married life. He thinks, for example, that he is demonstrating his brilliant business acumen when he gives her forty-five dollars with which to rent a house she tells *him* costs fifty, but which actually rents for thirty-five. "I figure if this Jack the Ripper wants fifty dollars he'll take forty-five," Bart says, proud of himself. "You've got to get up with the early birds to get ahead of me," he adds, unaware that his wife has not only duped him out of an extra ten dollars a month and manipulated him into renting a ten-room house he does not want, but that she also has managed to make him think that it is his idea to rent the extra rooms to boarders, who she has already decided will be her three sisters and their children (10).

The house transaction is part of the fiercely upwardly mobile Cleo's plan to move herself and her family away from Boston's South End and closer to the prosperity and prestige of the elite white suburb of Brookline, where her daughter, Judy, will not have to go to school with "knotty-head niggers" (5). Having manipulated her husband out of more than enough money to rent the big house in Brookline, Cleo sets about stocking the manor with her three sisters, whom she lures away from their own husbands through a series of lies and deceits. She becomes a kind of robber baron/grande dame who raids her husband's wallet to support the bulging household of women and children she holds mesmerized with her storytelling and artful manipulations. Her reign is short-lived, however, for just when it seems she has all the pawns placed where she wants them, the walls around Cleo Jericho's kingdom begin to come tumbling down. She loses her sisters to the individual sorrows, marital tragedies, and personal paranoias that her deceit and their weaknesses have brought them. Her daughter, a child wise beyond her years and already determined not to be like her mother, is spiritually lost to her as well. Her husband's business fails, and he too leaves her to seek his fortune in New York. As with Scarlett O'Hara, it is only as her husband is about to leave her that the manipulative wife recognizes both his value and her affection for him. But in this text, too, tomorrow is another day whose outcome is ambiguous. The novel closes on a solitary Cleo, left alone to stew in the destruction she has wrought.

   The Living Is Easy critiques, among other things, the elitism and pretensions of the black bourgeoisie. Mary Helen Washington suggests, in fact, that in her desperate need for status—her desire to attend the right parties, the right church—Cleo is a metaphor for the community of "emerging black professionals who pride themselves on the distance they can create between themselves and poor blacks." The daughter's ultimate rejection of the mother and her values, Washington argues, is similar to Dorothy West's rejection of "that insular and narrow community of elitist blacks."[5] But in reading Cleo as the mother (the precursor, perhaps, of "the mother" in Paule Marshall's *Brown Girl Brownstones* [1959]) and the mother as a metaphor for the black bourgeoisie, it is important to note that West's portrait is not simply that of a matriarch. Cleo would be *king*, not mother. In fact, she views motherhood and the domestic sphere as an "insufficient scope for her tremendous vitality" and envies her husband and other businessmen the public, "free-striding" male realm in which they operate (70–71). Cleo is trapped in the wrong body and locked into the wrong sex/gender role, as much a victim of biology and sociology—of genetic miscasting—as those around her who become her victims. She rules her weaker family members precisely because they are weak and to a certain extent need her strength. They feed on her vitality; she thrives on their foibles.

   The Living Is Easy, then, it seems to me, makes a complex and complicated statement not only about marital and mother-daughter relations but about male and female power: about father law and mother rule. Cleo, in her exaggerated villainy, becomes a grotesque, a monster for whom it is almost impossible to feel sympathy even as she is left alone to drown in the wake of the destruction that her thirst for absolute power, her pretensions, and her possessiveness have wrought. Yet the sins of oppression for which many critics believe the text condemns Cleo are the same virtues of aggression for which men are praised and promoted. Pride, strength, willfulness, subterfuge, authoritativeness, manipulation, craftiness, even deceit are the stuff of which tycoons are made—the tactics by which corporations prosper. Such men society calls successful, savvy; such women it labels grotesques, bitches, Sapphires, jezebels. Ironically, the ruthlessness Cleo employs in manipulating her extended family corporation is the kind of ruthlessness that might have saved the mild-mannered Bart Judson's business. Similarly, Bart's kindness and nurturance might have saved the family had he been in charge of the domestic realm. West's text seems to me, then, not simply an indictment of the bad mother and the manipulative wife, as many critics have argued, but a commentary on the male and the female, on the fallacies of separate spheres, and on the problematics of prescribed, often ill-fitting marital roles. Both Cleo and Bart are victims of the patriarchal ideology that defines the respective roles they must play in their marriage and in society. For black women writing in the 1930s and 1940s, claiming subjectivity and female authority meant disentangling the categories of woman and man from the shackles of patriarchal ideology and restrictive gender roles, as well as from what white psychoanalytical feminist Jessica Benjamin calls "the bonds of love"—bonds Cleo Judson fiercely resisted.

Zora Neale Hurston

The concern with the rising tide of black patriarchy and the bonds of love has a particularly dramatic presence in Zora Neale Hurston's work: in her autobiography, *Dust Tracks on a Road* (1942); in short stories such as "The Gilded Six-Bits," "Spunk," and "Sweat"; in her first novel, *Jonah's Gourd Vine* (1934); and especially in her best-known text, *Their Eyes Were Watching God* (1937). While its central characters are white, Hurston's last novel, *Seraph on the Suwanee* (1948), also is concerned with the problems of patriarchal ideology and the effects of unequal power relations on the marital union.

The remainder of this chapter explores the different aesthetic and political uses to which Hurston puts the coupling convention in her most acclaimed and perhaps most disclaimed texts, *Their Eyes Were Watching God* and *Seraph on the Suwanee*, respectively. I spend considerable time with *Seraph*, in particular, because the novel seems to me both to require and to deserve the same kind of close scrutiny and detailed interrogation that it gives the marital union. For many readers *Seraph on the Suwanee*—in large part because of its focus on white rather than black characters, on marital relations rather than race relations—represents an aberration in an otherwise brilliant literary career. I would argue, however, that Hurston's last novel—including its strategic deployment of white characters—represents a bold culmination in a novelistic career devoted almost exclusively to critiquing the marital relation and exploring female identity formation. (*Moses, Man of the Mountain* [1939] is a notable exception.) The focus on white men and women allows Hurston to take up in explicit detail the sexual subject matter her nineteenth-century precursors could only suggest. It allows her to scrutinize with unmatched intimacy the passions and problems of heterosexual coupling—including the previously unexamined issues of courtship and marital rape—without subjecting herself and her fiction to charges of pandering to white stereotypes of black sexuality.

In *Seraph on the Suwanee*, as in *Their Eyes Were Watching God*, Hurston explores the heart, mind, soul, and body of a woman searching for love *and* self and for love *of* self. And here, too, she undertakes her exploration within the folk milieu, capturing the idiom of the Florida "cracker" with the same meticulous attention to language that brings to life the rites and rhythms of black folk in *Their Eyes Were Watching God*.

Their Eyes Were Watching God

In *Their Eyes Were Watching God*, Nanny, who plays a major role in shaping the heroine's life, says to her sixteen-year-old granddaughter, Janie: "Dat's de very prong all us black women git hung on. Dis love! Dat's just what's got us uh pullin' and uh haulin' and sweatin' and doin' from can't see in de mornin' to can't see at night."[6] According to a number of critics, including Hurston's principal biographer, Robert Hemenway, *Their Eyes Were Watching God* is the story of Janie Crawford's search for "dis love," for the kind of sexual fulfillment—the "organic union," to use Hemenway's term—she first experiences vicariously as a teenager watching a bee pollinate a pear blossom. From *Their Eyes*:

> [Janie] was stretched on her back beneath the pear tree soaking in the alto chant of the visiting bees, the gold of the sun and the panting breath of the breeze when the inaudible voice of it all came to her. She saw a dust-bearing bee sink into the sanctum of a bloom; the thousand sister-calyxes arch to meet the love embrace and the ecstatic shiver of the tree from root to tiniest branch creaming in every blossom and frothing with delight. So this was a marriage! She had been summoned to behold a revelation. Then Janie felt a pain remorseless sweet that left her limp and languid. (24)

"Dust-bearing bee," "sanctum of a bloom," "creaming," "frothing with delight"—this explicitly orgasmic imagery seems far removed from the innuendo and submerged sexuality of nineteenth-century novels such as *Iola Leroy* and even the franker erotic encounters of *Plum Bun*, *Quicksand*, and *Passing*. At the same time, however, the use of such imagery links *Their Eyes* to a long-standing tradition of women's writing in which bees, birds, and blossoms are standard tropes used to signify both sexuality and the inherent inequality of heterosexual relations. Margaret Fuller wrote in her journal, for example: "Woman is the flower, man the bee. She sighs out of melodious fragrance, and invites the winged laborer. He drains her cup, and carries off the honey. She dies on the stalk; he returns to the hive, well fed, and praised as an active member of the community."[7] According to Elaine Showalter, the images invoked by Fuller and such white women writers as Mary Wilkins Freeman "decoy women into slavery, yet even drowning, [women] cannot escape from their seductiveness, for to ignore their claim is also to cut oneself off from culture, from the 'humming' life of creation and achievement."[8]

The visage of dust-bearing bees indeed serves as a decoy that lures Hurston's heroine into the seduction of orgasmic release and fantasies of matrimonial bliss. Few critics have failed to note that *Their Eyes Were Watching God* is in some way concerned with love and marriage, sex and sexuality (not necessarily in that order). The controversy over sex and the text has to do with the precise nature of that concern, with what it is that Hurston ultimately says about female independence, about sexuality, about the institution of marriage. Michael Awkward, for example, argues that in observing the pollination of the pear blossom, Janie witnesses what "God originally intended marriage to be" and begins her own quest for such a perfect union. He suggests that Hurston likens Janie to Adam—"a signal creation without a mate."[9] Blinded by the afterglow of her own orgasm, an overanxious Janie doesn't bother with God or ribs or dust; she fashions a mate of her own out of the first available male she sees: Johnny Taylor, the "shiftless" boy Nanny observes her kissing.

The Garden of Eden analogy is indeed implied by the text; however, I want to suggest a slight revision in what seems to me as it stands a rather masculinist reading of Janie as Adam. What Awkward calls Janie's "'pollinated' perception" of Johnny Taylor needs to be considered in light of Hurston's opening observation about the potentially destructive roles selective rememory, illusion, and ideology play in the lives of women: "Now, women forget all those things they don't want to remember, and remember everything they don't want to forget. The dream is the truth. Then they act and do things accordingly" (9). Hurston inverts and subverts the traditional androcentric creation myth as the first step in a woman-centered critique of the patriarchal character and perhaps the sexual disappointment of the marriage relation. While Awkward asserts that Janie witnesses what God intended marriage to be, I would argue that Janie merely *absorbs* the myth of what marriage is socially and ideologically constructed to be. Part of what *Their Eyes* confronts is the consequences for women of buying the myth, of seeking personal fulfillment in a primal male partner and equating sexual pleasure with marriage. Original sin in this text, after all, is not eating an apple proffered by woman but accepting a kiss proffered by man.

Made aware by that kiss of Janie's burgeoning womanhood and blooming sexuality, Nanny plots, in the fashion of Mrs. Bennet in *Pride and Prejudice*, to marry her granddaughter off with all deliberate speed to a single black man in possession of a comparatively great fortune. Like Mrs. Bennet, Nanny equates male marriageability with means and property. The root of Nanny's motives, however, is more tragic than comic. A former slave with painful personal knowledge of the sexual vulnerability of black women in a male-dominated, white supremacist society, Nanny acts swiftly to save Janie from the evils of men by placing her under the "big protection" and material support of a husband. To recommend him, Logan Killicks, the groom Nanny selects, has sixty acres and "de onliest organ in town" in his parlor (41). Nanny does not understand, however, that at sixteen and in beautiful sexual bloom, her granddaughter is interested in the organ in a man's pants, not in his parlor. Janie wants things sweet with her marriage, "Lak when you sit under a pear tree and think" (43). Her marriage to Logan Killicks does not "end the cosmic loneliness of the unmated." Nor does it "compel love like the sun the day" (38). In other words, the facts of Janie's daily married life do not live up to her romantic fantasies or fulfill her sexual desires. Instead, marriage to Logan

Killicks threatens to make her the very man-made mule of the world her grandmother wanted to protect her from becoming. This is the first of many disappointments, or as Hurston puts it: Janie learns from life with Logan Killicks that marriage does not make love. "Janie's first dream was dead, so she became a woman" (44). And being a woman, in the context of this story, means creating a new dream.

Out of the dust of bees, and pollen, and pear blossoms, Janie "creates" Joe Starks. She fashions him into the flesh-and-blood figure over which she drapes her private dream of pollination, even though she recognizes that he does not represent "sun-up and pollen and blooming trees" (50). He calls her "pretty doll-baby" and promises her a share in the kingdom he plans to create and rule over. Janie is attracted not so much by the material promises Joe makes her as by his self-confidence, the respect he commands *like a white man*. "Dazzled" by his shirt with the silk sleeve holders and by his self-confident strut, Janie endows this "citified, stylish dressed" black man with a stature equal to that of the most important white man she knows, Mr. Washburn, her grandmother's longtime employer. Joe was a "seal-brown color," we are told, "but he acted like Mr. Washburn or somebody like that to Janie" (47).

Janie is seduced by Joe Stark's glitter and spunk, by his "big-voice" and bravado, and by his willingness to work for her comfort in contrast to Killicks's plan to put her to work behind a plow. "You behind a plow," Joe exclaims at the idea of Janie's driving a mule. "You ain't got no mo' business wid uh plow than uh hog wid a holiday!" (49). One might argue that Janie is attracted to Joe because of the same middle-class aspirations that will later become the source of her own brand of the bourgeois blues. As impressed by Joe's rhetoric as she is depressed by Logan's, Janie succumbs to Starks's verbal lovemaking. Without a good-bye or a divorce, she eases on down the road with Jody, who like the black folk hero for whom he is nicknamed, has no qualms about skipping town with another man's wife.[10]

The great problem of this second marriage, however, is that Joe wants to command Janie like he does everyone else, to cow her like he cows the town. Janie soon learns that Joe's "big-voice" gains volume by silencing all other voices, including hers. As Sally Ferguson has noted, Janie ultimately learns what white women have known for some time: that "men who make women objects of their labor tend to treat them as things bought and owned" (189). Janie becomes yet another of Joe's possessions. The "like a white man" walk and big talk that she initially admired in Joe become the "like a white man" domination with which she must contend. Ironically, she has traded labor behind the plow in one husband's fields for work behind the counter in another's store. In spite of herself and her grandmother, Janie becomes a mule—a "classed-off" mule, to be sure, but a mule just the same. Hurston reinforces this point by having Janie defend Matt Bonner's mule in a way she has ceased to defend herself: "They oughta be shamed uh theyselves!" she says in disgust. "Teasin' dat poor brute beast lak they is! Done been worked tuh death; done had his disposition ruint wid mistreatment, and now they got tuh finish devilin' 'im tuh deat'h" (89). Joe overhears Janie's comments, and in a grand, magnanimous gesture he buys the mule and "frees" him. His gesture brings further ironic commentary from Janie, the meaning of which Joe misses:

> Jody, dat wuz uh mighty fine thing fuh you tuh do. 'Tain't everybody would have thought of it, 'cause it ain't no everyday thought. Freein' dat mule makes uh mighty big man outa you. Something like George Washington and Lincoln. Abraham Lincoln, he had de whole United States tuh rule so he freed de Negroes. You got uh town so you freed uh mule. You have tuh have power tuh free things and dat makes you lak uh king uh something. (92)

Joe just beams at what he hears as praise, unaware of the bitter edge to Janie's comment on her own enslaved condition and on the condition of the townspeople Joe has cowed.

As Janie and Joe's marriage wears on, the verbal lovemaking that characterized their courtship becomes verbal assault. Janie learns to accept most insults in silence, knowing that Joe "wanted her submission" and would keep on fighting until he felt he had it (111). Hurston makes it clear, however, that Joe's domination and Janie's passive resistance have a devastating effect on their intimate marital relationship. "The spirit of the marriage left the bedroom and took to living in the parlor," we are told. The marital bed ceases to be a "daisy-field" for Janie and Joe to play in and becomes simply a place to sleep.

When Joe at one point slaps Janie, the smoldering discord erupts into physical violence. The slap intensifies her silent resentment, but it is a verbal attack on her womanhood that finally forces Janie to give breath to her own resistance. She tells her big-voiced husband that all he is a big voice. "You big-bellies around here and put out a lot of brag," she says, "but 'tain't nothin' to it but yo' big voice. . . . When you pull down yo' britches, you look lak de change uh life" (123). So saying, Janie announces to his male subjects that their leader, the mighty Mayor Joe Starks, is sexually inadequate, that he can't get it up, that he's not enough man for "every inch" of woman she still is. It is significant, of course, that Janie reckons her sexuality by the male measurement of inches and makes it clear to all present that Joe's shriveled penis doesn't stand up. Hers is a series of well-placed punches that land below the belt, that not only rob Joe of "his illusion of irresistible maleness" but metaphorically feminize him by linking his impotence to female menopause — "de change uh life." In the wake of Janie's words, Joe's "vanity [bleeds] like a flood." It is a bloodletting that ultimately ends in the mayor's death, leaving Janie a financially well-fixed, independent, young widow.

Despite these two bad marriages, *Their Eyes Were Watching God* is most often read as a love story — "one of the most beautiful and convincing love stories in any literature"[11] — or, more recently, as a feminist text promoting a "new community based on sisterhood."[12] Bernard Bell, in effect, merges these two readings in his assessment of the novel. For him, Hurston's legacy to other novelists is "the most compelling modern feminist vision of an autonomous woman and inspirational love story in the tradition of the Afro-

American novel."[13] Indeed, in its portrayal of Janie's "liberating" third marriage to the wandering Tea Cake Woods, the text invites such readings. Tea
Cake seems at last the bee for Janie's blossom, someone with whom she can
be "petal-open," someone with whom she can be herself. Yet I would argue
that to interpret *Their Eyes* as a celebration of heterosexual love or as a
privileging of female independence and homosocial sisterhood is, respectively,
to under- or overread, if not completely misread, the novel.

Their Eyes Were Watching God is severely and profoundly critical not
necessarily of heterosexual relationships in and of themselves but of the power
imbalances—the relations of dominance and submission—such interactions
inspire in a patriarchal society. As Hortense Spillers has written of this would-
be love story: "[H]eterosexual love is neither inherently perverse nor necessarily dependence-engendering, except that the power equation between female
and male tends to corrupt intimacies."[14]

In her provocative discussion of literary matrilineage and the anxiety of
influence, Dianne Sadoff describes Janie Crawford Killicks Starks Woods as a
"dangerous woman"—a woman who abandons one husband, figuratively kills
a second, and literally kills a third. By novel's end all of Janie's male oppressors
have been eliminated, even—shockingly, for some readers—the beloved third
husband, Tea Cake.[15] However surprising his demise, Tea Cake's death at
Janie's hand is a narrative necessity—what critic Susan Willis describes as the
book's strongest statement, its most radical commentary on possible responses
to male domination. It demonstrates, Willis suggests, that no matter how
supportive the husband, "as long as relationships between men and women
are embraced by a larger system in which men dominate women, no woman
can expect to attain selfhood in marriage" (51–53).

In another powerful feminist reading of *Their Eyes*, Hortense Spillers argues
that the novel is "hurried, intense, and above all, haunted by an uneasy measure of control. One suspects that Hurston has not said everything she means
but means everything she says"—that an "awful scream" has been held back
(193–94). Yet for all the novel's forced "serenity," to use Spiller's word, rage
resides in this text. As Sadoff notes, Hurston, however covertly, rages against
male domination and ultimately liberates Janie from all men (22).

It is, however, not mere men who oppress in this novel but ideology—the
ponderous presence of an overarching system of patriarchal domination.
Janie's first and second husbands, Logan Killicks and Joe Starks, are surely
agents of this patriarchal oppression, but so is her grandmother. It is, after
all, Nanny who first turns Janie from the horizon and, hoping to protect her
from the consequences of her own sexuality, in effect sells her into a sexual
bondage sanctioned by marriage vows, even as Janie thirsts for that "foolishness" called love. Yet, if love (of men) is, as Nanny claims, "foolishness," "de
very prong all us black women gits hung on," love of self, as Janie seems to
have learned by novel's end, can be the prod that gets black women off the
hook: the power that liberates them from the bonds of loves. But where,
precisely, does liberated leave them? Foregrounding the friendship between

Janie and Pheoby, many feminist critics argue that such liberation as Janie achieves leaves women not alone without men but together with other women. Susan Willis, for example, suggests that the ultimate message of *Their Eyes* is not the impossibilities of heterosexual love but the possibilities of subversive sisterhood. Janie learns, according to Willis, that "although women must be with men and for men, they must also be with women and for women" (52). For Willis, the book's "most radical single statement" comes not from Janie but from Pheoby, who takes from the text of her friend's life a vision for altering her own marriage: "Lawd!" Pheoby says, "Ah done growed ten feet jus' listenin' tuh you, Janie. Ah ain't satisfied wid mahself no mo'. Ah means tuh make Sam take me fishing wid him after this" (284).

But this utopian notion of "a new community based on sisterhood" seems to me more Willis's than Hurston's and gives both Janie and Pheoby more agency than the text ultimately allows them. Pheoby says she aims to make her husband take her fishing with him; she does not say she plans to make him bake bread, wash his own underwear, and iron his own shirts. Nor does she say, "Let's *you and me* go fishing, Janie." And while it is certainly a wiser Janie on whom the book closes, it is a Janie who is largely without community—female or male—and whose final thoughts are not of self but of Tea Cake, who remains the essential medium of meaning in her life and, perhaps, the last illusion.

The novel's strongest statement, I would argue, lies not in Pheoby's resolve to go fishing with her husband but in the narrator's opening observation about forgetting and remembering, which reverberates throughout the text with a sense of the power of illusion and ideology in women's lives. Within the context of the novel, it is at least in part this selective remembering—a propensity for manipulating reality and for conflating dream and truth—that stifles women's self-realization.

Ultimately, then, like Mary Helen Washington, I cannot read *Their Eyes Were Watching God* as an "expression of female power,"[16] any more than I can read it as a celebration of heterosexual love. Indeed, *Their Eyes* critiques, challenges, and subverts male authority, ultimately eliminating the male oppressors, but female subjectivity does not win out over patriarchal ideology. I read this not as a failure in Hurston's fiction, as some critics do, but as its force. By way of explanation, let me underscore an important point Elliott Butler-Evans makes about Tea Cake as more patriarchal father than equal partner. When Joe Starks slaps Janie because his dinner isn't all he thinks it should be, the incident is presented by a disapproving narrator who takes the reader inside Janie's psyche and shares her reaction. Significantly, it is at this point that Janie realizes that her image of Joe has been a false one. It is here that she first sees that he "never was the flesh and blood figure of her dreams. Just something she had grabbed up to drape her dreams over" (*Their Eyes*, 112). Later, however, when Tea Cake beats Janie, the narrative voice, as Butler-Evans notes, "trivializ[es] the incident in the text ('No brutal beating at all. He just slapped her around a bit to show he was boss.')"—intervening in a way that *protects* Tea Cake from being viewed as an unsympathetic character; and the community chorus clearly approves—even envies Janie—his actions (*Desire*, 53–54).

Is narrative voice here parodic? Is part of the point the fact that society so endorses violence against women that even women themselves are conditioned—in some situations, anyway—to expect, accept, condone their own brutalization? Is Hurston demonstrating yet again how even independent-minded women can be captured, bound, diminished, and domesticated by patriarchal ideology and romantic mythology that suborne abuse in the name of "true love"? These questions take on even larger possibilities when viewed together with critical commentary on the ending to *Seraph on the Suwanee*, as well as to Larsen's *Quicksand* and *Passing* and Fauset's *Plum Bun* and *There Is Confusion*. All of these novels—written within a twenty-four-year period— have been described by critics as "copping out," squelching female subjectivity, ultimately either reducing otherwise resistant women to objects of male desire or killing them off.

Deborah McDowell, for example, argues that Fauset, Larsen, and Hurston all equivocate on the question of female independence and self-reliance, creating characters who seem for a time to act outside of convention but who ultimately opt for "marriage, motherhood, and domestic servitude." Can this be read not as obfuscation or, to use McDowell's words, as the apotheosis of marriage, home, and family, but as extending the texts' critique of these valorized institutions? As I read them, these ending are more in keeping with the ideology, polemics, and subversive politics of their texts than has been recognized.[17] "Happy endings," in which the female hero manages to outstride her male oppressors, resist the bonds of love, and escape the burdens of patriarchy, might make for powerful feminist manifestos, but they would represent ideological shifts inconsistent with the social conventions and material conditions out of which these texts were produced and which they necessarily inscribe.

Jessica Benjamin maintains that female submission must be acknowledged and considered concomitantly with male dominance. "How is domination," she asks, "anchored in the hearts of those who submit to it?"[18] This unasked question reverberates implicitly throughout *Their Eyes Were Watching God*. Hurston does not let us see Janie Crawford Killicks Starks single and independent for long, even though her inheritance from Jody leaves her far better able to survive alone than most women in her time and space. Is part of Hurston's message, then, that given the ubiquity of inculcated patriarchal values, few women are able to resist and escape the engendering that begins in infancy (or under a blooming pear tree)? What makes it possible for women to see options beyond their own submission, to resist the bonds of love, to distinguish "dream" from truth? Janie, after all, is much "freer" than most women of her time in ways other than her financial means: unlike Larsen, Hurston doesn't let her heroine get pregnant.

Their Eyes Were Watching God, then, is for me a novel as much about powerlessness as about power—about "women's exclusion from power," as

Mary Helen Washington has suggested. It is a text as much about submission as about self-fulfillment, as much about silence as about voice. Part of the novel's force lies in its exploration of the implications and effects of patriarchal values and male domination on the lives of black women. In the course of that examination, ideology itself functions as an unnamed but nonetheless important character—a character who, more than any other, demands Janie's submission.

Convinced that she "done been tuh de horizon and back"—seen "de light at daybreak" through Tea Cake—Janie at story's end chooses not to resume the search for the horizon but to return to the world she lived in with Jody. Reinstalled in that world, she is satisfied to "set heah in mah house and live by comparisons" (284). It is not clear, however, precisely what is being compared. What is remembered. What is forgotten.

Among the things forgotten, however, is the fact that with his last dying, rabid breath, a mad-dog Tea Cake bit Janie in the arm. "She was trying to hover him," the text says of Janie and Tea Cake's last moments together, "as he closed his teeth in the flesh of her forearm. . . . Janie struggled to a sitting position and pried the dead Tea Cake's teeth from her arm" (273). And while critics have taken little note of this scene (which is reminiscent of Tea Cake's own encounter with a rabid dog), the implications for Janie are potentially lethal. The danger is reinforced by the statement of the doctor who attended the hydrophobic Tea Cake. He testifies at Janie's trial to finding her "all bit in the arm, sitting on the floor and petting Tea Cake's head" (276).

In the concluding words of the novel, dream and truth merge for the last time in the image of Vergible (Truth) Tea Cake Woods prancing before Janie. "Of course he wasn't dead. He could never be dead," we are told, until Janie herself "had finished feeling and thinking. . . . She pulled in her horizon like a great fishnet. Pulled it from around the waist of the world and draped it over her shoulder" (286). Remembering the bite of the rabid Tea Cake, however, we must wonder whether this fishnet is shawl or shroud.[19]

Seraph on the Suwanee

However critical of patriarchal authority and gender conventions *Their Eyes Were Watching God* may be, Hurston's battle with male supremacy and the institution of marriage is actually most intense in her last and perhaps least-read novel, *Seraph on the Suwanee*, where the characters in love and patriarchal power struggle are white. Although initially well received,[20] *Seraph* has been dismissed by a great many contemporary critics—both male and female—for whom the novel is nothing more than a clinical study of a neurotic white woman whose various psychological problems undermine her marriage.

In one of the most insightful readings of *Seraph on the Suwanee*, Robert Hemenway asserts that the novel has little plot beyond the basic story of Arvay Henson, "whose life is defined by her marriage" and whose marriage is defined by "her uncertain sense of self and her husband's lusty, unthinking chauvinism."[21] I would argue, however, that this all-consuming, afflicted marriage is in itself quite a lot of plot. *Seraph* is a marriage story, a marriage story in some ways so conventional that it seems to mock the very tradition it invokes, even as it makes a dramatic statement about this other peculiar institution, which so governs the lives and loves of men and women and which is itself so governed by the respective roles society assigns its players. Here as in so many similarly plotted tales, a tall, dark, handsome white boy from a once genteel, now bankrupt family meets a repressed, blonde-haired, blue-eyed beauty from poor but honest country stock; the boy rapes, then marries, the girl; and they live not so happily ever after. What Hurston adds to this traditional plot, however, is an anatomical dissection of the psychosexual daily dramas and dilemmas of the marital here and now that disrupt the hearthside harmony of the "happy ever after."

Seraph on the Suwanee at once recounts and deconstructs the courtship and marriage of Arvay Henson and Jim Meserve and the conflicts that undermine their union. Arvay, whom we meet first, suffers from low self-esteem, a condition which many critics have dismissed as unexplained neurosis. The text is kinder and more clinical, however. Hurston takes pains to establish that Arvay, a shy and quiet child, has been neither the apple of her father's eye nor the favorite daughter of her community, Sawley, the turpentine-producing town in which she has been raised. She has been emotionally damaged by her family's indifference and the town's disdain—by their general, open preference for her older sister, Larraine:

> The Sawley people, eager to be amused at Arvay's expense, had no idea who or what Arvay Henson was. They had no way of knowing that Arvay was timid from feeling unsafe inside. Nor had anyone, not even her parents, the answer to Arvay's reactions to people. They did not suspect that the general preference for Larraine, Arvay's more robust and aggressive sister, had done something to Arvay's soul across the years.[22]

Lusty, virile Jim Meserve meets the shy, introverted Arvay Henson when she is twenty-one, a "spinster" by the standards of her community. By Arvay's reckoning as well as by that of the people of Sawley, she is five years past her prime, a fact which greatly concerns her parents, who are afraid of being stuck with the care and maintenance of an unmarriageable daughter. For the past several years Arvay has scared off any and all suitors by inducing hysterical fits and seizures, while carrying on an imaginary love affair—what she thinks of as "mental adultery"—with her sister's husband, Carl Middleton. It seems that, at sixteen, Arvay fell passionately in love with Sawley's then most eligible bachelor, the newly arrived, much-sought-after Reverend Carl Middleton. Though hotly pursued by most of the single women of the town, Middleton, it seemed to Arvay, singled her out for special attention, a sure sign of his deep affection. "She fell in love," Hurston writes, "and began to live a sweet and secret life inside herself" (11).

Arvay's sweet and secret life and dreams of matrimonial bliss with Reverend Middleton turned bitter, however, when her imaginary lover suddenly married her all-too-real older sister, Larraine. As jarring as this sudden marriage was to Arvay, it did not bring an end to the fantasies that continued to sustain her in her solitude. Believing that Middleton secretly loved her, Arvay continues to dream of the day when he will come to her, "kneel down on his knees, kiss the hem of her garment, tell her how it all happened and beg her to forgive and forget" (11). She is not certain precisely how it all happened—how the man she loves ended up married to the sister she hates—but in her fantasies she imagines that Larraine is somehow responsible, that it was through the "double-tongued lies and deceitfulness" of her sister that Middleton was parted from her. The truth of what happened will take more than twenty years to come out, but Arvay will ultimately discover that she was not mistaken in her assumption of duplicity on Larraine's part.

Into the midst of this family romance Hurston thrusts Jim Meserve, a proud and intensely chauvinistic Irish American who believes that the greatest measures of a man are in effect his penis and his pocketbook, his ability to provide for a woman physically and financially. The spirit of the inevitable clash between Jim's hubris and machismo and Arvay's insecurity and introversion—between sexual domination and psychological resistance (Hurston's version of pride and prejudice, perhaps)—is captured in the advice offered by Joe Kelsey, a black turpentine dipper whose work Jim Meserve supervises, to his soon-to-be-married foreman: "Most women folks will love you plenty if you take and see to it that they do. Make 'em knuckle under. From the very first jump, get the bridle in they mouth and ride 'em hard and stop 'em short. They's all alike, Boss. Take 'em and break 'em" (46).

Joe's advice suggests the degree to which black men, like white, operate under the influence of patriarchal ideology: women are beasts of burden—mules of the world—to be bridled, broken, and ridden. Indeed, black Joe's notion of gender relations is no different from that of white Jim, whose courtship of Arvay Henson is a matter of doing precisely what he pleases. Jim sees her, wants her, and decides that she is "worth the trouble of breaking in." He laughs off the notion, well known throughout the town, that Arvay, who has dedicated her life to missionary work, has renounced the world in general and men in particular. "Women folks don't have no mind to make up nohow," he tells Arvay in the midst of what is supposed to be a marriage proposal. "Lady folks were just made to laugh and act loving and kind and have a good man to do for them all he's able, and have him as many boy-children as he figgers he'd like to have" (25). Jim's chauvinistic philosophy of love and marital life is akin to that of Joe Starks in *Their Eyes Were Watching God*, and his sexist rhetoric is reminiscent of Stark's assertion that "somebody got to think for women and chillum and chickens and cows" (*Their Eyes*, 110). Even more so than Janie Starks, Arvay Meserve will learn to act out her resistance to being worked for, fetched for, and thought for in almost every nook and cranny of her marriage, including the bedroom, where she will feel most helpless, most possessed, most manipulated.

Jim's sexual aggression sets the tone for and rules the Meserve marriage, just as it culminated and consummated the courtship. Engaged to Arvay but unsure of her love for him, Jim set out to "break her in" by raping her in an assault Hurston describes in some detail: "In a fraction of a second she was snatched from the sky to the ground," we are told. "Her skirts were being roughly jerked upwards, and Jim was fumbling wildly at her thighs." Arvay protests, but to no avail; the assault continues, with Jim's ferocity only heightened by the barrier of her tight-legged drawers, which he summarily rips off: "A tearing sound of starched fabric, and the garment was being dragged ruthlessly down her legs. Arvay opened her mouth to scream, but no sound emerged. Her mouth was closed by Jim's passionate kisses, and in a moment more, despite her struggles, Arvay knew a pain remorseless sweet" (51).

The fact that the scene climaxes in a "pain remorseless sweet" (an orgasmic metaphor Hurston uses in *Their Eyes* as well) should not mask the degree of terror the rape inspires in Arvay or mitigate the impact that the violence of this assault has on the Meserve-Henson coupling. The rape confirms Arvay's fears that Jim's ardent courtship and marriage proposal are really part of a grand joke designed to bring her low. As Hurston writes, "[A]ll her old feelings of defeat and inadequacy came back on her. She was terribly afraid. She had been taken for a fool, and now her condition was worse than before" (51–52).

Critics—even feminist critics—have paid surprisingly little attention to this scene, often making casual or no mention at all of the rape or else mitigating the horror of the assault grammatically by calling it "seduction" or "lusty chauvinism." The word that Hurston uses, that Arvay uses, that Jim himself uses repeatedly is *rape*. "All I know is that I been raped," Arvay says to Jim after the deed is done. "You sure was," he boasts, "and the job was done up brown." He tells her that she is going to keep on getting raped every day for the rest of her life. Arvay, quite understandably, does not realize that Jim is referring to their future marital sexual relations, which he casts as rape, "rape in the first degree."

The site of this sexual assault (beneath the mulberry tree where Arvay played house as a child) is significant, for by raping her on the grounds of her childhood dollhouse retreat, Jim is forcing her—the devout Christian fundamentalist missionary—to, as the Bible says, put away all childish things, including her religion, and become a "wonderful woman" through the power invested in his penis. "No more missionarying [a pun?] around for you," he tells Arvay. "You done caught your heathen, baby." So saying, he carts her to the courthouse and marries her, but with such a beginning, readers should not be surprised that the Meserves do not easily live happily every after.

Date rape and marital rape are both relatively new concepts which feminism has forced upon a patriarchal society that has rarely called such examples of paternal sexual privilege by what many today recognize as their rightful name. Hurston's repeated use of the term "rape" to describe Jim Meserve's sexual violation of Arvay Henson seems ahead of its time, but the text also seems to send out mixed signals about how the rape is to be read. For as frightened as Arvay is, the assault is depicted as a not-altogether-unwelcome sexual awakening: as a *felix culpa*, my term for romantic fiction's frightening fixation with rape as a prelude to everlasting love.

In this fictive formula, fairly common in the popular romance, the innocent, virginal—but passionate—young heroine is raped by the handsome, rakish lord or sea captain with whom she invariably falls helplessly in love by the end of the novel. But the genre also presents a number of variations on this theme, such as the seemingly pleasurable marital rape portrayed in such texts as *Gone with the Wind* (1936). At one point in Margaret Mitchell's masterwork, an inebriated Rhett Butler, tired of being locked out of his wife's bedroom and jealous of her continued infatuation with Ashley Wilkes, sweeps Scarlett up into his arms, carries her up the stairs, kicks open the bedroom door, throws her on the bed, and presumably rapes her. The incident is particularly dramatic in the motion picture adaptation, where in the next scene, the morning after, Scarlett's enjoyment of the previous night's sexual escapade is visibly apparent. Vivien Leigh in the role of Scarlett O'Hara is so full of smiles and song that her colored mammy exclaims: "Lawd, lawd, Miss Scarlett, you sure is happy dis mornin'."

Perhaps because of what sexual vulnerability has meant for black women historically, rape as *felix culpa* is a phenomenon of white women's romantic fiction that rarely rears its problematic head in African American literature. A number of feminist scholars have suggested that the rape fixation persists in white popular fiction because women actually enjoy the experience of reading about sexual violence against their species. "[W]omen who couldn't thrill to male nudity in *Playgirl*," Ann Douglas writes, "are enjoying the titillation of seeing themselves, not necessarily as they are, but as some men would like to see them: illogical, innocent, magnetized by male sexuality and brutality."[23] While not discounting entirely the possibilities of Douglas's point, Janice Radway brings additional insight to the question. Drawing on Clifford Geertz's theory that all art forms render ordinary, everyday experience comprehensible, Radway argues that "the romance's preoccupation with male brutality is an attempt to understand the meaning of an event that has become almost unavoidable in the real world." The romance, then, she suggests, "may express misogynistic attitudes not because women share them but because they increasingly need to know how to deal with them."[24]

The use of white characters in *Seraph on the Suwanee* makes it possible for Hurston to deal with misogynistic attitudes and the issue of sexual violence in courtship and marriage without *directly* assigning to black men the politically and racially charged label of rapist. Latter-day black women writers such as Alice Walker and Gayl Jones will confront the issue of sexual violence against women without the veil of white (fore)skin. Their attempts to use the literary text both to expose and to come to terms with the threat and the reality of black-on-black sexual violence constitute a betrayal of the race in the eyes of many black readers, both male and female.

Even given the trope of white skin, however, black men are by no means placed outside patriarchy is Hurston's novel. Rather, as noted earlier, they are drawn under the oppressive miasma of sexism not only through the articulated misogyny of black characters like Joe Kelsey but also through the black community's general adoration of Jim as a "man's man" who knows how to treat a woman. Part of how a real man treats a woman—even in the eyes of the female members of this community—is to dominate her, to keep her, if not barefoot, by all means pregnant. Curiously, this view is expressed by, of all people, Joe Kelsey's black wife, Dessie. The first to notice that Arvay is "with child," Dessie exclaims with glee: "I declare! That husband you done married is *all parts of a man.* . . . *Youse knocked up*" (62; emphasis added). Manliness, a theme with which Hurston was perennially concerned, is defined even by the oppressed as dominance, the ability to impregnate, to "knock a woman up" as proof of sexual prowess. This ideology of manliness fosters a climate for rape.

In *Seraph on the Suwanee*, the mood shifts rather swiftly from Arvay's concern over her state of friendless ruination after she is raped to her in-spite-of-herself engagement with her own desire: "Some unknown power took hold of Arvay. She pressed her body tightly against his, fitting herself into him as closely as possible. . . . It seemed a great act of mercy when she found herself stretched on the ground again with Jim's body weighing down upon her. Even then she was not satisfied" (53–54). Perhaps it is in part this seemingly unproblematic shift from danger to desire that has helped to mask the trauma of the rape and to inspire a degree of critical silence about its impact on the text of the ensuing marriage. I read the juxtaposition of these two scenes of rape, on the one hand, and ecstacy, on the other, as a comment on the complexities of female subjectivity and human emotions: the ways in which love and sex, passion and power, danger and desire, anger and affection collide with each other and collapse whatever boundaries and separate spaces our emotions and desires are thought to occupy.[25]

The text generates additional confusion or ambivalence about its male protagonist because, even given his rape of Arvay, Jim Meserve is not depicted as a villain. It seems he is merely, in a word, a *man* or, as Anne Goodwyn Jones says of his counterpart, Rhett Butler: he is, from his large male body to his rational male mind, "the principle of masculinity."[26] There are in fact a number of similarities between Rhett Butler and Jim Meserve, as there are between *Gone with the Wind* and *Seraph on the Suwanee*. Both men function comfortably within a separate world of whiskey stills, juke joints, gambling houses, political payoffs, and not-always-quite-legal business deals—decidedly male spheres to which their wives in particular and women in general are denied access. Both men are often extremely gentle, profoundly patient, and selflessly generous. Rhett supports his mother and sisters, adores his daughter, and grieves heartbrokenly over the latter's death. Jim supports Arvay's mother after she is widowed, as well as his immediate family, and provides a home and employment for his colored friends, the Kelseys. While his daughter, Angeline, does not die like Bonnie Blue Butler, Jim is similarly enthralled with his girl child and, as with Rhett Butler, transfers to her the love and affection his wife seems neither to notice nor to appreciate.

But if the leading men of Mitchell and Hurston share some characteristics, so do their leading ladies. Arvay Henson, like Scarlett O'Hara, imagines herself in love with one man—who marries someone else—but is eventually hounded into marrying another whom she does not realize she loves. Neither wife functions in her role the way her husband wants, although Jim's reasons for concern over his wife's behavior are entirely different from Rhett's. Both female characters are depicted as small-minded and bigoted, in contrast to their husbands' kindness to, understanding of, and popularity with the colored folk. And both women ultimately drive their men away only to realize, after the fact, the depth of their affection for their lost mates. Significant similarities end here, for the most part, for in temperament and capacity for deceit and manipulation—at least for most of the novel—Arvay Henson is no Scarlett O'Hara (or Cleo Judson). Nor, however, is she a Janie Crawford—good, nice, easy on the reader's sympathies. For much of the novel, in fact, Arvay is presented as something less than likeable, while Jim is more positively constructed as a sensitive employer, as a generous friend, and even as a good husband, devoted to caring and providing for his wife and the three children they have together.

In fact, Jim Meserve is in some ways so positively drawn that literary critic Carole McAlpine Watson has been blinded by the glow from his halo. Erasing his proclivity for sexual coercion and the many other glaring signs of male supremacy, she argues that "Jim considers his marriage to Arvay a *partnership between equals.*"[27] Any of a number of scenes from the Meserve marriage would seem to contradict Watson's claim, however. In addition to what is only the first of a series of sexual assaults, there is, for example, Jim's boast to Arvay's father that he'll be able to handle her because a "woman knows who her master is all right, and she answers to his commands" (33). Or there is the later scene in which Jim orders Arvay to strip: "Don't you move!" he bellows at her. "You're my damn property, and I want you right where you are, and I want you naked" (216). This is hardly the rhetoric of a man who views his wife as an equal partner.

Yet, as contrary to the facts of the text as Watson's reading of Jim may be, she is not alone in offering what seems a masculinist interpretation of the novel's gender politics. As Hazel Carby points out, there is general confusion about who the hero of *Seraph* really is. "The difficulty for a feminist reading of *Seraph on the Suwanee*," Carby argues, "is that Jim Meserve, unlike Jody Starks, does not conveniently die so that his wife can get on with her life. In *Seraph* it is Arvay's expectations and desires that must be transformed to accommodate the demands of her husband" (xv). I might add that Jim Meserve, unlike Starks, is not figured as a one-dimensional, self-important despot, which also works against an easy feminist reading of the text.

Seraph's sexual politics and body language similarly complicate our ability to identify the hero or to polarize our loyalties along gender lines. As sexually engaged with her husband as Arvay quickly becomes, his physical aggressiveness and self-assurance reinforce rather than reduce his wife's lack of self-confidence. For Jim, their union is a true love match, but Arvay does not recognize it as such, in large part because her family's disdain and her sense of rejection have led her to hold herself beyond the pale of deep affection— unlovable, as a bad driver is uninsurable. Unfortunately for the potential quality of their coupling, Jim expresses his feelings in physical terms and with such unrelenting fervor that her body seems to Arvay the major medium of the marriage. In her mind, then, it is her *body* Jim loves, not her *being*; and she resents, rather than delights in, the degree to which her own body conspires against her by so hungrily craving his.

Arvay's resentment of what she reads as Jim's purely physical interest in her and his sexual hold over her runs deep and bitter. It rushes back not only to the moment he first raped her but to the insulting and awkward marriage proposal in which he informed her that women are mindless "play-pretties" meant for loving men and making boy babies. To Arvay, Jim's comment is a declaration of the terms of their marriage. While she does not overtly challenge those terms at the time, she will continue to resent and resist them throughout the first twenty years of her marriage. The text later translates Jim's words into what are supposed to be Arvay's thoughts about what he has said in so many words:

> Love and marry me and sleep with me. That is all I need you for. Your brains are not sufficient to help me with my work; you can't think with me. Let's get this thing straight in the beginning. Putting your head on the same pillow with mine is not the same thing as mingling your brains with mine anymore than crying when I cry is giving you the power to feel my sorrow. You can feel sympathy but not my sorrow. (35–36)

If Arvay, as a fictive invention of Hurston's, actually were characterized as capable of such rational, critical insight into herself, her husband, and her marriage, *Seraph on the Suwanee* would be a more credible novel than it ultimately is for many readers. On the contrary, Arvay is the model of irrationality, whose portrayal as insecure, introverted, and inferior-feeling belies her status as the female lead and narrative consciousness of the text. To Robert Hemenway this slippage between character and characterization represents a major flaw in the novel's narrative strategy. "Although narrated in the third person," he writes, "the story is told largely through Arvay's consciousness, and the book offers a number of acute insights as Zora explores her psyche." Ultimately, the novel is not successful, Hemenway maintains, "because Arvay is not given a stature that will support the psychological burden she is asked to bear" (310).

Indeed, Arvay Henson is no Janie Crawford—full of energy, imagination, wit, and humor, hungry for life, for love, for sexual passion but deterred from them by a well-intentioned but overprotective grandmother and a dominating, chauvinistic husband. On the contrary, Arvay lacks imagination, is almost completely without humor, and is scared to death of her husband's thundering sexuality, as well as of her own. The sexual passion and organic union for which Janie Crawford spends more than twenty years searching is thrust upon Arvay at the age of twenty-one. But the occasion of that initial "passion" is, after all, rape: an act of violence and brutality upon which we can hardly expect Arvay to build a healthy, loving relationship without ourselves endorsing the notion of rape as *felix culpa*. Part of what is troubling to me about

Seraph is that this is precisely what the text, at least at times, seems to ask us (and Arvay) to do. Whether by accident or design, Hurston has created for her character an emotional impasse (an impasse that is also the reader's) at the same time that the text seems to find fault in her resistance to the good loving of this "all parts of a man."

In a generous reading this kind of confusion could be taken as a brilliant narrative strategy, designed to reproduce in the reader the same psychological dilemma and internal turmoil that Arvay experiences. As a woman reader, for example, I undergo a crisis of feminist consciousness at those moments when I find myself pulling for this marriage—when I feel myself attracted to Jim's humor, devotion, tenderness, and (yes, forgive me) strength. Ultimately, however, I am no more able to just relax and enjoy living, loving, and sleeping with the enemy than Arvay is. In other words, in a generous interpretation of the text, we can argue that Hurston has skillfully manipulated our psyches so that Arvay's predicament becomes our predicament; her love-hate relationship with the man who both adores her madly and dominates her mercilessly is our relationship with a character we at once admire and abhor. Such critical generosity, however, requires us as readers to look beyond Arvay's faults (and perhaps the text's) and see her need, in the spirit of the hymn.

Among Arvay's most annoying faults are her small-mindedness and her irrational jealousy, which often rises to the rank of paranoia. After the birth of their first child, Earl, whose mental and physical deformity Arvay foolishly but humanly views as her punishment for having once coveted her sister's husband, the Meserves move from the turpentine town of Sawley on the Suwanee River to the citrus-growing community of Citrabelle, where they eventually have two more—this time healthy—children. Through hard work, ingenuity, political patronage, and a very profitable, highly illegal bootlegging business (run for him by former turpentine dipper Joe Kelsey), Jim succeeds rather splendidly, rising over the years from fruit-picker crew foreman to grove owner and moving his family from a rented cottage into their own home built at near-cost by colored carpenters whose admiration and respect he has won.

For Arvay, however, the Negro and Portuguese neighbors and workers whose goodwill and friendship Jim cultivates are just "niggers" and "furriners." She resents their presence in her husband's life and imagines all manner of conspiracies against her. The Corregios, the Portuguese family whose father, Alfredo, takes over managing the groves after Arvay's general nastiness drives the Kelseys away, become on sight the folks Arvay most loves to hate. She is immediately jealous of their pretty teenage daughter, Lucy Ann, and is convinced that either the girl or her mother is trying to seduce Jim Meserve with the "Geechy messes" they are always cooking and inviting her, as well as Jim, to eat (128).

The Corregios' greatest crime, however, is the fascination Lucy Ann holds for the Meserves' now-eighteen-year-old retarded son, Earl. Jim realizes that Earl is sexually attracted to Lucy Ann, but Arvay concludes that the Corregios "must have some different scent from regular folks and it make[s] Earl sick in some way or another" (125). Her corrective for Earl's wild, animal-like behavior and his fixation on Lucy Ann is to get rid of the Corregios. She is enraged when Jim suggests instead, as he has several times before, that Earl—who at one point tried to kill his younger brother—should be institutionalized for his own good and for the protection of the family. Tragedy seems inevitable, and except for Arvay no one—least of all the reader—is surprised that Earl's fascination with Lucy Ann Corregio ultimately proves a fatal attraction. He attacks her one night, knocking her down on the ground and biting her thigh like a mad dog in a move that seems reminiscent of the rabid Tea Cake who bites Janie in the arm, and perhaps even of Jim Meserve himself, whose similarly animalized passion for Arvay seems no more controllable than Earl's for Lucy Ann. Driven off by the approach of Lucy Ann's father, who has heard her screams, Earl steals a rifle from the house and runs into the swamp adjacent to the groves, where he is pursued and eventually killed by the sheriff's posse, just as he is about to shoot at his unarmed father a second time. For Earl's death, too, Arvay blames the Corregios.

The abundance and variety of Arvay's irrational fears and jealousies have led some critics to conclude that Hurston deliberately invested her heroine with a classic case of female hysteria, a type of neurosis particular to women, according to Freud, especially to those who are sexually repressed.[28] Hurston may well have been influenced by Freud, whose psychoanalytic theories were in great favor in her day, but she has given us a treatment of the female psychosexual self that moves beyond the master analyst. Arvay is emotionally ensnared in a state of suspended animation, caught between passion and resistance, desire and defiance. She *feels* the pressing weight of this dilemma but she does not *own* it or *know* it, nor can she call its name. She feels trapped in bondage to her husband, "tied and bound down in a burning Hell" from which she can see no way out, she says at one point, except to kill herself, which she threatens to do the next day. Jim's response to Arvay's "high and agonizing scream of desperation" is a kiss, planted "with a kind of happy arrogance," just before he falls into a peaceful sleep, snuggled against her breasts like a child (218–19).

Moments like this one—emotionally charged instants that cut open and lay bare the psychosexual dynamics of erotic coupling—keep *Seraph on the Suwanee* from being the failure many critics believe it to be. Arvay, in her very ordinariness, becomes extraordinary—becomes human. And if she is neurotic and hysterical in her fears, fantasies, and insecurities, it is that very neurosis that makes her interesting—and perhaps *familiar*. For hers is an archetypal and perhaps particularly female torment: to love him who violates and dominates her.

In an earlier emotionally charged moment, Arvay, pregnant with the couple's third child, misses the joke when Jim insists on a promise from her that the baby she is carrying is going to be a boy. "Just make up your mind to do as I tell you, and have that child a boy," Jim jokes. "I never did want no girls around the house" (97). Jim's teasing remarks are all the more obviously outrageous because he is so head-over-heels enamored of his daughter, their second-born. Arvay, however, takes his teasing seriously and suffers silently through the next five months of her pregnancy. When Jim finally becomes aware of his wife's distress over his long-since-forgotten joke, he is apologetic for having unintentionally put her through such needless agony. But when his contrition is met with anger and invectives, he retaliates by, in effect, pointing out Arvay's stupidity: "I thought anybody at all would see through a joke like that," especially, he points out, since "you know so well that I'd go to Hell for my daughter" (103). Not willing to let the matter go, an accusing, sullen Arvay tries Jim's patience when she responds tearfully that she thought he was just making up any old excuse to justify leaving her. "And me with three little bitty chillun on my hands to look after and do for. I was hurt-ed, Jim," she sobs. "Hurt-ed to my very heart, and felt like I was throwed clean away" (103). Her fears of impending desertion seem utterly unfounded, of course, since Jim's husbandly devotion is so overdetermined in the text.

Jim's understanding of who he is and how he loves and what he gives in his marriage is so different from Arvay's that he is at once deeply grieved to have caused his wife such needless pain and profoundly angry that the woman he thinks so much of could think so little of him and his love for her. For the first time in their troubled marriage, he thinks of leaving his impossible-to-please wife. After an hour of soul-searching, however, he decides that Arvay is too helpless to live without him and that he has gotten too "used to the comforts of a home through Arvay, and her tender loving care" to live without her. He concludes, in fact, that he is possessed by her, a condition which he decides he must keep from her, lest she use her power over him to her own advantage. "Twenty to twenty-five years later on, he could afford to let her know [the power she has over him]. No sense crowding his luck." Jim returns to his wife, and hugs and kisses her until she "succumb[s] to his love making." But long after their healthy son is born, long after the pregnancy prank seems forgotten, Arvay retains a "residue of resentment" and stubbornly blames Jim for having *deliberately* made a fool out of her (106).

I want to linger over this example a little longer because it speaks directly to the breakdowns in communication, residues of resentment, and failures in perception that plague the Meserve marriage. Jim is so caught up in his own manhood—in playing the role of patriarch—that he can neither see nor hear the woman he has married. And Arvay is so thoroughly blinded by her own insecurities that she invariably misreads the obvious and misunderstands the simple to the point that the reader, much sooner perhaps than her husband, loses patience with and sympathy for her myopia. Hurston, however, also tries her readers' patience: she shows us too much of Arvay's meanness and too little of the tender loving care and personal power to which Jim alludes for his reasoning to make sense. Rather, Arvay, as Hurston constructs her, is consistently so small-minded and meanspirited, petty and petulant that we at times have as much difficulty understanding why Jim loves her as she does.

At the same time, however, this is a text whose surplus of interpretability does not let either the characters or the reader off the hook easily. From the concave side of the double vision Hurston presents in this anatomy of a marriage, the text seems to argue in Arvay's defense that, given the tragic deformity of the Meserve's firstborn son Earl and the extent to which Arvay blames herself for that deformity, there *is* something thoughtless, if not cruel, about Jim's making her pregnancy the butt of his joke. And given the number of times that Jim has told Arvay that a wife's only function is to make her husband happy and to give him as many boy children as he wants, there is something inconsiderate in this particular mode of jest. Although by no means malicious, Jim's teasing is all the more thoughtlessly unkind because he knows from a long line of unappreciated pranks that Arvay does not enjoy a joke, particularly if it is on her.

But there is still more to Hurston's marital anatomy lesson. Approached from yet another angle, the pregnancy incident has imbedded in it an element of O'Henry's "Gift of the Magi." *Both* Jim and Arvay suffer greatly over their son's deformity, but neither talks through that suffering. Each is aware of the other's pain, but neither understands that the greater part of that pain is for the *other's* grief. Each wants to spare the other further suffering: Arvay by having a perfect child or by not getting pregnant at all, Jim by making light of her fears about the coming birth. Yet, in their unspoken wish to spare, to salve, to comfort, each hurts the other irreparably.

Like many couplings, the Meserve marriage is overripe with such misunderstandings and failures in communication—failures rooted, at least in part, in pride and insecurity. From correspondence with her publisher, we know that Hurston was particularly interested in exploring on paper what she saw as the almost archetypal insecurity of the "inferior wife," afraid of getting lost in the shuffle of her husband's achievements. In a letter to her editor at Scribner's, Hurston wrote rather disparagingly of Arvay Henson Meserve as such a fear-filled, inferior wife: "I get sick of [Arvay] at times myself," Hurston confessed. "Have you ever been tied in close contact with a person who had a strong sense of inferiority? I have, and it is hell. They carry it like a raw sore on the end of the index finger. . . . It colors *everything*." Marriages are smashed on the rocks of such insecurities, Hurston suggested. She offered as an example the businessman who works tirelessly to provide for the woman he loves, while his aggrieved partner sits home pouting and complaining about being neglected. The wife's misery stems, according to Hurston, from her fear of being drowned by the undertow of her husband's rising tide. "Millions of women," she concluded, "do not want their husbands to succeed for fear of losing him. It is a very common ailment. That is why I decided to write about it."[29]

Surprisingly, Hurston's analysis in her letter oversimplifies the same complex human dynamic her own novel complicates. For one thing, her comments obscure the fact that wife and family are frequently the excuses men claim for doing what their particular personalities and/or compulsive natures would drive them to do anyway. It also does not take into consideration the kind and quality of relationship these hardworking men may have with their discontented wives. Nor does it take into account the consequences for women of being "worked for": the possibility, for example, of themselves becoming property rather than equal partners, as with both Janie Starks and Arvay

Henson. The pouting, complaining, and nagging Hurston attributes to the wife's sense of her own inferiority may in some instances be acts of defiance and resistance rather than mere signs of insecurity. Hurston, it seems, may have written a far more psychologically sophisticated novel than even she realized.

In any case, whether Hurston intends it so or not, the insecurity that ultimately turns the tide of *Seraph* is not the wife's but the husband's, at least as I read the text. Arvay is called from her kitchen late one afternoon by the voice of her husband, lush with excitement. "Arvay! Arvay! Run here quick! I got something to show you! Run!" Arvay runs toward the sound of Jim's voice and is stopped in her tracks as she beholds the sight of her laughing husband holding captive at arm's length a fantastically gargantuan diamondback rattlesnake, perhaps eight feet long and proportionately thick. Arvay, who, as Jim is well aware, is deathly afraid of snakes and shrinks even from worms, is at once horribly frightened for her husband and profoundly angry that he has so recklessly placed himself in such needless jeopardy. This time Arvay's fears are not idle or ill founded, for this is one joke that will tragically turn in on Jim, very nearly costing him his life. In an instant the captive becomes the captor, as the writhing reptile begins to wrap the lower third of its immensely powerful body around Jim's waist, squeezing the breath out of the man like a boa constrictor as it struggles to free its head from between his fists. Arvay watches in helpless terror as her husband's usually beaming face becomes a "straining, gasping horror," his "eyes dilated with fear and pain." "Ar . . . vay! Help . . . me," she hears him breathe out in "agonizing gasps." But if Jim's pain is great in his immobility, so, too, is Arvay's, for she is frozen in place, and while in her mind she flies to his aid and frees him, in reality her feet never move (255).

Just as his strength is about to fail him, Jim is rescued by Jeff Kelsey, the now-grown son of Jim's colored friend, Joe. Jeff rushes to the aid of his beloved Mister Jim, grabbing the snake by the tail and unwinding the coils from around Jim's body. Together, the two men fling the snake through the air and it lands with a thud twenty feet away. Jeff wants to kill the stunned reptile, but Jim stops him. "He spied noble in the fight," Jim argues in response to Jeff's protests. "He put out the best he had, and it come mighty nigh being too damned much for me. . . . I tip my hat to a fighter, like that and leave him be" (258).

Arvay, on the other hand, has proven in her stasis that she is not a fighter, and neither Jeff nor Jim is about to tip his hat or even speak to her (though later Jim does try to cover for her in front of Jeff). Jeff, in fact, cuts her such a hateful, damning look that it stops her in her tracks toward her husband, forbidding her "to approach the person of Jim Meserve" and informing her that she has been judged and found unworthy. In her husband's eyes, however, as Jim himself informs her later that evening, it is not her immobility that makes her unworthy but her lack of understanding—her failure to see what he was really after in tackling the snake: "a chance to do something big and brave and full of manhood" to win her admiration and affection. He would have felt better, he tells Arvay, if she had said even one word to show him that she understood his intentions. "[B]ut you hated my guts," he says, "and then pitched in and helped the rattlesnake out. Not understanding is the part that I don't like" (262).

Not understanding is a disease — a blight on the marriage — with which both Arvay and Jim are infested. Stuffed stiff with his own sense of proud manhood, Jim does not understand that his grand attempt at snake charming was for Arvay a cruel taunt almost guaranteed to produce a conditioned response of paralysis, given her clinical case of herpetophobia. Though their marriage was hardly a Garden of Eden before this incident, a serpent seems once again to have driven man and woman from paradise. For, fed up with what he feels is Arvay's cowardly, "stand-still, hap-hazard kind of love," Jim announces that he is leaving her to go to live and work on the Florida coast, where he owns a successful shrimping business run for him by Alfredo Corregio.

The text seems to imply that Jim's decision to leave Arvay — precipitated as it is by her failure to come to his aid or to understand the finer purpose behind his folly with the snake — is justified. Indeed, Hurston herself "love[d] courage in every form" and "worship[ed] strength."[30] Her sympathies may well rest with Jim. For many, perhaps even most, readers, however, Jim's action with the snake and his expectations of Arvay are the aberrations of the encounter, not Arvay's inaction or her failure to understand the not-so-immediately transparent, boyish motives of this near-fifty-year-old man. In other words, the major and minor premises presented by the text do not necessarily force the conclusion the story seems to need in order to make sense of itself. Darwin Turner views this solipsism as a major weakness in the novel. Hurston "wished to suggest," he writes, "that, by failing to act, Arvay demonstrated to Jim that he cannot depend upon her when he needs help. Nevertheless, most readers will excuse Arvay for not perceiving that Jim's seizing the snake indicates his emotional need for her."[31] Turner's point is well taken; to it I would add the detail that Arvay's intense fear of snakes makes her inertia all the more tenable. However, since Hurston takes pains to inform us of Arvay's phobia, the text may not be as disdainful of her immobility as it appears.

As Robert Hemenway points out, the encounter with the rattlesnake is heavily laden with phallic and Christian symbolism. Distended, the snake recalls the penis that raped Arvay and her immobility at that moment as well, her sublimated resentment over the terms of her marriage, and, in Hemenway's perceptive assessment, "the evil that Jim's sexuality represents to her fundamentalist Christian conscience," as well as "her own pleasure — and guilt — in their tempestuous intercourse" (311).

Coiled, however, the snake becomes a *feminine* symbol, signifying the extent to which Jim has been encircled by Arvay's powerful grip, how the possessor has been the possessed. Like Arvay, the rattler has left its brand on Jim, as he demonstrates at one point by flinging open his bathrobe and revealing to his wife the battle scars of his war with the serpent: "From his short-ribs to his pelvis, was a band of raw-red abraded flesh. The crawling mechanics of the snake applied with such tremendous muscular tension had scoured Jim raw."

"Your kind of love," he tells Arvay, "don't seem to be the right thing for me. My feelings inside is just how I look outside" (266). So saying, Jim likens Arvay's hold on him to that of the snake: both strangleholds have left him raw and bleeding. Having thus made his point, he confirms his intentions to leave in the morning, giving Arvay a year in which to bring herself up to his expectations and come to him. For Jim and for Hurston, the onus is on Arvay; the next move is hers.

After months of miserable solitude in the wake of Jim's departure, Arvay is roused from oblivion and drawn back to her childhood home by the news that her mother is ill. At first the sudden trip home represents a chance to celebrate her cracker roots and to forget the man who is not her kind, whose ways are not her ways, and whose expectations of her she does not understand. The squalor, degradation, and abject poverty in which she finds her mother, sister, and once-beloved brother-in-law, however, make her count the blessings Jim's hard work has bestowed upon her. The Middletons are utterly without resources and have been living off the money and gifts Arvay and Jim send to Mrs. Henson. The once "neat, virile, vigorous and confident" Carl Middleton, with whom she lived in "mental adultery" for the five years preceding her own marriage, is now a pitiful, soiled, shapeless mass whose meanness and greed are as shocking as his altered appearance. Arvay beholds the specter of her miserable, "mule-faced and ugly" nieces and nephews and is filled with newfound gratitude toward her sister, for she realizes that "[b]ut for 'Raine's intervention, she might have been married to Carl. Been the mother of those awful-looking young men and women that he had fathered. Had to get in the bed with something like that" (289). She also learns from town gossip that Middleton was indeed in love with her all those years ago and saw himself as courting her. Realizing that she might be too young to understand his intentions, he tried to approach her through her sister, but Larraine brought back word that Arvay had turned down his proposal. As Middleton tells it, apparently to anyone who will listen, he lost interest in being a "big man" when he lost Arvay. Arvay's response upon hearing that Middleton considers her his long lost love is to burst into hysterical laughter. It is the first time in 295 pages that we have heard Arvay laugh. And it is good for her soul, an important step in making peace with the past.

Mrs. Henson dies, happy at having seen for one last time the daughter to whose prosperous marriage the Henson house has become a shrine, with gifts from Arvay arranged "museum-like" in the parlor. Arvay, with resistance rather than assistance from her sister and brother-in-law, sees her mother decently laid to rest, increasingly proud of the fact that her husband has provided for her so well that she can provide for her family. The Middletons, who wear their jealousy like their dirty skin, raid the Henson house the moment Arvay's back is turned, stripping it of its few meager possessions and then fleeing town like the thieves in the night they are. In a gesture that signifies closure, Arvay takes a torch to the old homestead and watches as the dry wooden frame burns quickly and completely to the ground.

Arvay's Sawley homecoming is presented as a leave-taking, a confrontation with the past designed to make the "ungrateful" Arvay see just how good her life with Jim Meserve has been, to make her appreciate what he has done on her behalf and what he has saved her from. Appreciation, she begins to understand, is that elusive, mysterious thing Jim seems so much to want, to need, and to expect from her. Confronting the realities of the impoverished past she had long glorified makes it possible for Arvay to embrace the present. Laughter, standing on her own and holding her own, and finally shedding — literally burning — the past all work conveniently together to give birth to a new Arvay. And the new Arvay is bound not out into the world, as some feminist readers may wish, but for the coast to reclaim her husband and "settle her fate."

As a rite of passage from "subconsciously" resistant to "consciously" submissive wife, this "you can't go home again" section of the novel is troubling to me, because of both its conciliatory function and the artificial way in which it serves that purpose. Arvay may be manipulated by the actual conditions of her long-romanticized home, but the reader is not. Home may have changed, but Jim Meserve is still "Lord Jim." Nevertheless, the reclamation of her marriage is the mission to which the text commits Arvay and at which she succeeds masterfully, over the objections of some readers who may want more for the new, improved Arvay than the "mothering" and "serving" to which she willingly gives herself at novel's end. "Jim was not the over-powering general that she had took him for," she realizes, lying in her husband's arms aboard his shrimp boat, the *Arvay Henson*. "Inside he was nothing but a little boy to take care of, and he hungered for her hovering." Her job, she decides, is to mother and hover the man she loves: "To keep on like that in happiness and peace until they died together, giving Jim the hovering that he needed" (351).

For many readers this romantic resolution makes for what Robert Hemenway describes as an unsatisfactory and unbelievable ending, expressed in terms that vitiate Arvay's struggle toward selfhood. "*Seraph on the Suwanee* is an unsuccessful work of art," Hurston's biographer asserts, "partially because Arvay's character promises a complexity and a subtlety of action that is never realized." Despite her enhanced self-confidence, Arvay is ultimately unable to define herself apart from her husband, Jim "Me-serve." "Just as Arvay begins to become interesting," Hemenway laments, "she is lost again to domestic service" (314–15).

Hemenway's point is certainly well taken, but I want to explore some of the problems that underpin this and other widely shared criticisms which read the text — and especially the ending — as realism. It seems to me that if we read this conclusion realistically — if we accept that Arvay *really* does commit herself to hovering and mothering the man she loves — condemning Arvay's choice carries with it an implicit devaluation of the domestic realm. One of the objects of at least some brands of feminist inquiry is not only to critique the unequal power relations of the patriarchal institution of marriage but to validate and legitimate woman's traditional role within that institution. Read realistically, Arvay, it seems to me, not only accepts the role of wife and mother at the end of *Seraph*, she affirms the importance of that role, of what she brings to, as well as what she receives from, the Meserve marriage.

But there is a second, more important point I want to make about the poetic closure of *Seraph on the Suwanee*, another level on which the ending can and, I think, should be read. While Hemenway maintains that the novel ultimately does not deliver the subtlety and complexity of action it promises, I want to argue that the ending is, in fact, so subtly complex that it invites misreadings. The happy ending takes on a much different cast once one ceases to take it seriously as realism or even as romance and begins to read it as the spoof its altered linguistic structure, tone, and characterizations suggest it may be. For example: Hemenway lists among the novel's faults the fact that Jim Meserve becomes a shrimp-boat captain "for the sole purpose of demonstrating Hurston's knowledge of shrimping" (310). Did Herman Melville make Moby Dick a whale solely to demonstrate his knowledge of whaling? Mister Jim's evolution into *Captain* Meserve is a narrative necessity required by the comic resolution Hurston offers. Jim's status as sea captain provides Hurston with a mechanism for rounding out her implicit critique not only of the marriage relation itself but of the ways in which the genre of the novel has romanticized and idealized that relation. *Seraph*'s own conclusion is romantic and idyllic, to be sure, but it is parodically so. And the particular model it seems to me most immediately to parody (and whose commercial success Hurston perhaps hoped to emulate) is *Gone with the Wind*.

As noted earlier, there are a number of similarities between *Seraph on the Suwanee* and *Gone with the Wind*—between Hurston's chauvinistic hero, Jim Meserve, and Mitchell's rakish sea captain, Rhett Butler. By the end of *Seraph*, Meserve, too, has become a daring sea captain, of the *Arvay Henson*, no less. Unlike Captain Butler, however, Captain Meserve *seems* to get his way with his wife by novel's end; he *seems* to have won her submission and appreciation. But if we read carefully the final scenes of the novel set aboard the *Arvay Henson*, what we see is Arvay seizing the helm of her marriage and figuratively, if not literally, steering the *Arvay Henson* and its captain, without his having any idea that he is not the one in control (a strategy Hurston admits to having herself adopted in dealing with male egos). For the first time in her more-than-twenty-year marriage, Arvay, with calculated determination, manipulates the situation to get what *she* wants.

What the new, improved Arvay has learned is some of the deviousness and duplicity that make the constantly calculating Scarlett O'Hara such an engaging character. We see Arvay put these newly acquired manipulative skills into action immediately after she leaves Sawley and returns to Citrabelle. Her new skills are evident in the way she goes about winning over Jeff Kelsey—an enemy since the rattlesnake incident—with a ham, a bag of pecans, and a "Hello there, Jeff, you old rascal. . . . You all look like new money in town to me. I sure am glad to see you." We have never heard Arvay talk to anyone like this before, certainly not to a "nigger," but she wants Kelsey on her side and a ride to the coast where Jim is. She gets both.

It is significant, as well, that at the end of the novel, in an effort to save her marriage, Arvay sets the stage, lures her husband to her cabin, and in effect seduces *him*, only to have him say, as he tears off his clothes and flings himself on the bunk: "And don't try to get cute and resist me, neither"—as if *he* is in control of the situation (348). Unlike Scarlett O'Hara, tomorrow is indeed for Arvay "another day." Perhaps in this romantic ending, Hurston, like her hero Jim Meserve, is "funnin'" her readers, pulling our legs. I imagine her writing the final pages of the novel with pen in hand and tongue in cheek. Let me explain further.

Hurston, so good at dialogue, especially repartee, in the final chapter of *Seraph on the Suwanee* suddenly indulges in a forced, stilted, even amateurish writing style that smacks of the popular romance at its most inept. Arvay's speech pattern, in particular, is completely altered. She speaks now not like the cracker she has been throughout the novel but like a coquette, a southern belle on the prowl, batting her eyelashes with her voice: "Oh, Jim! You got three boats already! And, my goodness! You got one named for me. . . . Oh, Jim, but you are doing well. . . . This is my first time to even see a boat as big as this. . . . Oh, Jim . . . I'm so proud and pleased with how you have done, that I want to go along with you and see you handle things." "Oh, Jim" this and "Oh, Jim" that. Every word out of Arvay's mouth is carefully calculated to get what *she* wants: her husband back. Her first night on board her name-sake shrimp boat, Arvay is unsure of her progress toward her goal. The day went pleasantly enough, but she's not sure whether she is "merely a guest on board and still parted from her husband" or whether she is a part of his life. For Jim, usually so sexually aggressive, sees her comfortably installed in his cabin, but then goes below to sleep in the crew's quarters.

As the *Arvay Henson* sets sail the next morning, we realize that Mrs. Captain is not the only one on board given to "Ohs." The crew members call Jim "My Captain," and the passage is full of "Oh, Captain, My Captains." Jim's decision to take his boat across the bar, despite dangerously rough waters, is met with pleas from a terrified first mate who at one point drops to his knees, grabs Jim's leg, and cries: "Captain! My Captain! You gone crazy? Turn back! This bar too rough to cross right now. Oh, Captain!" In a scene that I think can only be read comically, Arvay, who has been watching from below, flings the hatch open, leaps upon the mate, grabs him by the hair, and pulls him away from Jim's leg. "Let go my husband's leg!" she says, pounding the mate with her fists. "You want to make him wreck his boat? Turn loose!"

The mate is gotten under control, and captain, wife, and crew make a safe crossing into the calm waters of the Atlantic just in time for a spectacular sunrise, which occasions another set of "Oh, Jims!" The fear she felt (but did not show) crossing the bar gone and forgotten "like a birth-pain," Arvay asks Jim, "in a soft maiden voice," if he took the awful chance of crossing when he did so that she could see the sunrise on her first sight of the ocean. When Jim confirms her suspicion, Arvay tells him precisely what his ego needs to hear: "Then, Jim, you're the boldest and the noblest man that ever forked a pair of pants. You'se a monny-ark, Jim, and that's something like a king, only bigger and better. I'm proud enough to die" (331). Arvay's use of hyperbole is not unlike Janie Starks's when she, with wonderful, undetected sarcasm, tells Joe that he is "something like George Washington and Lincoln . . . lak uh king uh something" for freeing Matt Bonner's mule (*Their Eyes*, 92). Arvay's motivation is certainly different from Janie's, but both wives are playing parts and neither husband is even aware of the game.

Determined not to let Jim spend another night below with his crew, Arvay lures him into her cabin, wishing she had some "silk female things on board to adorn herself with" instead of the blue work shirt she puts on—the only thing she puts on. She rehearses a speech, as she lies in wait for her prey: "Jim, your loving Arvay has thrown off every hindering weight so as to follow you along in an easy way. Whither thou goest, I will go along too. Thy kind of people shall be my kind of people, and thy God shall be my God." But clad only in a shirt that stops halfway between her hips and her knees (a point to which Jim's eyes are drawn immediately) and with a new air of self-confidence through which she says to Jim, "I was born with all I ever needed to handle your case," Arvay doesn't need the speech. Suffice it to say, as Hurston does in undulating sexual overtones: "The *Arvay Henson* rode gently on the bosom of the Atlantic. It lifted and bowed in harmony with the wind and the sea. It was acting in submission to the infinite, and Arvay felt its peace" (349).

On the surface, *Their Eyes Were Watching God* and *Seraph on the Suwanee* seem to pose very different possibilities for women in the realm of heterosexual coupling. As Hazel Carby writes: "Arvay's discovery that she needs to be a mother to her husband long after her own children have grown is a vision of female fulfillment that is very different from, and more controversial than, the vision of female autonomy that Hurston created in *Their Eyes Were Watching God*" (xvi). But the difference between these two visions is not only one of autonomy versus service; it is also one of solitary selfhood versus enlightened or calculated, seeming submission. Janie outlives her male oppressors and is left alone with the memory of perfect love, which, as I have argued, can be read as yet another illusion. Arvay rides the waves with her husband, in "submission to the infinite" powers of patriarchy, and finds peace or, at least, a way to keep the peace. But is this peace also an illusion? Or is its purchase price—*seeming* submission—higher than anyone should have to pay? The text's answer to the latter question may rest in the fact that the more self-assured Arvay who chooses to actively submit to Jim Meserve in the final pages of *Seraph* is not the same insecure Arvay Henson who has passively resisted his domination throughout the novel.

Yet, to the extent that "active submission" is necessarily a contradiction in terms, Arvay's surrender can be read as tragic—as a forced conclusion—for the limitations of her time and space leave her little place to go except to her husband. To the extent that Arvay reinvents herself as an actor in a marriage *she* wants to maintain, however, her reconciliation with Jim can be read not merely as romantic or conventional but as what I might call "heroically comic": a joke on her husband, a claiming, rather than a surrendering, of self.

Is Hurston, then, arguing for a kind of duplicitous female acquiescence in the fact of "quintessential maleness"? A feigned submission? An enlightened collaboration with "the enemy" for the sake of hearthside harmony, domestic security, male companionship, and sexual pleasure? Is her advice to visible, independent women the same advice Grandfather—the "spy in the enemy's country"—gives the Invisible Man in Ralph Ellison's novel: play the game, but don't believe in it? "Live with your head in the lion's mouth. . . . [O]vercome 'em with yeses, undermine 'em with grins."[32] Is the difference between Janie and Arvay the fact that Janie never really stops believing in the game of love, in the dream as truth as man as Tea Cake? Arvay, on the other hand, not only learns how to play the love game, she learns that winning the game means *not* believing in it. The dream is a lie, and Arvay acts and does things accordingly: "Oh, Jim." "Yes, Jim." "My Jim." Love, like life, is a war in which women must be "spies" not only in the enemy's country, perhaps, but in his bed. This, then, is the way Hurston's fictional world ends: not only with a bang, but with a wink.

Conclusion

Marriage, Tradition, and the Individualized Talent

> In his daydream he pulled up to his house, a stately mansion with cherry-red brick chimneys and matching brick porch and steps, in a long chauffeur-driven car. . . . Brownfield's wife and children — two girls and a boy — waited anxiously for him just inside the door in the foyer. They jumped all over him, showering him with kisses. While he told his wife of the big deals he'd pushed through that day she fixed him a mint julep. After a splendid dinner . . . , he and his wife, their arms around each other, tucked the children in bed and spent the rest of the evening discussing her day (which she had spent walking in her garden), and making love.
>
> — ALICE WALKER, *The Third Life of Grange Copeland*

If *Pride and Prejudice* suggests the degree to which the gentry of Jane Austen's era was preoccupied with money and marriage, the novels of African American writers from William Wells Brown to Zora Neale Hurston suggest the extent to which black Americans have been similarly concerned with the social, economic, and erotic arrangements of this other peculiar institution. Moreover, the "hard times, tough love" stories of contemporary writers such as Alice Walker, Toni Morrison, Gayl Jones, Gloria Naylor, and Terry McMillan suggest that coupling is not a convention only of the literary past. In fact, the popularity and commercial success of Walker's *The Color Purple* (1982) and McMillan's *Waiting to Exhale* (1992), both involved in some way with love struggles and erotic relations, indicate not only that the coupling convention is alive and kicking in African American fiction but that black men and women in love and trouble just may be the story contemporary audiences most want to read.[1]

As I have argued in this study, however, the particular history of African Americans has complicated the marriage stories black authors have told and continue to tell. Alice Walker's first novel, *The Third Life of Grange Copeland* (1970), for example, highlights the disparity between the implicit promises of the marriage ideal of Austen's fiction and the explicit impossibilities of the actual social and material conditions of most Americans, especially most black Americans. Ignored as a child by a troubled, seemingly indifferent father and a caring but hopelessly burdened and brutalized mother, a young Brownfield Copeland consoles himself with his own imagined version of the white American dream, a dream that romanticizes and idealizes marriage and family:

perfect wife, perfect children, perfect house replete with servants and a chauf-
feur-driven limousine. Brownfield's dream, however, is very much a "dream
deferred" — an impossible dream of prosperity and storybook romance that
shrivels in the midst of crippling poverty, racism, and paternalism. Bitterly
ashamed of his own ignorance, illiteracy, and immobility, Brownfield wages
war not on the irrepressible socioeconomic forces that have brought and keep
him low but on his wife and children. For them, life with Brownfield Copeland
becomes a reign of terror that ultimately ends in death.

For black men and women in America, the acting out of traditional male-
female marital roles, as defined by hegemonic ideologies at given historical
moments, has been dramatically disrupted by the same social structures that
both prescribe and proscribe those roles. The literary history I have attempted
to trace thematically in this study is rooted in and reflects these disruptions.
From early representations of marriage as a bourgeois ideal to be aspired to,
to modern renderings of wedlock as a stranglehold to be escaped from, the
novels of African American women writers have been sites of intense social
and cultural critique.

In the mid-nineteenth century, Harriet Wilson and Harriet Jacobs, along
with William Wells Brown, appropriated and revised the form of conventional
sentimental literature, turning the genre in on itself by exposing both the
ideological limitations of "true womanhood" and genteel femininity and the
hypocrisy of a patriarchal system that privileged the institution of marriage
while denying its sanctity to the black men and women on whose enslavement
the system depended. In their experimentations with the novel and the coupling convention, these early black writers were interested less in scrutinizing
marriage as a social relation than in claiming the marriage ideal for African
Americans as a civil liberty. Representations of marriage in their novels, I
have argued, have little to do with the intricacies and intimacies of heterosexual coupling and everything to do with literary convention, social practice,
and racial and sexual ideology. At the turn of the century, black writers,
activists, and intellectuals such as Frances Harper, Pauline Hopkins, and Anna
Julia Cooper laid siege to womanhood, to desire, and to democracy by claiming for their heroines and female constituencies the right to marry — the freedom "not to need permission for desire," as Toni Morrison says in *Beloved*.
Escorting in a new, modern moment, Jessie Fauset, Nella Larsen, Dorothy
West, and Zora Neale Hurston in the twenties, thirties, and forties showed
that the *legal* right to desire was not the same thing as sexual and reproductive
freedom or public and professional viability. Beginning with Fauset and picking up force in the fiction of first Larsen and then Hurston, African American
women writers began to look closely at the marital relation itself, identifying
it as a site of confinement and oppression for women. For their female characters, love, eros, romance, coupling, sexual intercourse all carry with them
their own bonds and bogeys: male domination, domestic drudgery, perpetual
pregnancy, eternal motherhood, sexual violence, and even death. Far removed
from the utopian partnerships theorized by nineteenth-century black women

novelists, coupling in the modern black feminist text is more often fictionalized as marital horror than as hearthside harmony.

Representations of love and struggle—even desire and death—are not unique, of course, to modern black women's fiction. It would be a mistake for me to imply by this study that black women writers represent problematic erotic relations between African Americans as something altogether separate and divorced from the marital relations and gender conventions of other men and women. On the contrary, as I have argued, coupling is consistently used as a metaphor in these texts, as the outward and visible sign of the inward and systemic ills that plague American society. What these writers present as problematic about heterosexual coupling among African and European Americans is potentially problematic for all social relations conceived within the confines and conventions of a racist, patriarchal society and under the prescriptions of models of domination and submission.

In *The Bonds of Love*, Jessica Benjamin attempts to explain why positions of subject/object, master/slave persist between the sexes. Domination, she argues, is a deeply inculcated proclivity that begins in infancy and is reinforced by almost every aspect of social and cultural relations through puberty into adulthood, where it manifests itself in erotic relations. Breaking the cycle of domination and submission means maintaining a healthy tension between "self-assertion and mutual recognition"—a delicate balance that allows "self and other to meet as sovereign equals."[2] Such a meeting is possible, according to Benjamin, only if women claim their subjectivity, thus offering men the possibility of "becoming alive in the presence of an equal other" (221). Benjamin readily admits that even on the theoretical level such an intersubjective equality is a utopian vision (very much like that of black women writing in the 1890s). Yet she suggests one avenue of hope: "The conception of equal subjects has begun to seem intellectually plausible only because women's demand for equality has achieved real social force" (221). The work of black women novelists—from Harriet Wilson to Zora Neale Hurston to Alice Walker and Toni Morrison—has been an important part of that social force.

As I have also argued, however, literary studies have been slow to come alive in the presence of an equal black female other. Neither the tales of perfect love (of good black patriarchs and equal partnerships) nor the narratives of male dominance and female oppression (of brutal black men and deadly coupling) have easily found places of honor within what is commonly called the African American literary tradition. Dominated until recently by male voices, this tradition has often ignored, dismissed, and otherwise marginalized the work of black women, unfavorably comparing novels such as Harper's *Iola Leroy* to Brown's *Clotel*, Larsen's *Quicksand* and *Passing* to McKay's *Home to Harlem*, Petry's *The Street* to Wright's *Native Son*, and Hurston's *Their Eyes Were Watching God* to Ellison's *Invisible Man*. With the exception of *Their Eyes* and Morrison's *Beloved* and *Song of Solomon*, few texts by black women have been able to cross over securely into the mainstream of either Anglo- or Afro-American canon construction.

At the same time, however, black feminist critics have been actively engaged in establishing a countertradition of African American women writers. While it has often privileged the "authentic" voices and experiences of black women of the rural South such as Hurston's Janie Crawford, this "womanist" tradition has also begun to carve out crevices for the stories of poor black women of the urban North such as Petry's Lutie Johnson and even of bourgeois black women such as Larsen's Helga Crane and Irene Redfield. Like the larger African American literary tradition, however, this woman-centered canon has not yet found a comfortable place for novels such as *Seraph*, with its white heroine, or for *Megda* and *Four Girls at Cottage City*, with their racially ambiguous leading ladies, or for *Comedy: American Style* and *The Living Is Easy*, with their dastardly female antiheroes who are more victimizers than victims.

Alice Walker, for example, so instrumental in reclaiming Hurston's work from obscurity, has actually panned *Seraph on the Suwanee*, along with such novels as *Iola Leroy*, *Megda*, and *Contending Forces*, for what she sees as their structured colorism. As Walker reads it, Hurston's later work became "reactionary, static, shockingly misguided and timid." This is particularly true of Hurston's last novel, she maintains, "which is not even about black people, which is no crime, but *is* about white people for whom it is impossible to care, which is."[3] Similar dismissals and omissions can be found throughout both black feminist and mainstream African American literary criticism. Bernard Bell's definitive study, *The Afro-American Novel and Its Tradition* (1987), to cite one important contemporary example, makes no mention of either *Megda* or *Four Girls at Cottage City*; *Seraph on the Suwanee* fares only slightly better. Noting that Hurston's last novel is "neither comic, nor folkloric, nor about blacks," Bell maintains that the text's "focus on whites places it outside the scope of [his] study."[4]

The exclusion of *Seraph on the Suwanee* from a so-called African American literary tradition or from a tradition of black women writers largely because of its move away from black folklore and its use of white figures suggests just how highly problematic the concept of tradition is in African American literary criticism. Race—that is to say, "blackness"—or, in black feminist criticism, race and gender are the foundations on which the temple of tradition is built. As the example of *Seraph on the Suwanee* suggests, however, neither the racial identity nor the gender of its author is necessarily enough to qualify a text for what I might call, borrowing from Barbara Christian, "the race for tradition."

Tradition, as this study has attempted to demonstrate, is a troubled and troubling term—"a word that nags the feminist critic," Mary Helen Washington has said.[5] Part of its polemic, at least in the context of African American literary studies, is that it is constantly invoked but rarely defined, generally assumed but seldom delineated. In black feminist criticism, for example, does the claim of an identifiable tradition of black women writers refer to a uniquely black female expressive modality or to a historical scheme of chronologically ordered works? Or both? What links these works? Race? Theme? Material condition? Common female experience? An essential black female consciousness? According to Henry Louis Gates, "Literary works configure into a tradition not because of some mystical collective unconscious determined by the biology of race or gender, but because writers read other writers and *ground* their representations of experience in models of language provided largely by other writers to whom they feel akin. It is through this mode of literary revision," he argues, "that a 'tradition' emerges and defines itself."[6]

While I readily agree that authors read and revise each other across cultures, times, and traditions, I would argue that such revisionism does not spontaneously generate or autonomously define a particular literary tradition. Traditions and the canons that confirm them are made not born, constructed not spawned. I would also argue that mythologies of race, gender, and class have a great deal to do with the invention of such traditions and that there is a great deal at stake in the creation myths of literary canons. Cornel West has suggested that while it has the positive effect of bringing important texts to the fore, African American canon construction "principally reproduces and reinforces prevailing forms of cultural authority in our professionalized supervision of literary products."[7] In other words, like its European and Anglo-American counterparts, the African American literary canon is an exclusive club whose roster is determined by the tastes of a handful of intellectuals.

What is at stake in canonizing black texts, however, is not just who determines what we read and how we read it but who *we* are — what *authentic* African American culture is. For all our rhetoric about race as socially constructed rather than biologically determined, much of our critical and cultural theory still treats race as natural and transhistorical. To a large extent, contemporary tradition building and canon construction are rooted in reified notions of culture as based on race, encapsulated in race. Other imperatives of identity formation, including gender, often become excess baggage not only in the invention of an African American literary tradition but also in the development of a black feminist canon based on the belief in an essential, definitively black female experience and language.

Again, let me use the critical rejection of *Seraph on the Suwanee* to illustrate my point. For all that it says about gender, power, and marital relations, about courtship and marital rape, and about female psychology and male domination, *Seraph on the Suwanee* should be an interpretive gold mine for feminist critics in particular. But in the race for tradition, *Seraph* actually upsets the canonical apple cart because it de-essentializes the "always already essentialized." Within the confines of the mainstream African American and black feminist literary traditions, Hurston is authorized to write about women's experience so long as the women she writes about are black. Similarly, in the Anglo-American and white feminist literary traditions, Hurston's authority is limited to "the black experience," even if her characters are women and even if her women are white. In other words, in what seems to me a particularly paradoxical reversal, the racial assumptions of feminists (black and white) and the gender blind spots of African Americanists (male and female) have conspired in placing *Seraph* and other seemingly nonconformist, unauthorized texts under erasure, outside of tradition. Put yet another way: the race for tradition has become a race for race—a race run on a track that is not only a dead end for black literary studies, as Gates has argued, but a maze.[8]

How do we get out of the maze, out of the black hole of our own essentialism, the racial fix of our fixation on race? Do we shelve the idea of an African American literary canon and leave the representation of "authentic" black life to Mark Twain and William Faulkner? My own project would prove me a fraud, I'm afraid, if in the eleventh hour of this study I were to debunk entirely the notion of tradition and canon or to advocate the complete abandonment of cultural moorings and racial markers. I do want to suggest, however, that black literary studies must put its practice where its theory is. Critics and theorists of African American literature must conceptualize race, class, culture, and experience, as well as traditions and canons, in terms far less natural, absolute, linear, and homogeneous than we have in the past.

What I have argued for throughout this study is a critical practice that moves beyond the assumption and promotion of a single, seamless master narrative; a particular, privileged black experience; or a solitary, individualized black talent. I hope that this study of coupling and convention—of the shifts, ironies, and ambiguities within the marriage tradition in black women's fiction—will contribute to a reconsideration of the African American novel and its traditions.

Notes

Introduction

1. Evelyn J. Hinz maintains that this line from *Pride and Prejudice* "is as famous for its enunciation in socially critical terms of the marriage theme as the entire work is exemplary of the conventions of the novelistic tradition." See Evelyn J. Hinz, "Hierogamy Versus Wedlock: Types of Marriage Plots and Their Relationship to Genres of Prose Fiction," *PMLA* 91 (1976): 900–913.

2. See Leslie Fiedler, *Love and Death in the American Novel* (New York: Stein and Day, 1960; rpt. New York: Anchor, 1992).

3. Claudia Tate has done groundbreaking work on representations of marriage and the family in nineteenth-century domestic fiction. Her book *Domestic Allegories of Political Desire: The Black Heroine's Text at the Turn of the Century* (New York: Oxford University Press, 1992), appeared while my own volume was in production. To my knowledge Sybille Kamme-Erkel's 1988 dissertation "Happily Ever After? Marriage and Its Rejection in Afro-American Novels," published in book form by Peter Lang, is the only other full-length study of the treatment of matrimony in African American fiction. Surveying a staggering number of novels, from *Clotel* to *The Color Purple*, Kamme-Erkel's dissertation examines both representations of and attitudes toward marriage in African American fiction. My study differs from hers in its concern with marriage as both a social and a literary convention and in its overall approach to the novels it examines. While Kamme-Erkel defines her approach as "purely descriptive," devoid of any attempt to force "certain theories from linguistics or literary criticism onto the interpretations of the novels," I am admittedly as intrigued by (and preoccupied with) the theoretical questions surrounding the texts I treat as by the texts themselves. Where Kamme-Erkel asserts that in her study "the novels will be allowed to speak for themselves," I argue that texts are produced by their readings and are largely mute without the voices and critiques of their interpretive communities. See *Happily Ever After? Marriage and Its Rejection in Afro-American Novels* (Frankfurt am Main: Peter Lang, 1989). For a comment on Kamme-Erkel's reading of *Clotel*, see chapter 1, note 11, of this study.

4. Nina Baym, *Woman's Fiction: A Guide to Novels by and About Women in Amer-

ica, 1820–1870 (Ithaca, NY: Cornell University Press, 1978), 11–12. Baym argues that the novels written by American women between 1820 and 1870 all offer variations of a single tale: the story of a young girl who, deprived of the support and sustenance she needs, is forced to make her own way in the world—usually into a marriage. Though she does not qualify them as such, Baym is speaking exclusively of white women authors and white heroines.

5. However popular *Their Eyes Were Watching God* has become in recent years, it was not so well received when it was published in 1937. It promptly went out of print and, for the most part, remained so until it was reissued in 1978 by the University of Illinois Press. For a detailed account of the publication history and critical reception of *Their Eyes*, see the editor's introduction to *New Essays on "Their Eyes Were Watching God,"* ed. Michael Awkward (New York: Cambridge University Press, 1991), 1–27.

6. Harriet Jacobs, *Incidents in the Life of a Slave Girl* (1861), edited and with an introduction by Jean Fagan Yellin (Cambridge, MA: Harvard University Press, 1987), 201. Given the analogy some of her white women contemporaries drew between marriage and slavery, Jacobs's remark may be doubly subversive.

7. Toni Morrison, *Beloved* (New York: New American Library, 1987), 162.

8. Installed in New York City after finally escaping from the cruelty and sexual coercion of her owner, Jacobs was eventually purchased, against her will, by friends wanting to spare her further pursuit and persecution as a fugitive slave. Jacobs objected to the sale because "being sold from one owner to another"—even to one who intended to manumit her—"seemed too much like slavery" (199). Without Jacobs's knowledge, her friends went ahead with the transaction, obtaining a bill of sale for her in the free city of New York.

9. Harriet Wilson, *Our Nig . . .*, 1859; reprinted with an introduction and notes by Henry Louis Gates, Jr. (New York: Vintage, 1983), 5.

10. See, among others: Hazel Carby, "Slave and Mistress: Ideologies of Womanhood Under Slavery," in *Reconstructing Womanhood: The Emergence of the Afro-American Woman Novelist* (New York: Oxford University Press, 1987), 20–39; P. Gabrielle Foreman, "The Spoken and the Silenced in *Incidents in the Life of a Slave Girl* and *Our Nig*," *Callaloo* 13 (Spring 1990): 313–24; Harryette Mullen, "Runaway Tongue: Resistant Orality in *Uncle Tom's Cabin*, *Our Nig*, *Incidents in the Life of a Slave Girl*, and *Beloved*," paper presented at the annual meeting of the American Studies Association, New Orleans, LA, November 1990; Jane Campbell, "Celebrations of Escape and Revolt," in *Mythic Black Fiction: The Transformation of History* (Knoxville: University of Tennessee Press, 1986), 1–17.

11. Mullen, "Runaway Tongue," 1. Echoing Jane Tompkins, Mullen notes that sentimental novels instructed "women how to submit to their culturally defined roles in order to exercise the power available to bourgeois white women operating within the limits of true womanhood." Slave narratives, on the other hand, promoted not submission but resistance to and flight from patriarchal oppression. For a description and discussion of the prescriptive nineteenth-century ideology Barbara Welter identified, see her essay "The Cult of True Womanhood" in *Dimity Convictions: The American Woman in the Nineteenth Century*, ed. Barbara Welter (Athens: Ohio State University Press, 1975), 21–41.

12. This claim has perhaps been most clearly articulated by black lesbian feminist critic Barbara Smith, who argues that "thematically, stylistically, and conceptually Black women writers manifest common approaches to the act of creating literature as a direct result of the specific political, social, and economic experience they have been obliged to share." Smith suggests as well that these writers use "specifically Black fe-

male language" to convey their messages and incorporate "traditional Black female activities" into their texts. See Barbara Smith, "Toward a Black Feminist Criticism," in *The New Feminist Criticism: Essays on Women, Literature, and Theory*, ed. Elaine Showalter (New York: Pantheon, 1985), 174. Smith's essay appeared originally in *Conditions: Two* 1, no. 2 (October 1977) and has been widely reprinted and anthologized.

13. See, for example, Barbara Christian's antitheory manifesto, "The Race for Theory," and Michael Awkward's rebuttal, "Appropriative Gestures: Theory and Afro-American Literary Criticism," both in *Gender and Theory: Dialogues on Feminist Criticism*, ed. Linda Kauffman (New York: Basil Blackwell, 1989), 225–46. See also the at-times vitriolic exchange between Joyce Joyce, on the one hand, and Houston Baker, Jr., and Henry Louis Gates, Jr., on the other, in *New Literary History* 18 (Winter 1987): 335–84; and Audre Lorde, "The Master's Tools Will Never Dismantle the Master's House," in *Sister Outsider* (Trumansburg, NY: Crossing Press, 1984), 110–13.

14. For interesting discussions of this point see Carby, *Reconstructing Womanhood*, 3–19; Cornel West, "Minority Discourse and the Pitfalls of Canon Formation," *Yale Journal of Criticism* 1 (Fall 1987): 193–201; Henry Louis Gates, Jr., *Figures in Black: Words, Signs, and the "Racial" Self* (New York: Oxford University Press, 1989), xxii.

15. Houston A. Baker, Jr., *Workings of the Spirit: The Poetics of Afro-American Women's Writing* (Chicago: University of Chicago Press, 1991), 25.

16. The *Colored American Magazine* was published by the Colored Cooperative Publishing Company, which also published Hopkins's first novel, *Contending Forces*. Both the publishing company and the journal sought specifically and deliberately to develop a black membership and readership.

17. Hazel Carby, introduction to *Iola Leroy, Shadows Uplifted*, by Frances E. W. Harper (1892; rpt. Boston: Beacon, 1987), xvi, xxi–xxii. While Carby speaks specifically of Harper, I argue in chapters 2 and 3 that much the same claim can be made for Brown and Hopkins. It is also worth noting that even where the target audience for a text was white—as with so-labeled "abolitionist novels" like *Clotel*—the authors wrote *on behalf of* a black constituency.

18. Barbara Christian, *Black Women Novelists: The Development of a Tradition, 1892–1976* (Westport, CT: Greenwood, 1980), 40–44.

19. Barbara E. Johnson, response to an essay by Henry Louis Gates, Jr., "Canon-Formation and the Afro-American Tradition," in *Afro-American Literary Studies in the 1990s*, ed. Houston A. Baker, Jr., and Patricia Redmond (Chicago: University of Chicago Press, 1989), 42.

20. See Fredric Jameson, *The Political Unconscious: Narrative as a Socially Symbolic Act* (Ithaca, NY: Cornell University Press, 1981), 9–23.

21. Indira Karamcheti, "Post-Coloniality and the Internationalization of Cultural Studies," paper presented at the Mainstreams and Margins Conference, University of Massachusetts-Amherst, April 3, 1992.

22. Linda Gordon, "What's New in Women's History," in *Feminist Studies/Critical Studies*, ed. Teresa de Lauretis (Bloomington: Indiana University Press, 1986), 29.

23. Rita Felski, *Beyond Feminist Aesthetics: Feminist Literature and Social Change* (Cambridge, MA: Harvard University Press, 1989), 12.

24. For an etymology of the term "feminism" and a history of the concept, see Nancy F. Cott, *The Grounding of Modern Feminism* (New Haven, CT: Yale University Press, 1987).

25. Gerda Lerner, *The Creation of Patriarchy* (New York: Oxford University Press, 1986), 239.

26. C. L. R. James, *Notes on Dialectics: Hegel, Marx, Lenin* (1948, 1965; rpt. London: Allison & Bushby, 1980), 15.

Chapter 1

1. Molefi Kete Asante, *The Afrocentric Idea* (Philadelphia, PA: Temple University Press, 1987), 6–7. Asante is widely regarded as one of the nation's leading proponents of Afrocentricity, a critical perspective that interprets African diasporic cultures in the context of African rather than Western social and cultural belief systems. While there is much to be gained from such a perspective, Afrocentricity also runs the risk of replacing one monocentrism with another, exchanging one form of cultural myopia for another. It is unclear in this discussion what Asante means by "traditionally," particularly since he uses the present tense. Certainly contemporary African novels in English and French by both men and women writers are concerned with romantic themes. Asante's cited source, Charles Larson, makes a stronger case than the one Asante presents. He describes love as a different concept for Africans, for whom the principal purpose of marriage is procreation. "Romantic love, seduction, sex—these are not the subjects of African fiction," Larson writes. I would argue, however, that they are indeed the subtexts of numerous African novels. While it does not present a pure love plot, like a number of African novels, Chinua Achebe's *Man of the People*, for example, works its theme of political corruption through portrayals of personal, sexual relationships, as well as political confrontations. See Charles Larson, "Heroic Ethnocentrism: The Idea of Universality in Literature," *The American Scholar* 42 (Summer 1973): 463–75.

2. Evelyn Hinz has identified two types of obstacles that complicate the plot and forestall the eventual union in British and Anglo-American fiction: (1) the prejudices either of the couple themselves or, more typically, of their family and friends; and (2) unequal status, different backgrounds, or membership in different social classes. Even in the European and Anglo-American novel, other types of obstacles appear, and the African American novel adds considerably to this list.

3. Claudia Tate, "Allegories of Black Female Desire; or, Rereading Nineteenth-Century Sentimental Narratives of Black Female Authority," in *Changing Our Own Words: Essays on Criticism, Theory, and Writing by Black Women*, ed. Cheryl A. Wall (New Brunswick, NJ: Rutgers University Press, 1989), 103. Tate offers a provocative, compelling reading of the discourse on marriage in the novels of several nineteenth-century black women writers. She enlarges upon this discussion in her comprehensive study *Domestic Allegories of Political Desire* (New York: Oxford University Press, 1992).

4. Herbert Gutman, *The Black Family in Slavery and Freedom, 1750–1925* (New York: Vintage, 1976), 412–18. See also Jacqueline Jones, *Labor of Love, Labor of Sorrow: Black Women, Work, and the Family from Slavery to the Present* (New York: Vintage, 1985); Jessie Bernard, *Marriage and Family Among Negroes* (Englewood Cliffs, NJ: Prentice-Hall, 1966) (Bernard uses birth registrations as an admittedly crude index to determine marriage trajectories among blacks between 1860 and 1960); Benjamin A. Botkin, *Lay My Burden Down* (Chicago: University of Chicago Press, 1945); and E. Franklin Frazier, *The Negro Family in the United States*, rev. ed. (New York: Holt, Rinehart & Winston, 1948).

5. While the issue needs further research, it does seem to have been primarily *freedmen* who had the right of choice. Bernard foregrounds in her analysis an important

issue Gutman largely sidesteps: the institutionalization of enforced monogamy. In an effort to rebut the findings of Daniel P. Moynihan, Gutman is concerned in his study with documenting the existence of double-headed households and long-term marriages among slaves and freedmen and freedwomen. In the process, he largely elides the question of serial and perhaps not entirely "voluntary" monogamy. As Deborah Gray White warns: "Statistics on long-lived marriages must be approached with caution. The length of a slave marriage does not necessarily indicate how voluntary it was, nor the circumstances under which it occurred." Christie Farnham adds that the term "double-headed," as Gutman uses it, is misleading because it "obscures the fact that many men were not the biological fathers of all the children present in the family." See Deborah Gray White, Ar'n't I a Woman? Female Slaves in the Plantation South (New York: Norton, 1985), 150; and Christie Farnham, "Sapphire? The Issue of Dominance in the Slave Family, 1830–1865," in "To Toil the Livelong Day": America's Women at Work, 1780–1980, ed. Carol Groneman and Mary Beth Norton (Ithaca, NY: Cornell University Press, 1987), 73.

6. Jacqueline Jones, Labor of Love, 69. Without meaning to invoke a protracted debate about African cultural retention, it might be worth noting that these former slaves often came from cultures in which marriage and family were extremely important institutions, societies in which marriage rites and wedding ceremonies were occasions for great gaiety and expansive color long before contact with whites. With this in mind it becomes possible to view the "dressing out" and "acting up" Jones notes not as strictly reactive, imitative actions but as acts of reclamation in keeping with the expressive cultures from which African Americans were taken—cultures in which clothing was colorful and celebrative, works of an art that was everywhere, including worn on the body.

7. Charles Chesnutt, "The Wife of His Youth," in The Wife of His Youth and Other Stories of the Color Line (New York: Houghton Mifflin, 1899; rpt. Ann Arbor: University of Michigan Press, 1968), 15.

8. Joseph Boone, Tradition Counter Tradition: Love and the Form of Fiction (Chicago: University of Chicago Press, 1987), 1.

9. Boone's abbreviated but sensitive and compelling reading of Naylor's Women of Brewster Place suggests that there is much readers might have gained from his insight had he included the African American novel under the rubric of American literature.

10. To his credit, Boone does acknowledge that representations and critiques of marriage are central to the work of a number of modern black women writers. (He cites specifically Hurston, West, and Morrison.) He also makes the point that because black women writers have a cultural understanding of the family and a doubled relation to the romantic other quite different from notions of "hearthside harmony" held by the dominant class, the relation of black fiction to the middle-class marriage tradition is highly problematic (24).

11. Brown published revised versions of this narrative under different titles in 1861, 1864, and 1867; my discussion here is of the original 1853 version. In her published dissertation, Happily Ever After?, Sybille Kamme-Erkel offers a critique of the 1864 version of Brown's narrative, with mention of the alternate ending presented in the final edition, Clotelle; or, The Colored Heroine: A Tale of the Southern States (Boston: Lee and Shepart, 1867). Kamme-Erkel states in a footnote that the 1867 text "shows only few changes to the earlier versions" (41). She seems to confuse or conflate the original text with subsequent versions published in the United States. These later narratives—especially the last two—are, in fact, quite different from the original version published in London, where Brown had greater freedom to exploit the rumor that

a daughter of the president of the United States had been sold on the auction block for one thousand dollars. See, for example, Arthur Davis's introduction to *Clotel* or Farrison's biography of Brown.

12. Christian, *Black Women Novelists*, 22–23.

13. Alice Walker, "If the Present Looks Like the Past, What Does the Future Look Like?" in *In Search of Our Mothers' Gardens* (New York: Harvest, 1984), 301–2, 310 (emphasis added). The fact that Walker refers to Brown's heroine as "Clotelle" suggests that she, too, is relying on the later versions of the novel. It may also be worth noting that, however inadvertently, Walker's argument seems to condemn as unnatural a large segment of the nation's "black" population. According to census records, by 1850 there were nearly 250,000 *light-skinned* mulatto slaves, just slightly less than 10 percent of the slave population. How, then, is the mulatta figure unnatural? Precisely the "natural phenomenon" with which Brown and Fauset and Larsen toy is the fact that "white" *is* one of the colors in which "blacks" exist. (I emphasize "light-skinned" because, according to John Hope Franklin, census takers at the time "counted as mulattoes only those who appeared to be of mixed parentage." See John Hope Franklin and Alfred E. Moss, *From Slavery to Freedom*, 6th ed. [New York: Knopf, 1988], 128.)

14. Brown at one point refers to Clotel as a "true woman."

15. William Wells Brown, *Clotel; or, the President's Daughter: A Narrative of Slave Life in the United States* (London: Patridge & Oakey, 1853; rpt. New York: Macmillan, 1975), 37–38.

16. Part of a dowry of 135 slaves Jefferson acquired at the time of his marriage, Dashing Sally, as Hemings was known around Monticello, was in fact the half sister of Martha Wayles Jefferson, the president's wife. A young Sally accompanied the widower Jefferson and his daughter Maria to France, where Hemings indeed became pregnant, giving birth to a son she named Tom after her return to Monticello. Sally had five more children, all born after Jefferson retired to Monticello in 1794. Jefferson did not free Hemings or her children in his will, a fact some scholars read as an indication he was neither her "lover" nor the father of her offspring. Hemings and her remaining children were freed by Jefferson's daughter Martha Randolph two years after his death in 1826. Scholars continue to debate the particulars of Jefferson's sexual politics, but as Catherine Clinton argues, the issue is not only whether the third president slept with and impregnated one of his slaves, but "about American history itself." As William Farrison has pointed out, Jefferson's personal history does not quite fit with the chronology Brown establishes in *Clotel*. The immediate inspiration for the principal plot of *Clotel*, Brown acknowledged, was the supposedly true story of a Virginia slaveholder named Carter who sold his longtime colored mistress and their daughter at the time of his marriage to a respectable white woman. Brown, Farrison writes, replaced the obscure figure of Carter with that of the well-known statesman Thomas Jefferson. See Catherine Clinton, *The Plantation Mistress: Woman's World in the Old South* (New York: Pantheon, 1982), 217–20; and William Farrison's introduction to *Clotel* (New York: Carol Publishing Group, 1989), 7–9. See also Joel Williamson, *New People: Miscegenation and Mulattoes in the United States* (New York: Free Press, 1980); Fawn Brodie, *Thomas Jefferson: An Intimate History* (New York: Norton, 1974); and Barbara Chase-Riboud, *Sally Hemings* (New York: Viking, 1979).

17. Brown takes pains to establish that once Clotel becomes aware of Green's legal marriage, she denies him further carnal knowledge, despite Green's attempts to continue the affair. This seemingly minor point becomes important when taken together with the biting criticism from many feminist readers who see Brown only as maligning

black womanhood. Here and elsewhere, Brown goes to some lengths and strains credibility to endow his heroine with more morality than the system that enslaved her. In subsequent versions of the novel, the injured wife is much more sympathetically drawn (perhaps to elicit the support of such injured wives and their white sisters). It is the wife's mother who enslaves her son-in-law's colored child. In fact, the last two versions attempt to unindict the wronged wife. "I blamed my wife for your being sold away," Henry Linwood says upon being reunited with Mary, who is now named Clotelle, "for I thought she and her mother were acting in collusion; But I afterwards found that I blamed her wrongfully. Poor woman! she knew that I loved your mother, and feeling herself forsaken, she grew melancholy and died in a decline three years ago" (*Clotelle; or, The Colored Heroine*, 102). The characterization of the wife as an innocent, long-suffering victim is more in keeping with Lydia Maria Child's story "The Quadroons," from which Brown borrowed liberally.

18. Some skilled slaves were allowed to market their expertise or "hire their time" out on a fee-for-services basis, so long as their owners were reimbursed for their time away. William is such as slave. His characterization becomes important because many critics have complained that Brown's colored characters are "clowns" and "buffoons," while his quadroons and mulattoes are noble, heroic, and well spoken. Brown's colorism is hard to deny, but he himself also critiques the color and caste consciousness among slaves and creates several characters who defy the stereotypes assigned to him. William, a tall, dark, "full-bodied negro, whose very countenance beamed with intelligence," is one such character. "Being a mechanic," Brown writes, "he had, by his own industry, made more than what he paid his owner; this he laid aside, with the hope that some day he might get enough to purchase his freedom."

19. In 1848 Ellen and William Craft, who had "married" two years earlier, escaped from slavery in Georgia by posing as a white gentleman (Ellen) traveling with his black slave (William). The couple was legally married in 1850 and forced by the Fugitive Slave Law to flee to England the same year. Brown knew and admired the Crafts and incorporated their story into his novel. In a letter to William Lloyd Garrison in 1849, Brown outlined the ingenious disguises employed by the Crafts (including Ellen's man's dress and bandaged hand that excused her from having to write her name) and praised Ellen Craft in particular as a true heroine. For the text of Brown's letter see Dorothy Sterling, *Black Foremothers: Three Lives*, 2nd ed. (New York: The Feminist Press, 1988), 22–23.

20. As Clotel makes her way to Richmond, Brown takes up one of the novel's numerous subplots. We learn that Clotel's younger sister, Althesa, was rescued from slavery by Henry Morton, a white doctor from Vermont who purchased and legally married her. Both Althesa and her husband die in the New Orleans yellow fever epidemic of 1831, leaving behind two daughters. Upon their parents' deaths, the daughters, who had no knowledge of their Negro heritage, are sold as slaves—a sale made possible by the fact that Morton neglected to manumit his wife, assuming that their legal marriage made her free. By law and by custom, the children followed the condition of the mother, who in this instance was a slave. One daughter commits suicide rather than submit to the concubinage for which she is purchased; the other dies of a broken heart after watching helplessly as her young lover is shot and killed trying to rescue her.

21. Brown, *Clotel*, 177. This fictive incident, too, has had other factual and fictional lives. Clotel's leap from Long Bridge resembles an incident memorialized by the abolitionist Grace Greenwood in a poem published in 1851 entitled "The Leap from the Long Bridge: An Incident in Washington." Brown incorporates (and rewrites some-

what) the poem into his text, making it appear to be written in response to his character's suicide.

22. Ibid., 177–78. Brown's choice of words here is cleverly, ironic. He crafted his
white-skinned heroine so that she should be, quite literally, *within* "the pale of sympathy." It is worth noting as well that, as is often the case, Brown borrows from and
poeticizes the popular abolitionist rhetoric of the day in remarking that in America,
charity does not begin at home. A somewhat similar commentary on America's greater
fondness for the "heroism" of Hungarian refugees than for the survival instincts of its
own runaway slaves appears in chapter 17 of *Uncle Tom's Cabin:* "When despairing
Hungarian fugitives make their way, against all the search-warrants and authorities of
their lawful government, to America, press and political cabinet ring with applause
and welcome. When despairing African fugitives do the same thing,—it is—what *is*
it?" In her remarkable biography, *Harriet Beecher Stowe: A Life* (New York: Oxford
University Press, forthcoming), Joan Hedrick traces Stowe's source to a commentary
that appeared in the New York *Independent* in January 1851. See Harriet Beecher
Stowe, *Uncle Tom's Cabin* (New York: Signet, 1966), 216.

23. Addison Gayle, Jr., *The Way of the New World: The Black Novel in America*
(Garden City, NY: Anchor Press/Doubleday, 1976), 6–8. Gayle's critique of Brown is
a scathing one that includes the suggestion that "[c]ensure must be leveled against him
for his failure, as a black novelist, to undertake the war against the American imagists."
The idea that a black novelist writing in the mid-nineteenth century should be censured
by modern readers for not living up to the black nationalist standards of the 1960s and
1970s seems to me absurdly anachronistic. Gayle's indictment ultimately says more
about him as a critic than about Brown as a novelist. It properly places him squarely in
the camp of the black aestheticians who since the 1960s have made *their* definition of
cultural nationalism the principal index by which they evaluate the texts of African
American writers.

24. Christian, *Black Women Novelists*, 14.

25. Brown, *Clotelle; or, The Colored Heroine*, 5.

26. Jean Fagan Yellin, *The Intricate Knot: Black Figures in American Literature,
1776–1863* (New York: New York University Press, 1972).

27. Since he had instigated their attempted escape from St. Louis, Brown blamed
himself for his mother's sale. In 1834 he succeeded in escaping alone. See *Narrative of
the Life of William Wells Brown, a Fugitive Slave* (Reading, MA: Addison-Wesley,
1969), originally published in 1847 and revised in 1848 and 1849.

28. In *The Black Man, His Antecedents, His Genius, and His Achievements*, the
first of four histories of African Americans, Brown claimed Daniel Boone as his maternal grandfather. However, William Edward Farrison, Brown's principal biographer,
suggests that Brown's grandfather was more likely a black revolutionary soldier named
Simon. See William Edward Farrison, *William Wells Brown: Author and Reformer*
(Chicago: University of Chicago Press, 1969), 11. See Farrison also for a detailed
accounting of the sources from which Brown borrowed liberally in crafting *Clotel.*

29. As Brown recorded in his own autobiographical narrative, he was one of seven
children born to his mother; each of those seven children had a different father.

30. Richard Yarborough, introduction to *Contending Forces*, by Pauline Hopkins
(New York: Oxford University Press, 1988), xxxiv.

31. Brown practiced considerable intertextuality within his own oeuvre. Sam, for
example, a dark-skinned slave in *Clotel*, is much the same character as Cato, who
appears in Brown's play *The Escape; or, A Leap for Freedom: A Drama in Five Acts*
(1858). Sam and Cato both work for white doctors and are allowed to "treat" other

slaves, eventually acquiring the title "Black Doctor." While both characters provide considerable comic relief in their respective texts in a way that may make them seem prototypical black buffoons, Cato, in particular, is no fool. Rather, he wears what poet Paul Laurence Dunbar called "the mask that grins and lies." When the opportunity arises, he makes good his escape and has, if not quite the last laugh, the last "shout loudly for freedom." Brown deals a bit more harshly with Sam, who, despite the gift of literacy (and gab), regards his dark skin color as "a great misfortune." See William Wells Brown, *The Escape; or, A Leap for Freedom*, anthologized in *Black Theater, USA*, ed. James Hatch and Ted Shine (New York: Free Press, 1974), 36–58.

32. Catharine Maria Sedgwick, *Hope Leslie; or Early Times in Massachusetts*, ed. Mary Kelley (New Brunswick, NJ: Rutgers University Press, 1987), 225.

33. Henry Louis Gates, Jr., *The Signifying Monkey: A Theory of Afro-American Literary Criticism* (New York: Oxford University Press, 1988), 122.

34. Mullen, "Runaway Tongue."

35. The second version, *Miralda; or, The Beautiful Quadroon: A Romance of American Slavery Founded on Fact*, was serialized in *The Weekly Anglo-African* between November 1860 and March 1861. In this version Clotel is Isabelle, Mary is Miralda, and white-skinned George is dark-skinned Jerome. The plot is not quite so thick with what critics such as Robert Bone have called crude abolitionist propaganda, but much of the discourse on marriage is also removed.

36. Brown, *Clotelle; or, The Colored Heroine*. This final (1867) version of Brown's novel was first reprinted in 1969 by Mnemosyne Publishing. (Subsequent page references are to the reprint edition, although its pagination is identical to the original.)

37. Brown's first book, his autobiography, *Narrative of William Wells Brown, a Fugitive Slave, Written by Himself* (1847), was, according to its own press, a stunning best-seller whose popularity necessitated an immediate second printing. Following perhaps too hotly on the heels of *Uncle Tom's Cabin*, published the year before, *Clotel* did not do as well in either the antislavery or the popular market. (Even *Narrative*, however, sold only 3,000 copies in less than six months, as opposed to the 300,000 copies of *Uncle Tom's Cabin* sold in the United States in its first year, not to mention the 1.5 million copies sold overseas.)

Chapter 2

1. Christina Crosby, *The Ends of History: Victorians and "The Woman Question"* (New York: Routledge, 1991), 1.

2. Nancy F. Cott, "Passionlessness: An Interpretation of Victorian Sexual Ideology, 1790–1850," in *A Heritage of Her Own: Toward a New Social History of American Women*, ed. Nancy F. Cott and Elizabeth H. Pleck (New York: Simon & Schuster, 1979), 162–81.

3. Ann Allen Shockley, "The Black Lesbian in American Literature: An Overview," in *Home Girls: A Black Feminist Anthology*, ed. Barbara Smith (New York: Kitchen Table/Women of Color Press, 1983), 83.

4. Carolyn Sylvander, *Jessie Redmon Fauset, Black American Writer* (Troy, NY: Whitson, 1981), 5.

5. Elizabeth Ammons, *Conflicting Stories: American Women Writers at the Turn into the Twentieth Century* (New York: Oxford University Press, 1991), 23.

6. Elizabeth V. Spelman, *Inessential Woman: Problems of Exclusion in Feminist Thought* (Boston: Beacon, 1988), 13.

7. In his recent study *The Afro-American Novel and Its Tradition* (Amherst: University of Massachusetts Press, 1987), Bernard Bell likens Harper's *Iola Leroy* to William Dean Howells's racist period piece *An Imperative Duty*, labeling Harper's work a "melodramatic study of the color line" (58). He refers to Hopkins's work in the midst of making several points but offers no actual analysis of *Contending Forces* itself, thereby missing an opportunity to discuss not only the author's treatment of such feminist concerns as black women's political activism and the particular vulnerability of black women to rape and sexual coercion but her depiction of such social issues as slavery, racism, miscegenation, lynching, and discrimination as well.

8. Barbara Bardes and Susan Gossett, *Declarations of Independence: Women and Political Power in Nineteenth-Century American Fiction* (New Brunswick, NJ: Rutgers University Press, 1990), 11. In a footnote Bardes and Gossett direct their readers to the Schomburg Library of Nineteenth-Century Black Women Writers for examples of this allegedly afeminist fiction (191, n. 36).

9. Of the bitter, at times vitriolic, debate over black manhood rights versus female suffrage, Harper reportedly remarked: "When it was a question of race, she let the lesser question go. But the white women all go for sex, letting race occupy a minor position. . . . If the nation could handle only one question, she would not have the black women put a single straw in the way, if only the men of the race could obtain what they wanted." Harper's comment cuts to the core of a differential that continues to divide black and white feminists: different social and political imperatives. See Eleanor Flexner, *Century of Struggle: The Woman's Rights Movement in the United States*, rev. ed. (Cambridge, MA: Harvard University Press, 1975), 147.

10. Elizabeth Cady Stanton, Susan B. Anthony, and M. J. Gage, eds., *History of Woman Suffrage* (Rochester, NY: Fowler & Wells, 1881), 1:567–68. See also Gerda Lerner, *Black Women in White America* (New York: Pantheon, 1972), 569–72.

11. Themselves silenced by the angry indictments and heckling of white ministers arguing against woman's rights, many of the white women attending the Akron Woman's Rights Convention did not want Sojourner Truth, "that colored woman," to be allowed to speak. Many different versions of Truth's address exist, and I have drawn from more than one source in the excerpt offered here. For the text as recorded by Matilda Joslyn Gage, who presided over the convention and allowed Truth to speak (or at least did not stop her), see Stanton, Anthony, and Gage, *History of Woman Suffrage*, 1:116. See also Bert James Loewenberg and Ruth Bogin, eds., *Black Women in Nineteenth-Century American Life* (University Park: Pennsylvania State University Press, 1976), 235–36; and Jacqueline Bernard, *Journey Toward Freedom: The Story of Sojourner Truth* (New York: Norton, 1967; reprinted with an introduction by Nell Irvin Painter, New York: The Feminist Press, 1990), 163–67.

12. As white feminist historian Phyllis Marynick Palmer has pointed out: "White feminists who may know almost nothing else about black women's history are moved by Truth's famous query. . . . They take her portrait of herself . . . as compelling proof of the falsity of the notion that women are frail, dependent, and parasitic. They do not, we may notice, use Sojourner Truth's battle cry to show that *black* women are not feeble." See Phyllis Marynick Palmer, "White Women/Black Women: The Dualism of Female Identity and Experience in the United States," *Feminist Studies* 9, no. 1 (Spring 1983): 152.

13. The antilynching and temperance crusades came into direct conflict when British journalists asked Wells if WCTU president Frances Willard, who was also in England at the time, supported her campaign. Wells responded that not only had Willard not

joined the antilynching cause, she herself had spoken disparagingly of black men as a threat to white women. "The colored race multiplies like the locusts of Egypt," Willard asserted in a published interview. "The grogshop is its center of power. The safety of women, of children, the home, is menaced in a thousand localities at this moment, so that men dare not go beyond the sight of their own roof-trees." Willard's words, as Wells read them, painted black men as drunken rapists and white lynch mobs as defenders of home, hearth, and white womanhood. For discussions of the Wells-Willard debate see, among other sources, Paula Giddings, *When and Where I Enter: The Impact of Black Women on Race and Sex in America* (New York: Bantam, 1984), 90–92; Ida B. Wells [Barnett], *On Lynchings: Southern Horrors; A Red Record; Mob Rule in New Orleans* (New York: Arno Press, 1969).

14. Pauline Hopkins, *Contending Forces: A Romance Illustrative of Negro Life North and South* (Boston: Colored Co-operative Publishing House, 1900), 13. The novel has been reprinted twice, as far as I can determine: first in 1978 by Southern Illinois University Press, as part of its Lost American Fiction Series, and most recently in 1988 by Oxford University Press, as part of the Schomburg Library of Nineteenth-Century Black Women Writers. All references to the text are to the original edition. Hopkins wrote three other novels, which were serialized in the *Colored American Magazine* between March 1901 and November 1903: *Hagar's Daughter. A Story of Southern Caste Prejudice; Winona. A Tale of Negro Life in the South and Southwest;* and *Of One Blood. Or, the Hidden Self.* For a full and fascinating discussion of Hopkins and her work, including her magazine fiction, see Hazel Carby's, *Reconstructing Womanhood* and her introduction to *The Magazine Novels of Pauline Hopkins* (New York: Oxford University Press, 1988). See also Elizabeth Ammons's discussion of Hopkins in *Conflicting Stories.*

15. While Howells, the son of abolitionists on both sides of his family, undoubtedly saw himself as taking up for the Negro, his stereotyped, monolithic portraits of blacks made his fiction reek with racism, a perception that inspired response from more than one black writer. In fact, as noted elsewhere, *Iola Leroy* includes an implied critique, if not a rewriting, of Howell's *An Imperative Duty.* In J. McHenry Jones's *Hearts of Gold* (1896), the critique is direct, however arguable. Addressing Howells's racial monolithism, Jones wrote: "Among these people [Negroes], as elsewhere, the marks of class differences are severely drawn; but worth, not complexion, forms the barrier of demarcation." Jones went on to cite Howells as one of many white writers who err on this "point of public observation." See J. McHenry Jones, *Hearts of Gold* (1896; rpt. Miami: Mnemosyne, 1969), 66–67.

16. Anna Julia Cooper, *A Voice from the South* (Xenia, OH: Aldine, 1892; reprinted with an introduction by Mary Helen Washington, New York: Oxford University Press, 1988), 31.

17. It is significant that members of the League have met en masse specifically for the purpose of determining what action to take in response to the rash of lynchings in the South. Some, especially some white members, advocate reason and restraint; others, like Luke Sawyer, argue eloquently against conservativism and blindness to the suffering of blacks in both the South and the North.

18. Hopkins leaves ambiguous the question of Grace Montford's racial heritage, pointing out that in many instances "African blood had become diluted from amalgamation with the *higher races*, and many of these 'colored' people became rich planters or business men (themselves owning slaves) through the favors heaped upon them by their white parents" (22; emphasis added). Pointing out the constructedness (rather than the

biological determination) of race, Hopkins adds: "[T]here might even have been a strain of African blood polluting the fair stream of Montford's vitality, or even his wife's, which fact would not have caused him one instant's uneasiness."

19. Hopkins, who herself worked as a stenographer and typist off and on throughout her adult life, makes a point of noting that good as she is at her job, Sappho is forced to bring her work home to transcribe and type in order to circumvent the objections of white office personnel who refuse to work with even a white-skinned Negro. J. McHenry Jones's novel *Hearts of Gold* makes a similar point through a black woman character who is also a stenographer.

20. Langley represents an exception to the popular notion that patriarchy in nineteenth-century novels is exclusively white. His mother was a slave and his father lower-class southern white—a coupling bound, in this text, to spawn evil. In addition to betraying friend and fiancée alike, Langley also betrays his race by accepting bribes from white businessmen to foster conservatism among the black professional community. Later, black women writers will examine the ways in which patriarchy and masculinist ideology, as systems of domination, embrace black men as well as white. For this literary moment, however, black men, like Will Smith, are *benevolent* patriarchs, whose "manliness" is admired.

21. In Twain's troubling text, Roxana, a mulatta slave who is herself only one-sixteenth "Negro," exchanges her infant son Chambers with her master's boy Tom, so that her child may enjoy the benefits and blessings of the institution that "daily robbed [her] of an inestimable treasure—[her] liberty." Despite the privileges of position and the luxuries of wealth, Roxy's son—the false heir apparent—grows up to be a thief and a murderer who sells his slave mother down the river and kills his "father." On the other hand, the rightful heir—reared as a slave, speaking the folk English of the slave, is no less a "good guy." The troublesome nature of the text's racial and identity politics is captured in Roxy's evaluation of her son: "Thirty-one parts o' you is white, en on'y one part nigger, en dat po' little one part is yo' *soul*." Instead of avenging herself and her people on the system that enslaves them, Roxana creates a monster, but the great tragedy of the text is that whatever his intentions, Twain implies not only that even a gram of Negro blood is bad blood but that heredity, rather than condition, determines character. Unfortunately, there are several moments in *Contending Forces* as well where the Smiths' excellent "address and manner" and their "superior intelligence" are represented as the legacy of their white aristocratic ancestry, just as Langley's perfidy is the product of his poor-white and black slave heritage. See Mark Twain, *Pudd'nhead Wilson and Those Extraordinary Twins*, ed. Sidney E. Berger (New York: Norton, 1980).

22. Narrowly focused on the Smiths' well-entitled, rightfully claimed $150,000 in reparations from the U.S. government, Hopkins elides the fact that the Montfords' original fortune was acquired through the labor of slaves. She makes much of the Smiths' proud, noble lineage, when in fact their heritage is one of owning and exploiting other human beings.

23. Dr. Lewis is patterned after Booker T. Washington, and Will after W. E. B. Du Bois. Lewis is a conservative who believes that "industrial education and the exclusion of politics will cure all our race troubles" (124). He maintains that "women should be seen and not heard, where politics is under discussion"—a position which makes Sappho call him an "insufferable prig." He seems a fitting mate for Dora, however, who is "not the least bit of a politician." Will, like Du Bois, is much more radical and nationalistic in his views. Hopkins puts in Will's mouth some of the text's most fiery political rhetoric, borrowed from some of the nation's best-known public speakers. Sappho is

also politically minded and well spoken on social and educational matters. Regrettably, however, *her* fiery political rhetoric is confined to the private sphere of her sitting room.

24. Tate, "Allegories of Black Female Desire," 118–19.

25. Richard Yarborough, "The Depiction of Blacks in the Early Afro-American Novel" (Ph.D. diss., Stanford University, 1980), 486.

26. See chapter 4 for a discussion of Freud's "dark continent" metaphor for female sexuality and its relationship to the primitivist ideology of the era.

27. Gloria Naylor, "Love and Sex in the Afro-American Novel," *The Yale Review* 78, no. 1 (Spring 1989): 19–31. The quotation appears on page 22.

28. Jean Fagan Yellin, introduction to *Incidents in the Life of a Slave Girl*, xxxi.

29. While Bernard Bell implies that Harper borrowed from William Dean Howells's *An Imperative Duty* (serialized in *Harper's* in 1891) in crafting her novel, I would argue that *Iola Leroy* rewrites and subverts Howells's racist construction. In Howells's novella the white-skinned colored "heroine," Rhoda Aldgate, who exists only as an object of male desire, accepts the proposal and protection of the white Dr. Olney under the condition that no one is to ever know of the "colored connections" of which she herself has learned. Confronted with a similar dilemma of sudden "colored connections," Iola Leroy makes quite a different choice—one of affirmation rather than denial. See William Dean Howells, *An Imperative Duty* (1891; rpt. Bloomington: Indiana University Press, 1970), 96–97.

30. Carby, introduction to *Iola Leroy*, xxv.

31. Frances E. W. Harper, *Iola Leroy; or, Shadows Uplifted* (Philadelphia: Garrigues Brothers, 1892; reprinted with an introduction by Hazel Carby, Boston: Beacon, 1987), 270–71.

32. See Naylor, "Love and Sex in the Afro-American Novel," and Walker, "If the Present Looks Like the Past." Walker accuses Harper, Hopkins, and Kelley of "turn[ing] away from their own *selves*" in depicting white-skinned heroines instead of "identifiably 'colored,'" working-class women.

Chapter 3

1. For a text of Harper's World Congress speech from which this phrase comes, see "Woman's Political Future" as recorded in *World's Congress of Representative Women*, ed. May Wright Sewall (Chicago, 1983), 344–47, and anthologized in Loewenberg and Bogin, *Black Women in Nineteenth-Century American Life*, 244–47. In an essay published in 1888, Harper attributes the term "woman's era" to Victor Hugo. "Victor Hugo has spoken of the nineteenth century as being 'woman's era,'" she wrote, "and among the most noticeable epochs in this era is the uprising of women against the twin evils of slavery and intemperance." See "A Double Standard" and "The Woman's Christian Temperance Union and the Colored Woman," both in *A Brighter Coming Day: A Frances Ellen Watkins Harper Reader*, ed. Frances Smith Foster (New York: The Feminist Press, 1990), 281, 344–46.

2. Cott, "Passionlessness," 173.

3. See Carby, introduction to the reprint of *Iola Leroy*, xxiv. See also Carby's discussion of the absence of the patriarchal father in *Reconstructing Womanhood*, 143–44.

4. Cooper, *A Voice from the South*, 134–35.

5. James Oliver Horton, "Freedom's Yoke: Gender Conventions Among Antebellum Free Blacks," *Feminist Studies* 12 (Spring 1986): 51–76.

6. N. F. Mossell, *The Work of the Afro-American Woman* (Philadelphia: Ferguson Company, 1894; reprinted with an introduction by Joanne Braxton, New York: Oxford University Press, 1988), 118–19.

7. Of this fiery black orator and activist, Marilyn Richards writes: "Likely the first black American to lecture in defense of women's rights, Stewart constructed a spirited series of arguments citing feminist precedents drawn from biblical, classical, and historical sources. A bold and militant orator, she called on black women to develop their highest intellectual capacities, to enter into all spheres of the life of the mind, and to participate in all activities within their community, from religion and education to politics and business, without apology to notions of female subservience." As Richardson notes, Maria Stewart's melding of abolitionist and feminist concerns (as well as religious issues) places her squarely at the helm of a tradition of black female political and literary activism, the significance of which is only now beginning to be addressed. See Marilyn Richardson, ed., *Maria W. Stewart, America's First Black Woman Political Writer: Essays and Speeches* (Bloomington: Indiana University Press, 1987), xiii–xiv. The quotation from Stewart appears on page 38.

8. Louise Newman, "Ideologies of Womanhood at the Turn of the Century: A Re-examination of Anna Julia Cooper's *A Voice from the South*," paper presented at the annual meeting of the American Studies Association, November 1990. As Newman notes, Cooper attributed what she called the blighted mental and moral life of Asian women to the degraded state in which they had been forced to live for centuries in accordance with China's oppressive, patriarchal laws and customs, in effect warning her audience of colored clergymen that they will not be successful in uplifting their race if they bind the feet, clip the tongues, and sexually exploit their women as China and Turkey have done theirs. See Cooper, *A Voice from the South*, 9–20.

9. Anna Julia Cooper, "Address Before the World Congress of Representative Women," 1893; anthologized in Loewenberg and Bogin, *Black Women in Nineteenth-Century American Life*, 329.

10. Deborah E. McDowell, introduction to *Four Girls at Cottage City*, by Emma Dunham Kelley-Hawkins (Boston: James H. Earle, 1898; reprinted with an introduction by McDowell, New York: Oxford University Press, 1988), xxix.

11. Molly Hite, introduction to *Megda*, by Emma Dunham Kelley (Boston: James H. Earle, 1891; reprinted with an introduction by Hite, New York: Oxford University Press, 1988). Kelley's *Megda* and *Four Girls at Cottage City* and Mrs. A. E. Johnson's *Clarence and Corinne* and *The Hazeley Family* were all reprinted in 1988 as part of the Schomburg Library of Nineteenth-Century Black Women Writers. References to *Megda* are to the original edition, although the pagination remains the same in the Schomburg reprint.

12. Ethel Lawton, the most spiritually pure and devoutly Christian of Megda's friends, is also the "whitest," and the text abounds with passages commenting on her goodness and whiteness. At one point, however, Megda explains that Ethel's fair complexion is an inherited trait: "[A]ll her people on her mother's side have very white skin" (108). Interestingly, Megda makes this remark to her brother, who seems to be not so good with colors (at least in women's suits): he mistakes seal brown for deep red and emerald green for black.

13. Henry Louis Gates, Jr., "Writing 'Race' and the Difference It Makes," in *"Race," Writing, and Difference*, ed. Henry Louis Gates, Jr. (Chicago: University of Chicago Press, 1985), 5.

14. Hortense Spillers, introduction to *Clarence and Corinne*, by Amelia Johnson

(Philadelphia: American Baptist Publication Society, 1890; reprinted with an introduction by Hortense Spillers, New York: Oxford University Press, 1988), xxviii.

15. In her provocative study of Victorian sexual ideology, Smith-Rosenberg explores the nineteenth-century phenomenon of long-lived, intimate, loving friendships among women. She identifies a subculture, steeped in "uniquely female rituals [that] drew women together during every stage of their lives, from adolescence through courtship, marriage, childbirth and child rearing, death and mourning." While by the 1890s, New (white) Women writers had largely abandoned and were even somewhat disdainful of the restrictions of "women's culture," black women writers such as Kelley and Johnson were still rooted in and influenced by the ethos of both the female world of love and ritual and the ideology of passionlessness. Kelley's work, in particular, looks back with nostalgia on that world, even as it seems at moments to want to venture outside the confines of women's community, into the professional world and other public realms. See Carroll Smith-Rosenberg, "The Female World of Love and Ritual: Relations Between Women in Nineteenth-Century America," *Signs* 1 (Autumn 1975): 1–29; also in Cott and Pleck, *A Heritage of Her Own*, 311–42.

16. *Megda*, Kelley's first novel, is drawn into the text of *Cottage City* as Garnet realizes that the cottage they are inhabiting is the same one described in *Megda* and that their room is very likely the same one Megda and her friends occupy in the novel. From here the girls go on to discuss which characters they like best and why. Significantly, given her professed intentions never to marry, Jessie asserts that May is her favorite, "for she was brave enough to live and die an old maid for the sake of someone else." Vera, ever the voice of mature reason, announces that there is going to be a sequel to *Megda* and suggests that Jessie should wait and see what happens to May, who might be married in the next book. If Kelley ever completed a sequel to *Megda*, as this passage suggests she intended, it has yet to be discovered.

17. Baym, *Woman's Fiction*, 234.

18. In the final moments of the novel we learn that Maude made a tragic marriage to a man who turned out to be a drunken heathen whose evil ways and lack of character pull her down with him. She calls Megda and Arthur Stanley to her deathbed and makes them promise to raise her daughter. As proof of his depravity, Maude's husband offers to sell his daughter to Stanley for fifty dollars. This particular turn seems to serve the double purpose of pointing out the wages of sin, hypocrisy, and marrying outside the Christian fold and, as Megda reads it, of giving her an opportunity both to atone for the great sin of having disliked Maude and to know "the blessedness of 'returning good for evil'" (394) through the great Christian service of raising the child of her nemesis.

19. Josephine Bruce, "What Has Education Done for Colored Women," *The Voice of the Negro*, July 1905, 295. Quoted by Giddings in *When and Where I Enter*, 100.

20. Frances Harper, "The Two Offers," anthologized in *Afro-American Women Writers, 1746–1933: An Anthology and Critical Guide*, ed. Ann Allen Shockley (New York: New American Library, 1989), 64. "The Two Offers" was serialized in the *Anglo-African* in 1859.

21. Welter, "The Cult of True Womanhood," 271. See also Foster, *A Brighter Coming Day*, which presents Harper's work in historical context. Foster has argued convincingly against the assumption that Harper's characters are necessarily white. See, for example, "Researching and Reinterpreting the Reconstruction of Literature of Frances Ellen Watkins Harper," paper presented at the annual meeting of the American Studies Association, Costa Mesa, CA, November 1992.

Chapter 4

1. Robert Hayden, *Collected Prose*, ed. Frederick Glaysher, with a foreword by William Meredith (Ann Arbor: University of Michigan Press, 1984), 144–45.

2. Hazel Carby, "'It Jus Be's Dat Way Sometime': The Sexual Politics of Black Women's Blues," in *Unequal Sisters: A Multicultural Reader in U.S. Women's History*, ed. Ellen Carol DuBois and Vicki L. Ruiz (New York: Routledge, 1990), 239. The essay originally appeared in *Radical America* 20 (1986).

3. Houston A. Baker, Jr., *Blues, Ideology, and Afro-American Literature: A Vernacular Theory* (Chicago: University of Chicago Press, 1984), 3–4.

4. Hazel Carby, "Reinventing History/Imagining the Future," review of *Specifying: Black Women Writing the American Experience*, by Susan Willis, *Black American Literature Forum* 23, no. 2 (Summer 1989): 381–87. The quotation appears on p. 384.

5. Baker, *Workings of the Spirit*, 23.

6. Carby, "'It Jus Be's Dat Way Sometime,'" 238.

7. While Hull's remark is somewhat ambiguous, by "sensational mainstream" she appears to mean what she sees as the dominant (licentious) discourse of the black Harlem moment, rather than the cultural production of the period in general. See Gloria T. Hull, *Color, Sex, and Poetry: Three Women Writers of the Harlem Renaissance* (Bloomington: Indiana University Press, 1987), 25.

8. Barbara Christian, "Afro-American Women Poets: A Historical Introduction," in *Black Feminist Criticism: Perspectives on Black Women Writers* (New York: Pergamon, 1985), 122; Cheryl A. Wall, "Poets and Versifiers, Singers and Signifiers: Women of the Harlem Renaissance," in *Women, the Arts, and the 1920s in Paris and New York*, ed. Kenneth W. Wheeler and Virginia Lee Lussier (New Brunswick, NJ: Transaction, 1982), 75. Hull quotes essentially the same passages from Christian and Wall.

9. Sandra Lieb, *Mother of the Blues: A Study of Ma Rainey* (Amherst: University of Massachusetts Press, 1981), 81.

10. Originally, white minstrel shows and blackface vaudeville acts, which gained almost phenomenal popularity in the 1840s, were attempts on the part of white entertainers to represent what they viewed as authentic black plantation life, to imitate blacks in their "natural habitat," as it were. Black minstrels began to appear a decade later, and a number of black troupes toured the South in the 1860s. Many of the more successful groups, however, were eventually forced out of the business or taken over by significantly more successful and resourceful white companies. A number of blues stars, including Ma Rainey and Bessie Smith, began their careers touring in minstrel shows and tent performances that followed black migrant workers from harvest to harvest. See, for example, Lieb, *Mother of the Blues*, 4–5; LeRoi Jones [Amiri Baraka], *Blues People: The Negro Experience in White America and the Music That Developed from It* (New York: Morrow, 1963), 81–94.

11. Lawrence W. Levine, *Black Culture and Black Consciousness: Afro-American Folk thought from Slavery to Freedom* (New York: Oxford University Press, 1977), 225.

12. Ralph Ellison, "Blues People," in *Shadow and Act* (New York: Vintage, 1972), 256–57. There are many differing opinions on the nature of both traditional and classic blues. In *Blues People*, for example, LeRoi Jones distinguishes between classic blues as public entertainment and traditional, or "primitive," blues as folklore. Ralph Ellison argues, however, that Jones's distinction is a false one: classic blues were both entertainment *and* folklore. "When they were sung professionally in theatres, they were entertainment," Ellison writes; "when danced to in the form of recordings or used as a means of transmitting the traditional verses and their wisdom, they were folklore."

13. "Race records," as recordings of jazz, blues, ragtime, spirituals, gospel, and sermons were called, were marketed almost exclusively in black neighborhoods.

14. See Mary Ann Doane's chapter "Dark Continents: Epistemologies of Racial and Sexual Difference in Psychoanalysis and the Cinema" in her *Femmes Fatales: Feminism, Film Theory, Psychoanalysis* (New York: Routledge, 1991), 209–48.

15. Sander L. Gilman, "Black Bodies, White Bodies: Toward an Iconography of Female Sexuality in Late Nineteenth-Century Art, Medicine, and Literature," in *"Race," Writing, and Difference*, ed. Henry Louis Gates, Jr. (Chicago: University of Chicago Press, 1986), 223, 228, 232. This essay originally appeared in *Critical Inquiry* (August 1985).

16. Nella Larsen, *Quicksand*, edited and with an introduction by Deborah McDowell (New Brunswick, NJ: Rutgers University Press, 1986), 87. Of the racial mythology that propels Olsen, Cheryl Wall writes: "Olsen knows nothing of African women, but that does not shake his belief in their exotic primitivism. Black women, he feels, are completely sentient, sexual beings. Helga Crane should confirm that belief. When she does not, it proves she has been contaminated by the West, has suffered the primordial female corruption." See Cheryl Wall, "Passing for What? Aspects of Identity in Nella Larsen's Novels," *Black American Literature Forum* 20 (Spring–Summer 1986): 104.

17. It is interesting to note that black men sang raunchy, man-proud folk and traditional blues long before black women began to record what came to be called classic blues for such major production companies as Columbia, Paramount, and Okeh. In the early 1920s black composer Perry Bradford finally succeeded in convincing General Phonograph to permit black vocalist Mamie Smith, a veteran of the minstrel circuit, to record his "Crazy Blues" on the Okeh label. The commercial success of "Crazy Blues" spawned other recordings and the signing of other blues women throughout the music industry. By 1922 both race records and the race for records were on; the blues was big business, and blues women quickly became a prized commodity over which phonograph companies fought, at times bitterly, while bluesmen remained largely unrecorded, perhaps because sex, the quintessential theme of the blues, was a subject more safely sung by black women than by black men.

18. Paul Oliver, *Screening the Blues: Aspects of the Blues Tradition* (London: Cassell, 1968); quoted in Daphne Duval Harrison, *Black Pearls: Blues Queens of the 1920s* (New Brunswick, NJ: Rutgers University Press, 1988), 105.

19. "I'm a Mighty Tight Woman" was recorded and made popular by Sippie Wallace; "Put a Little Sugar in My Bowl" was popularized by Bessie Smith.

20. David Littlejohn, *Black on White: A Critical Survey of Writing by American Negroes* (New York: Grossman, 1966), 50–51.

21. Jessie Fauset, *There Is Confusion* (New York: Boni & Liveright, 1924; reprinted with an introduction by Thadious M. Davis, Boston: Beacon, 1989), 103.

22. As quoted by David Levering Lewis, who adds: "This was the voice of the Salon Negrotarian—not always distinguishable from that of professional primitivist of the Vachel Lindsay or Julia Peterkin variety." See David Levering Lewis, *When Harlem Was in Vogue* (New York: Knopf, 1979; rpt. New York: Oxford University Press, 1989), 98–99.

23. Carl Van Vechten, "A Rudimentary Narration," Columbia Oral History, Columbia University, New York, 1963; quoted by Bruce Keller, "Carl Van Vechten's Black Renaissance," in *The Harlem Renaissance: Revaluation*, ed. Amritjit Singh, William S. Shiver, and Stanley Brodwin (New York: Garland, 1989), 26.

24. Cardy D. Wintz, *Black Culture and the Harlem Renaissance* (Houston, TX: Rice University Press, 1988), 101.

25. To Fauset's younger half brother, Arthur Huff Fauset, published reports of his sister's prosperous middle-class background were ironic mythology, for whatever valuable property his family may once have owned in Philadelphia was long lost by the time he was born in 1899, and his family struggled to get by on the meager income his father, an African Methodist Episcopal minister, managed to squeeze out of the church collection plate and the tithes of his poor parishioners. Having distinguished herself as an exceptional student at Philadelphia High School for Girls, Jessie Fauset was awarded a scholarship to Cornell University, from which she received a bachelor of arts degree in 1905. One of the first, if not the first, black women to graduate from Cornell, she was elected to Phi Beta Kappa the same year. She received a master's degree from the University of Pennsylvania in 1919 and accepted an appointment as literary editor of *Crisis*, resigning her position at the M Street School (later known as Dunbar High School) in Washington, D.C., where she had taught for fourteen years. The class privilege and "old money" that so many critics have attributed to Fauset were actually the products of hard work and determination. It was not "old money," then, that backed Fauset but the "new money" she *earned*, with which she supported herself and, for a time at least, one of her sisters. See Carolyn Sylvander's biography, *Jessie Redmon Fauset*.

26. Of his literary mentors Hughes wrote: "Jessie Fauset at *Crisis*, Charles Johnson at *Opportunity*, and Alain Locke in Washington were the three people who midwifed the so-called New Negro literature into being. Kind and critical—but not too critical for the young—they nursed us along until our books were born." See Langston Hughes, *The Big Sea* (New York: Hill & Wang, 1963), 218.

27. *There Is Confusion* and *Plum Bun* were far more successful, both critically and commercially, than either of Fauset's last two novels, both of which remain out of print.

28. The same year, Larsen's faith in her writing was irrevocably shaken by a devastating charge of plagiarism leveled against her by a reader who noted striking similarities between her short story "Sanctuary," published in *Forum*, and one by Sheila Kaye-Smith, which had appeared in *Century* eight years earlier. While the similarities between the two stories are dramatic, most scholars maintain that any "intertextualizing" on Larsen's part was almost certainly unconscious. None of her subsequent work matched the promise of either *Quicksand* or her second novel, *Passing*; a third novel, *Mirage*, written during her Guggenheim Fellowship year in Europe, was rejected by Knopf, as were two other manuscripts.

29. Gwendolyn Bennett, review of *Quicksand*, by Nella Larsen, *Opportunity*, May 1928, 153.

30. Thadious M. Davis, introduction to Nella Larsen, in *The Gender of Modernism: A Critical Anthology*, ed. Bonnie Kime Scott (Bloomington: Indiana University Press, 1990), 211.

31. Opinions vary as to the genuineness of and motivation behind Carl Van Vechten's interest in black culture. Because my own reading has positioned him among the primitivists, I want to be careful to point out that Van Vechten himself reportedly never used the term. Additionally, his interest in black art and culture predated the Negro vogue of the twenties. It is worth mentioning as well that the James Weldon Johnson Memorial Collection of Negro Arts and Letters at Yale University was founded and funded by Van Vechten and initally stocked with literature and artifacts from Van Vechten's personal collection.

32. Floyd Calvin, "Harlem Society Repudiated," *Pittsburg Courier*, January 23, 1932, 2; quoted by Sylvander, *Jessie Redmon Fauset*, 79.

33. Giddings, *When and Where I Enter*, 193.

34. Richard Wright, "Between Laughter and Tears," *New Masses*, October 5, 1937, 22–25.

35. Cheryl A. Wall, "Zora Neale Hurston: Changing Her Own Words," in *American Novelists Revisited: Essays in Feminist Criticism*, ed. Fritz Fleischmann (Boston: G. K. Hall, 1982), 371.

36. See McDowell's review of *Specifying* in *Signs* 14 (Summer 1989): 952.

37. Michael Awkward, *Inspiriting Influences: Tradition, Revision, and Afro-American Women's Novels* (New York: Columbia University Press, 1989), 12.

38. See Dianne Sadoff's essay "Black Matrilineage: The Case of Alice Walker and Zora Neale Hurston," *Signs* 11 (Autumn 1985): 4–26. Sadoff argues that both Harold Bloom's "masculinist and Gilbert and Gubar's Victorian-feminist paradigms of anxiety and influence" must be dramatically revised before they can be applied to the work of black women writers. "In celebrating her literary foremothers," Sadoff writes, "the contemporary black woman writer covers over more profoundly than does the white writer her ambivalence about matrilineage, her own misreadings of precursors, and her link to an oral as well as a written tradition" (5). See also Valerie Smith's summary and critique of Sadoff's argument in "Black Feminist Theory and the Representation of the 'Other,'" in Cheryl A. Wall, *Changing Our Own Words* (New Brunswick, NJ: Rutgers University Press, 1989), 38–57.

39. Sandra Gilbert and Susan Gubar, *The Madwoman in the Attic: The Woman Writer and the Nineteenth-Century Literary Imagination* (New Haven, CT: Yale University Press, 1979), 49.

40. Elliott Butler-Evans, *Race, Gender, and Desire: Narrative Strategies in the Fiction of Toni Cade Bambara, Toni Morrison, and Alice Walker* (Philadelphia, PA: Temple University Press, 1989), 44.

41. See Hazel Carby's essay "'On the Threshold of Woman's Era': Lynching, Empire, and Sexuality in Black Feminist Theory," in *"Race," Writing, and Difference*, ed. Henry Louis Gates, Jr. (Chicago: University of Chicago Press, 1985), 301–16. Carby's essay offers an excellent discussion of the 1890s as the "woman's era" and the roles of women artists, activists, and intellectuals in shaping the decade. Carby speaks specifically of the 1890s, and I suppose I take some liberties in extending her commentary into the early twentieth century. However, as Gloria Hull, Cheryl Wall, Claudia Tate, Thadious Davis, and others have documented, the 1920s and 1930s were no more eras of black male creative and intellectual genius alone than were the 1890s.

42. *Home to Harlem*, for example, is propelled by the protagonist's search for the "particularly sweet piece of business" who not only satisfied him sexually during their one night together but who also returned his money. In *Banana Bottom*, McKay's indictment and ultimate rejection of Western civilization and Christian values is achieved through the rape, seduction, engagement, affair (with a playboy named Hopping Dick, no less), and eventual marriage of the heroine, a Jamaican peasant girl named Bita Plant. Of Bita and the physical encounters that frame her story Robert Bone writes: "McKay uses sex as the chief means of dramatizing his theme. He understands that the major conflicts in a woman's life will be sexual, and that Bita's struggle with the Craigs [the white missionaries who raise and educate her] will naturally assume this form" (73). It is interesting to note that this insight comes from the same critic who dismisses as neurosis Nella Larsen's exploration of female sexual conflict.

43. Elizabeth Ammons, "New Literary History: Edith Wharton and Jessie Redmon Fauset," *College Literature* 13 (Fall 1987): 208–9. See also Ammons's *Conflicting Stories*.

44. See Alice Dunbar-Nelson, "A Modern Undine," in *The Works of Alice Dunbar Nelson*, vol. 2, with an introduction by Gloria T. Hull (New York: Oxford University

Press, 1988). Hull notes in her introduction that "A Modern Undine" exists only in a seventy-nine-page typed draft which Dunbar-Nelson evidently worked on between 1898 and 1903. As Hull also notes, in folklore an undine is a female water sprite who could gain a soul through marriage to a human. Perhaps even the titles of these two works—"A Modern Undine" and "Seraph on the Suwanee"—suggest another connection between Dunbar-Nelson's water spirit and Hurston's river-bound cherub.

45. I am thinking in particular of recent film representations of Baker's life, which include a 1987 British documentary, *Chasing a Rainbow*; a 1991 made-for-cable television movie, *The Josephine Baker Story*; and a second television movie and a feature film, both in the planning stage. In addition, two of Baker's French films from the 1930s, *Princess Tam-Tam* and *Zou-Zou*, have been rereleased with subtitles and shown to capacity crowds in theaters throughout the United States, as well as marketed on videocassette. See Phyllis Rose, "Exactly What Is It about Josephine Baker?" *New York Times*, March 10, 1991, H31.

Chapter 5

1. This descriptive phrase come from Claude McKay, who viewed his often sexually explicit descriptions of black life as an "artistic truth" that his detractors were not yet intellectually advanced enough to appreciate. Quoted by Wayne Cooper in his biography *Claude McKay: Rebel Sojourner in the Harlem Renaissance, A Life* (Baton Rouge: Louisiana State University Press, 1987), 247.

2. Elaine Showalter, "Tradition and the Female Talent: *The Awakening* as a Solitary Book," in *New Essays on "The Awakening*," ed. Wendy Martin (New York: Cambridge University Press, 1988), 34–35.

3. It would be several decades, however, before literature would become as explicit as the blues in its representations of female sexuality. Interestingly, Gayl Jones, one of the first contemporary black women writers to undertake a fuller examination of the intimate sexual self, would do so through the medium of the blues, by writing the story of a black woman blues singer's struggle to define herself sexually and artistically. Despite the groundwork laid by blues singers and fiction writers in the twenties and thirties, Jones's frank representation of female sexuality would be no more welcome in some circles in the mid-1970s than Chopin's was at the turn of the century or than Bessie Smith's was in some realms of renaissance Harlem. See Gayl Jones, *Corregidora* (New York: Random House, 1975).

4. Jessie Fauset, *Comedy: American Style* (New York: Frederick A. Stokes, 1933; rpt. New York: McGrath, 1969), 308–9.

5. Christian, *Black Women Novelists*, 46.

6. Robert Bone, *The Negro Novel in America* (New Haven, CT: Yale University Press, 1969), 102.

7. In this instance fiction has spawned fact. Not only has a black designer in Ohio started making such garments, she calls her business "Miss Celie's Pants."

8. See Giddings, *When and Where I Enter*, 187–89.

9. Davis, introduction to *There Is Confusion*, xi.

10. Carby, "It Jus Be's Dat Way Sometime," 221.

11. Larsen, *Quicksand*, 74.

12. Jessie Fauset, *The Chinaberry Tree* (New York: Frederick A. Stokes, 1931; rpt. College Park, MD: McGrath Publishing, 1969), x.

13. Significantly, while a number of critics have assumed that Laurentine's mother,

Sal Strange, is an ex-slave once owned by Laurentine's father, Captain Halloway, Fauset takes pains to establish otherwise. We are told explicitly that Sal was born in Mississippi *after* slavery and came north to work for Halloway's mother at the urging of a relative (72). Fauset, in fact, makes quite a point of romanticizing Halloway and Sal's affair as a "true love match, the kind you read about—Heloise and Abelard and all that kind of thing. She wasn't a slave—she didn't have to yield to him" (160). While the power dynamics between a wealthy white college boy and a poor black housemaid hardly suggest easy refusal, to read Halloway as master and Sal as slave denies the latter the degree of agency with which the text endows her and robs Fauset of the credit due her for her counterconventional representation of other than coercive sex between white men and black women.

14. Ammons, "New Literary History," 213.

15. See chapter 3.

16. Melissa Paul is the daughter of Judy Strange, Laurentine's aunt, and the product of an illicit affair between Judy and her best friend's husband, Sylvester Forten. Unaware of her actual parentage, Melissa falls in love with and becomes engaged to Malory Forten, who, unbeknownst to either of the young lovers, is her half brother.

17. Missy Dehn Kubitschek, *Claiming the Heritage: African American Women Novelists and History* (Jackson: University of Mississippi Press, 1991), 104.

18. Deborah McDowell, introduction to *Plum Bun* by Jessie Fauset (New York, 1929; rpt. Boston: Pandora, 1985), xx. McDowell's introduction includes a particularly provocative, insightful reading of this much-misunderstood text.

19. Deborah E. McDowell, introduction to *Quicksand* and *Passing*, xxvi–xxvii. This is as quoted by McDowell; I will return to the actual letter a little later.

20. Lauren Berlant, "National Brands/National Body: *Imitation of Life*," in *Comparative American Identities: Race, Sex, and Nationality in the Modern Text*, ed. Hortense Spillers (New York: Routledge, 1991), p. 111.

21. Wall, "Passing for What?" 106.

22. Bone, *The Negro Novel in America*, 102.

23. Margaret Perry, *Silence to the Drums: A Survey of the Literature of the Harlem Renaissance* (Westport, CT: Greenwood, 1976).

24. Deborah McDowell, "New Directions for Black Feminist Criticism," in *The New Feminist Criticism: Essays on Women, Literature, and Theory*, ed. Elaine Showalter (New York: Pantheon, 1985), 190. In "Toward a Black Feminist Criticism," Barbara Smith suggests that "if in a woman writer's work a sentence refuses to do what it is supposed to do, if there are strong images of women and if there is a refusal to be linear, the result is innately lesbian literature" (175). Smith takes Toni Morrison's *Sula* (1973) as a case in point, arguing that *Sula* works as a lesbian text "because of Morrison's consistently critical stance toward the heterosexual institutions of male-female relationships, marriage, and the family." McDowell criticizes this definition, arguing that Smith has "simultaneously oversimplified and obscured the issue of lesbianism." See Barbara Smith, "Toward a Black Feminist Criticism," 168.

25. Frank Kermode, *The Classic: Literary Images of Permanence and Change* (New York: Viking, 1975), 140.

Chapter 6

1. Larsen, *Quicksand*, 117.

2. Perhaps an allusion to Edith Summers Kelley's 1923 novel, *Weeds*, in which the

weeds grow with "such lustiness and vigor" that they overtopped the corn. *Quicksand* shares with *Weeds* a concern about the plight of married women, including the consequences for women of passion and sexual intimacy: endless children.

3. See, for example, Glasgow's *Barren Ground* (1925) and Edith Summers Kelley's *Weeds* (1923), as well as Edith Wharton's *House of Mirth* (1905) and *Custom of the Country* (1913), Kate Chopin's *The Awakening* (1899), and Agnes Smedley's *Daughters of the Earth* (1929). Similarities of plot and theme run throughout these and other novels and short stories of the 1920s and 1930s, making these works overripe for intertextual analysis. Important intertextual expeditions have been undertaken by a number of feminist critics, most notably, perhaps, Elizabeth Ammons and Thadious Davis.

4. Dorothy West, *The Living Is Easy* (Boston: Houghton Mifflin, 1948; rpt. Old Westbury, NY: The Feminist Press, 1982), 71.

5. Mary Helen Washington, "I Sign My Mother's Name: Alice Walker, Dorothy West, and Paule Marshall," in *Mothering the Mind: Twelve Studies of Writers and Their Silent Partners*, ed. Ruth Perry and Martine Watson Brownley (New York: Holmes & Meier, 1984), 153. West, who lived out her apprenticeship as a writer in the heyday of the Harlem literary uprising as the "little sister" of those who were or would be the "big guns" of the era—Hurston, Hughes, Cullen, and McKay—ultimately retreated to Martha's Vineyard, where she wrote *The Living Is Easy*. Herself a properly bred Bostonian, West has acknowledged that her father, known as the "Black Banana King," was the prototype for Bart Judson and that her mother's strength, dominance, and desire for control were part of the inspiration behind her portrait of Cleo Judson.

6. Zora Neale Hurston, *Their Eyes Were Watching God* (Philadelphia: Lippincott, 1937; reprinted with a foreword by Sherley Anne Williams, Urbana: University of Illinois Press, 1978), 41.

7. Quoted by Showalter in "Tradition and the Female Talent," 53.

8. Ibid.

9. Awkward, *Inspiriting Influences*, 19.

10. In calling Joe Starks "Jody," Hurston links him to "Jody the Grinder," the sexually adept folk hero who makes a life's work out of seducing other men's wives. For an excellent discussion of the Jody myth see Sally Ann Ferguson, "Folkloric Men and Female Growth in *Their Eyes Were Watching God*," *Black American Literature Forum* 21, nos. 1–2 (Spring–Summer 1987): 185–97. Ferguson argues that Hurston rewrites and appropriates for her own use three folkloric motifs in her creation of her three leading men in *Their Eyes:* (1) the May-December, young girl–old man pattern reflected in Janie's marriage to Logan Killicks; (2) the Jody myth represented by Janie's second marriage to Joe (Jody) Starks; and (3) the Stagolee figure of which the gambling, fun-loving Tea Cake Woods is reminiscent.

11. Barbara Johnson, "Metaphor, Metonymy and Voice in *Their Eyes Were Watching God*," in *Black Literature and Literary Theory*, ed. Henry Louis Gates, Jr. (New York: Methuen, 1984).

12. Susan Willis, *Specifying: Black Women Writing the American Experience* (Madison: University of Wisconsin Press, 1987), 52.

13. Bernard Bell, *The Afro-American Novel and Its Tradition*, 128.

14. Hortense J. Spillers, "A Hateful Passion, A Lost Love," in *Feminist Issues in Literary Scholarship*, ed. Shari Benstock (Bloomington: Indiana University Press, 1987), 192.

15. Sadoff, "Black Matrilineage," 22.

16. For an insightful reading of silence and powerlessness in *Their Eyes Were*

Watching God, see Mary Helen Washington's essay on the novel in *Invented Lives: Narratives of Black Women, 1860–1960*, ed. Mary Helen Washington (New York: Anchor, 1987), 237–54.

17. McDowell, "New Directions for Black Feminist Criticism," 193. I read in *Their Eyes Were Watching God* the same potentially tragic undercurrent that I read in *Seraph on the Suwanee* (despite its seemingly happy ending) and Hurston's autobiography, *Dust Tracks on a Road*. In a patriarchal society where male dominance is the norm, the price of female independence and self-possession is often the kind of aloneness that undercut Hurston's own life. And the marital accord that Arvay Henson finally achieves (on her husband's terms) in *Seraph* is often at the expense of the female self.

18. Jessica Benjamin, *The Bonds of Love: Psychoanalysis, Feminism, and the Problem of Domination* (New York: Pantheon, 1988), 52.

19. Opinions abound as to the meaning of this final passage. Michael Awkward reads it positively, as the reconciliation of the divided self (*Inspiriting Influences*, 56). Hortense Spillers, on the other hand, suggests that the passage can be interpreted as "a eulogy for the living; Janie has been 'buried' along with Teacake" ("Passion," 196). Obviously, I am inclined toward—even beyond—Spiller's view. (She does not address the issue of Janie's contracting rabies from Tea Cake.) Since the text presents no overt signs of hydrophobia in Janie, perhaps the double mention of the virulent bite is meant merely to reinforce the justifiable nature of the homicide. Perhaps, however, this final passage can be read as a eulogy not for the living, as Spillers suggests, but for the dead and dying.

20. Reviews in the *New York Times* and the *New York Herald Tribune*, for example, offered qualified praise, commenting on the novel's contradictions and need for honing, as well as its Freudian psychology and picaresque metaphors. Long out of print, *Seraph* was reissued in 1991 by HarperCollins. A month before the book's original publication in October 1948, Hurston was arrested and charged with sodomy based solely on the accusations of a disturbed ten-year-old boy. The claim was eventually proven false, but by the time the charges were dismissed six months later, immense damage had been done to Hurston both personally and professionally. She was devastated, driven to contemplate suicide, though she ultimately rallied. The *Baltimore Afro-American* used as a headline a passage from *Seraph*, I'm "just as hungry as a dog for a knowing and doing love," speculating that Hurston was similarly hungry. Hemenway maintains, however, that because it went unreported by the white press, the morals charge did little damage to the promising initial sales of *Seraph on the Suwanee*. See Robert Hemenway, *Zora Neale Hurston: A Literary Biography* (Urbana: University of Illinois Press, 1988), 319–23.

21. Hemenway, *Zora Neale Hurston*, 309. Lillie P. Howard also includes a chapter on *Seraph on the Suwanee* in her study, *Zora Neale Hurston* (Boston: G. K. Hall, 1980), 133–48. See also Hazel Carby's foreword to the 1991 HarperCollins edition of *Seraph*.

22. Zora Neale Hurston, *Seraph on the Suwanee* (New York: Scribner's, 1948; reprinted with an introduction by Hazel Carby, New York: HarperCollins, 1991), 9.

23. Ann Douglas, "Soft-Porn Culture," *New Republic*, August 30, 1980, 25–29; quoted by Janice A. Radway in *Reading the Romance: Women, Patriarchy, and Popular Literature* (Chapel Hill: University of North Carolina Press, 1984), 71.

24. Clifford Geertz, "Notes on the Balinese Cockfight," in *The Interpretation of Culture* (New York: Basic Books, 1973), 443. Geertz writes: "Like any art form . . . the cockfight renders ordinary, everyday experience comprehensible by presenting it in terms of acts and objects which have had their practical consequences removed

and been reduced . . . to the level of sheer appearances, where their meaning can be more powerfully articulated and more easily perceived." See Radway, *Reading the Romance*, 72.

25. Alice Walker, it seems to me, captures this same elusive spirit of conflicting desires in her description of the sexual encounters between the twelve- to fifteen-year-old Meridian Hill and the local undertaker, whose "hobby" is seducing young girls. Walker writes of Meridian's reaction to her own violation: "She hated him but was fascinated. . . . The Assistant would manipulate her breasts and cram her between his legs and rub her so against him that her *panties became flooded with the residue of her resistance*" (emphasis added). See Alice Walker, *Meridian* (New York: Washington Square Press, 1976), 66.

26. Anne Goodwyn Jones, *Tomorrow Is Another Day: The Woman Writer in the South, 1859–1936* (Baton Rouge: Louisiana State University Press, 1981), 347.

27. Carole McAlpine Watson: *Prologue: The Novels of Black American Women, 1891–1965* (Westport, CT: Greenwood, 1985), 94 (emphasis added).

28. One reviewer suggested that Hurston "took a textbook on Freudian psychology and adapted it to her needs, perhaps with her tongue in her cheek while doing so." See Frank Slaughter, review of *Seraph on the Suwanee*, *New York Times Book Review*, October 31, 1948, 24.

29. Zora Neale Hurston to Burroughs Mitchell, October 2, 1947, Charles Scribner's Sons Archives, Author File 3. Quoted by Robert Hemenway in *Zora Neale Hurston* (312) and by Hazel Carby in her introduction to *Seraph on the Suwanee* (xvi), among others.

30. "Zora Neale Hurston," in *Twentieth Century Authors*, ed. Stanley Kunitz and Howard Haycraft (New York: H. W. Wilson, 1942), 695; also quoted in Hemenway, *Zora Neale Hurston*, 314.

31. Darwin Turner, *In a Minor Chord: Three Afro-American Writers and Their Search for Identity* (Carbondale: Southern Illinois University Press, 1971), 115.

32. Ralph Ellison, *Invisible Man* (New York: New American Library, 1952), 19.

Conclusion

1. Walker's Pulitzer Prize–winning novel, *The Color Purple*, was released as a motion picture in 1986. The paperback rights to McMillan's third novel, *Waiting to Exhale*, were sold for $2.64 million, one of the highest prices ever paid for a reprint, according to the *New York Times*, and a major studio is negotiating for the film rights. See Daniel Max, "McMillan's Millions," *New York Times Magazine*, August 9, 1992, 20–26.

2. Benjamin, *The Bonds of Love*, 12.

3. Alice Walker, "Zora Neale Hurston: A Cautionary Tale and a Partisan View," in *In Search of Our Mothers' Gardens*, 89–90.

4. Bernard Bell, *The Afro-American Novel and Its Tradition*, 128.

5. Washington, *Invented Lives*, xvii.

6. See p. xviii of Gates's introduction to any one of the volumes of the Schomburg Library Collection of Nineteenth-Century Black Woman Writers.

7. Cornel West, "Minority Discourse," 198.

8. See Gates, *Figures in Black*, xxii.

Bibliography

Primary Sources

Novels, Short Stories, and Drama

Austin, Doris Jean. *After the Garden*. New York: New American Library, 1987.

Bambara, Toni Cade. *Gorilla My Love*. New York: Vintage, 1972.

_____. *The Salt Eaters*. New York: Random House, 1980.

_____. *The Sea Birds Are Still Alive*. New York: Random House, 1974.

Bonner, Marita. *Frye Street & Environs: The Collected Works of Marita Bonner*. Edited and with an introduction by Joyce Flynn and Joyce Occomy Stricklin. Boston: Beacon, 1987.

Brooks, Gwendolyn. *Maud Martha*. New York: Harper & Row, 1953.

Brown, William Wells. *Clotel; or, The President's Daughter: A Narrative of Slave Life in the United States*. London: Patridge & Oakey, 1853; rpt. New York: Macmillan, 1975; reprinted with an introduction by Arthur Davis. New York: Collier Books, 1970; reprinted with an introduction by William Farrison. New York: Carol Publishing Group, 1989.

_____. *Clotelle: A Tale of the Southern States*. Boston: James Redpath, 1864.

_____. *Clotelle; or, The Colored Heroine. A Tale of the Southern States*. Boston: Lee & Shepard, 1867; rpt. Miami, FL: Mnemosyne, 1969.

_____. *The Escape; or, A Leap for Freedom*. In *Black Theater, USA*, ed. James Hatch and Ted Shine. New York: Free Press, 1974.

_____. *Miralda; or, The Beautiful Quadroon: A Romance of American Slavery Founded on Fact*. In *The Weekly Anglo-African*, November 1860–March 1861.

Butler, Octavia E. *Kindred*. Boston: Beacon, 1979.

Chase-Riboud, Barbara. *Sally Hemings*. New York: Viking, 1979.

Chesnutt, Charles W. *The House Behind the Cedars*. 1900; rpt. New York: Collier, 1969.

_____. *The Wife of His Youth, and Other Stories of the Color Line*. 1899; rpt. Ann Arbor: University of Michigan Press, 1968.

Dunbar-Nelson, Alice. "A Modern Undine." In *The Works of Alice Dunbar Nelson*.

Vol. 2. Publication of the Schomburg Library, edited by Henry Louis Gates, Jr., with an introduction by Gloria T. Hull. New York: Oxford University Press, 1988.

Edwards-Yearwood, Grace. *In the Shadow of the Peacock*. New York: McGraw-Hill, 1988.

Fauset, Jessie Redmon. *The Chinaberry Tree*. New York: Frederick A. Stokes, 1931; rpt. College Park: MD: McGrath Publishing, 1969.

———. *Comedy: American Style*. New York: Frederick A. Stokes, 1933; rpt. College Park, MD: McGrath Publishing, 1969.

———. *Plum Bun*. New York: Frederick A. Stokes, 1929; rpt. Boston: Pandora, 1985.

———. *There Is Confusion*. Boni & Liveright, 1924; reprinted with an introduction by Thadious M. Davis. Boston: Beacon, 1989.

Gaines, Ernest. *Of Love and Dust*. New York: Bantam, 1967.

Glasgow, Ellen. *Barren Ground*. Garden City, NY: Doubleday, Page, 1925.

Golden, Marita. *A Woman's Place*. New York: Ballantine, 1986.

Guy, Rosa. *Ruby*. New York: Bantam, 1976.

Hale, Sarah Josepha. *Northwood*. New York: H. Long & Brother, 1852.

Harper, Frances Ellen Watkins. *Iola Leroy; or, Shadows Uplifted*. Philadelphia: Garrigue Brothers, 1892; reprinted with an introduction by Hazel Carby. Boston: Beacon, 1987.

Hopkins, Pauline. *Contending Forces: A Romance Illustrative of Negro Life North and South*. Boston: Colored Co-operative Publishing House, 1900.

———. *Contending Forces: A Romance Illustrative of Negro Life North and South*. Publication of the Schomburg Library, edited by Henry Louis Gates, Jr., with an introduction by Richard Yarborough. New York: Oxford University Press, 1988.

———. *The Magazine Novels of Pauline Hopkins*. Publication of the Schomburg Library, edited by Henry Louis Gates, Jr., with an introduction by Hazel Carby. New York: Oxford University Press, 1988.

Howells, William Dean. *An Imperative Duty*. Originally serialized in *Harper's* in 1891; rpt. Bloomington: Indiana University Press, 1970.

Hunter, Kristin. *God Bless the Child*. New York: Scribner's, 1964; reprinted with an introduction by Darwin Turner. Washington, D.C.: Howard University Press, 1986.

Hurston, Zora Neale. *Jonah's Gourd Vine*. New York: Lippincott, 1934; reprinted with an introduction by Larry Neal. New York: Lippincott, 1971.

———. *Moses, Man of the Mountain*. Philadelphia: Lippincott, 1939; reprinted with an introduction by Blyden Jackson. Urbana: University of Illinois Press, 1984.

———. *Seraph on the Suwanee*. New York: Scribner's, 1948; reprinted with an introduction by Hazel Carby. New York: HarperCollins, 1991.

———. *Spunk: The Selected Short Stories of Zora Neale Hurston*. Berkeley: Turtle Island Foundation, 1985.

———. *Their Eyes Were Watching God*. Philadelphia: Lippincott, 1937; reprinted with a foreword by Sherley Anne Williams. Urbana: University of Illinois Press, 1978.

Johnson, Mrs. A. E. *Clarence and Corinne; or, God's Way*. Philadelphia: American Baptist Publication Society, 1890; reprinted. Publication of the Schomburg Library, edited by Henry Louis Gates, Jr., with an introduction by Hortense Spillers. New York: Oxford University Press, 1988.

———. *The Hazeley Family*. Philadelphia: American Baptist Publication Society,

1894; reprinted. Publication of the Schomburg Library, edited by Henry Louis Gates, Jr., with an introduction by Barbara Christian. New York: Oxford University Press, 1988.

Jones, Gayl. *Corregidora*. New York: Random House, 1975.

_____. *Eva's Man*. New York: Random House, 1976.

_____. *White Rat*. New York: Random House, 1977.

Jones, J. McHenry. *Hearts of Gold*. Wheeling, WV: Daily Intelligencer Steam Job Press; rpt. Miami, FL: Mnemosyne, 1969.

Kelley, Edith Summers. *Weeds*. New York: Harcourt, Brace, 1923; rpt. Carbondale: Southern Illinois University Press, 1972.

Kelley, Emma Dunham. *Four Girls at Cottage City*. Boston: James H. Earle, 1898; reprinted. Publication of the Schomburg Library, edited by Henry Louis Gates, Jr., with an introduction by Deborah E. McDowell. New York: Oxford University Press, 1988.

_____. *Megda*. Boston: James H. Earle, 1891; reprinted. Publication of the Schomburg Library, edited by Henry Louis Gates, Jr., with an introduction by Molly Hite. New York: Oxford University Press, 1988.

Kincaid, Jamaica. *Annie John*. New York: New American Library, 1983.

Larsen, Nella. *Quicksand* and *Passing*; reprinted in one volume, edited and with an introduction by Deborah E. McDowell. New Brunswick, NJ: Rutgers University Press, 1986.

Lee, Andrea. *Sarah Phillips*. New York: Penguin, 1984.

McMillan, Terry. *Disappearing Acts*. New York: Viking, 1989.

_____. *Mama*. Boston: Houghton Mifflin, 1987.

_____. *Waiting to Exhale*. New York: Viking, 1992.

Marshall, Paule. *Brown Girl, Brownstones*. 1959; rpt. Old Westbury, NY: The Feminist Press, 1981.

_____. *The Chosen Place, The Timeless People*. 1969; rpt. New York: Vintage, 1984.

_____. *Praisesong for the Widow*. New York: Dutton, 1984.

_____. *Reena and Other Stories*. Old Westbury, NY: The Feminist Press, 1983.

_____. *Soul Clap Hands and Sing*. New York: Atheneum, 1961.

Merriweather, Louise. *Daddy Was a Numbers Runner*. New York: Jove Publications, 1970.

Morrison, Toni. *Beloved*. New York: New American Library, 1987.

_____. *The Bluest Eye*. New York: Washington Square Press, 1970.

_____. *Song of Solomon*. New York: New American Library, 1977.

_____. *Sula*. New York: Bantam, 1973.

_____. *Tar Baby*. New York: New American Library, 1981.

Murry, Pauli. *Proud Shoes*. New York: Harper & Row, 1956.

Naylor, Gloria. *Linden Hills*. New York: Penguin, 1986.

_____. *Mamma Day*. New York: Ticknor & Fields, 1988.

_____. *The Women of Brewster Place*. New York: Penguin, 1982.

Petry, Ann. *Country Place*. Boston: Houghton Mifflin, 1947.

_____. *Miss Muriel and Other Stories*. Boston: Houghton Mifflin, 1971; rpt. Boston: Beacon, 1989.

_____. *The Narrows*. Boston: Houghton Mifflin, 1954; reprinted with a foreword by Nellie Y. McKay. Boston: Beacon, 1988.

_____. *The Street*. Boston: Houghton Mifflin, 1946; rpt. Boston: Beacon, 1985.

Polite, Carlene Hatcher. *The Flagellants*. Boston: Farrar, Straus & Giroux, 1987; rpt. Boston: Beacon, 1987.

Sedgwick, Catharine Maria. *Hope Leslie; or Early Times in Massachusetts*. New York: White, Gallaher, and White, 1827; reprinted; edited and with an introduction by Mary Kelley. New Brunswick, NJ: Rutgers University Press, 1987.

_____. *The Linwoods; or, "Sixty Years Since" in America*. New York: Harper & Row, 1835.

Shange, Ntozake. *Betsy Brown*. New York: St. Martin's, 1985.

_____. *Sassafrass, Cypress, and Indigo*. New York: St. Martin's, 1982.

Shockley, Ann Allen. *Loving Her*. New York: Avon, 1974.

_____. *Say Jesus and Come to Me*. Tallahassee, FL: Naiad Press, 1982.

Toomer, Jean. *Cane*. New York: Liveright, 1923; rpt. New York: Norton, 1988.

Walker, Alice. *The Color Purple*. New York: Harcourt Brace Jovanovich, 1982.

_____. *In Love and Trouble: Stories of Black Women*. New York: Harcourt Brace Jovanovich, 1973.

_____. *Meridian*. New York: Washington Square Press, 1976.

_____. *The Temple of My Familiar*. New York: Harcourt Brace Jovanovich, 1989.

_____. *The Third Life of Grange Copeland*. New York: Harcourt Brace Jovanovich, 1973.

_____. *You Can't Keep a Good Woman Down*. New York: Harcourt Brace Jovanovich, 1981.

Walker, Margaret. *Jubilee*. Boston: Houghton Mifflin, 1966.

West, Dorothy. *The Living Is Easy*. Boston: Houghton Mifflin, 1948; rpt. Old Westbury, NY: The Feminist Press, 1982.

Wharton, Edith. *The Custom of the Country*. New York: Scribner's, 1913; reprinted with an introduction by Anita Brookner. New York: Penguin, 1984.

_____. *Ethan Frome*. New York: Scribner's, 1911.

_____. *The House of Mirth*. New York: Scribner's, 1905.

Williams, Sherley Anne. *Dessa Rose*. New York: Morrow, 1986.

Wilson, Harriet. *Our Nig; or, Sketches from the Life of a Free Black*. 1859; reprinted with an introduction and notes by Henry Louis Gates, Jr. New York: Vintage, 1983.

Wright, Sarah. *This Child's Gonna Live*. 1969; rpt. New York: The Feminist Press at The City University of New York, 1986.

Narratives, Interviews, and (Auto)Biographies

Andrews, Williams L., ed. *Sisters of the Spirit: Three Black Women's Autobiographies of the Nineteenth Century*. Bloomington: Indiana University Press, 1986.

Angelou, Maya. *I Know Why the Caged Bird Sings*. New York: Random House, 1970.

Bambara, Toni Cade, ed. *The Black Woman: An Anthology*. New York: Norton, 1981.

Bernard, Jacqueline, ed. *Journey Toward Freedom: The Story of Sojourner Truth*. New York: Norton, 1967; reprinted with an introduction by Nell Irvin Painter. New York: The Feminist Press, 1990.

Brown, William Wells. *Narrative of the Life of William Wells Brown*. Reading, MA: Addison Wesley, 1969.

Cooper, Anna Julia. *A Voice from the South*. 1892; reprinted. Publication of the Schomburg Library, edited Henry Louis Gates, Jr., with an introduction by Mary Helen Washington. New York: Oxford University Press, 1988.

Cooper, Wayne. *Claude McKay, Rebel Sojourner in The Harlem Renaissance: A Life*. Baton Rouge: Louisiana State University Press, 1987.

Davis, Charles, and Henry Louis Gates, Jr., eds. *The Slave's Narrative*. New York: Oxford University Press, 1985.

Evans, Mari, ed. *Black Women Writers (1950–1980): A Critical Evaluation*. Garden City, NY: Anchor, 1984.

Farrison, Edward. *William Wells Brown: Author and Reformer*. Chicago: University of Chicago Press, 1969.

Foster, Frances Smith, ed. *A Brighter Coming Day: A Frances Ellen Watkins Harper Reader*. New York: The Feminist Press, 1990.

Gates, Henry Louis, Jr., ed. *Collected Black Women's Narratives*. Publication of the Schomburg Library, with an introduction by Jean Fagan Yellin. New York: Oxford University Press, 1988.

Hayden, Robert. *Collected Prose*. Edited by Frederick Glaysher, with a foreword by William Meredith. Ann Arbor: University of Michigan Press, 1984.

Hemenway, Robert. *Zora Neale Hurston: A Literary Biography*. Urbana: University of Illinois Press, 1977.

Hughes, Langston. *The Big Sea*. New York: Hill & Wang, 1963.

Hurston, Zora Neale. *Dust Tracks on a Road*. 1942; reprinted with an introduction by Robert Hemenway. Urbana: University of Illinois Press, 1984.

Jacobs, Harriet A. *Incidents in the Life of a Slave Girl*. 1861; reprinted with an introduction by Jean Fagan Yellin. Cambridge, MA: Harvard University Press, 1987.

Lerner, Gerda, ed. *Black Women in White America*. New York: Pantheon, 1972.

Loewenberg, Bert James, and Ruth Bogin, eds. *Black Women in Nineteenth-Century American Life*. University Park: Pennsylvania State University Press, 1976.

Lorde, Audre. *A Burst of Light*. Ithaca, NY: Firebrand Books, 1988.

_____. *Sister Outsider: Essays and Speeches*. Trumansburg, NY: The Crossing Press, 1984.

_____. *Zami: A New Spelling of My Name*. Trumansburg, NY: The Crossing Press, 1982.

McKay, Nellie. *Jean Toomer, Artist: A Study of His Literary Life and Work, 1894–1936*. Chapel Hill: University of North Carolina Press, 1984.

O'Brien, John. *Interviews with Black Writers*. New York: Liveright, 1983.

Smith, Barbara, ed. *Home Girls: A Black Feminist Anthology*. New York: Kitchen Table/Women of Color Press, 1983.

Sterling, Dorothy, ed. *We Are Your Sisters: Black Women in the Nineteeth Century*. New York: Norton, 1986.

Sternberg, Janet, ed. *The Writer on Her Work*. New York: Norton, 1980.

Stetson, Erlene, ed. *Black Sister: Poetry by Black American Women, 1746–1980*. Bloomington, IN: Indiana University Press, 1981.

Tate, Claudia, ed. *Black Women Writers at Work*. New York: Continuum, 1986.

Washington, Mary Helen, ed. *Black-Eyed Susans: Classic Stories by and About Black Women*. Garden City, NY: Anchor, 1975.

_____. *Invented Lives: Narratives of Black Women, 1860–1960*. Garden City, NY: Anchor, 1987.

_____. *Memories of Kin: Stories About Family by Black Writers*. New York: Anchor, 1991.

_____. *Midnight Birds: Stories of Contemporary Black Women Writers*. Garden City, NY: Anchor, 1980.

Woodward, C. Vann, ed. *Mary Chesnut's Civil War*. New Haven, CT: Yale University Press, 1981.

Secondary Sources

Books

CRITICISM, THEORY, AND LITERARY HISTORY

Abel, Elizabeth, ed. *Writing and Sexual Difference*. Chicago: University of Chicago Press, 1982.

Abel, Elizabeth, Marianne Hirsch, and Elizabeth Langland, eds. *The Voyage In: Fictions of Female Development*. Hanover, NH: University Press of New England, 1983.

Ammons, Elizabeth. *Conflicting Stories: American Women Writers at the Turn into the Twentieth Century*. New York: Oxford University Press, 1991.

Ardis, Ann. *New Women: Feminism and Early Modernism*. New Brunswick, NJ: Rutgers University Press, 1990.

Armstrong, Nancy. *Desire and Domestic Fiction: A Political History of the Novel*. New York: Oxford University Press, 1987.

Armstrong, Nancy, and Leonard Tennenhouse. *The Imaginary Puritan: Literature, Intellectual Labor, and the Origins of Personal Life*. Berkeley: University of California Press, 1992.

Asante, Molefi Kete. *The Afrocentric Idea*. Philadelphia, PA: Temple University Press, 1987.

_____. *Afrocentricity: The Theory of Social Change*. Buffalo, NY: Amulefi, 1980.

Auerbach, Nina. *Communities of Women*. Cambridge, MA: Harvard University Press, 1978.

Awkward, Michael. *Inspiriting Influences: Tradition, Revision, and Afro-American Women's Novels*. New York: Columbia University Press, 1989.

Baker, Houston, Jr. *Blues, Ideology, and Afro-American Literature: A Vernacular Theory*. Chicago: University of Chicago Press, 1984.

_____. *The Journey Back: Issues in Black Literature and Criticism*. Chicago: University of Chicago Press, 1980.

_____. *Long Black Song: Essays in Black American Literature and Culture*. Charlottesville: University Press of Virginia, 1972.

_____. *Modernism and the Harlem Renaissance*. Chicago: University of Chicago Press, 1987.

_____. *Workings of the Spirit: The Poetics of Afro-American Women's Writing*. Chicago: University of Chicago Press, 1991.

Baker, Houston, Jr., and Patricia Redmond, eds. *Afro-American Literary Studies in the 1990s*. Chicago: University of Chicago Press, 1989.

Bakhtin, Mikhail. *The Dialogic Imagination*. Translated by Cary Emerson and Michael Holquist and edited by Michael Holquist. Austin, TX: University of Texas Press, 1981.

Bardes, Barbara, and Susan Gossett. *Declarations of Independence: Women and Political Power in Nineteenth-Century American Fiction*. New Brunswick, NJ: Rutgers University Press, 1990.

Bauer, Dale M. *Feminist Dialogics: A Theory of Failed Community*. Albany: State University of New York Press, 1988.

Baym, Nina. *Novels, Readers, and Reviewers: Responses to Fiction in Antebellum America*. Ithaca, NY: Cornell University Press, 1984.

_____. *Women's Fiction: A Guide to Novels by and About Women in America, 1820–1870*. Ithaca, NY: Cornell University Press, 1978.

Bell, Bernard W. *The Afro-American Novel and Its Tradition*. Amherst: University of Massachusetts Press, 1987.

Bell, Roseanne P., Bettye J. Parker, and Beverly Guy-Sheftall, eds. *Sturdy Black Bridges: Visions of Black Women in Literature*. New York: Anchor, 1979.

Belsey, Catherine. *Critical Practice*. New York: Routledge, 1980.

Belsey, Catherine, and Joan Moore, eds. *The Feminist Reader: Essays in Gender and the Politics of Literary Criticism*. New York: Basil Blackwell, 1989.

Benstock, Shari, ed. *Feminist Issues in Literary Scholarship*. Bloomington: Indiana University Press, 1987.

———. *The Private Self: Theory and Practice of Women's Autobiographical Writings*. Chapel Hill: University of North Carolina Press, 1988.

Berzon, Judith. *Neither White nor Black: The Mulatto Character in American Fiction*. New York: New York University Press, 1978.

Bloom, Harold. *The Anxiety of Influence: A Theory of Poetry*. New York: Oxford University Press, 1973.

———, ed. *Modern Critical Views: Zora Neale Hurston*. New York: Chelsea House, 1986.

Bone, Robert. *The Negro Novel in America*. New Haven, CT: Yale University Press, 1969.

Bontemps, Arna, ed. *The Harlem Renaissance Remembered*. New York: Dodd, Mead, 1972.

Boone, Joseph Allen. *Tradition Counter Tradition: Love and the Form of Fiction*. Chicago: University of Chicago Press, 1987.

Bowers, Bege K., and Barbara Brothers, ed. *Reading and Writing Women's Lives: A Study of Novels of Manners*. Ann Arbor: UMI Research Press, 1990.

Braxton, Joanne. *Black Women Writing Autobiography: A Tradition Within a Tradition*. Philadelphia, PA: Temple University Press, 1990.

Braxton, Joanne M., and Andree Nicola, eds. *Wild Women in the Whirlwind: Afra-American Culture and the Contemporary Literary Renaissance*. New Brunswick, NJ: Rutgers University Press, 1989.

Brittan, Arthur, and Mary Maynard. *Sexism, Racism and Oppression*. New York: Basil Blackwell, 1984.

Butler, Judith. *Gender Trouble: Feminism and the Subversion of Identity*. New York: Routledge, 1990.

Butler-Evans, Elliott. *Race, Gender, and Desire: Narrative Strategies in the Fiction of Toni Cade Bambara, Toni Morrison, and Alice Walker*. Philadelphia, PA: Temple University Press, 1989.

Callahan, John F. *In the African-American Grain: Call-and-Response in Twentieth-Century Black Fiction*. Middletown, CT: Wesleyan University Press, 1988.

Campbell, Jane. *Mythic Black Fiction: The Transformation of History*. Knoxville: University of Tennessee Press, 1986.

Carby, Hazel. *Reconstructing Womanhood: The Emergence of the Afro-American Woman Novelist*. New York: Oxford University Press, 1987.

Christian, Barbara. *Black Feminist Criticism: Perspectives on Black Women Writers*. New York: Pergamon, 1985.

———. *Black Women Novelists: The Development of a Tradition, 1892–1976*. Westport, CT: Greenwood, 1980.

Cocks, Joan. *The Oppositional Imagination: Feminism, Critique and Political Theory*. New York: Routledge, 1989.

Cohen, Ralph, ed. *The Future of Literary Theory*. New York: Routledge, 1989.

Collins, Patricia Hill. *Black Feminist Thought: Knowledge, Consciousness, and the Politics of Empowerment*. New York: Routledge, 1990.

Crosby, Christina. *The Ends of History: Victorians and "The Woman Question."* New York: Routledge, 1991.

Culler, Jonathan. *Framing the Sign: Criticism and Its Institutions*. Norman: University of Oklahoma Press, 1988.

_____. *On Deconstruction: Theory and Criticism After Structuralism*. Ithaca, NY: Cornell University Press, 1982.

Dearborn, Mary. *Pocahontas's Daughters: Gender and Ethnicity in American Culture*. New York: Oxford University Press, 1985.

de Lauretis, Teresa, ed. *Feminist Studies/Critical Studies*. Bloomington: Indiana University Press, 1986.

de Man, Paul. *Resistance to Theory*. Minneapolis: University of Minnesota Press, 1986.

Diamond, Arlyn, and Lee R. Edwards, eds. *The Authority of Experience: Essays in Feminist Criticism*. Rev. ed. Amherst: University of Massachusetts Press, 1988.

Diamond, Irene, and Lee Quinby, eds. *Feminism and Foucault: Reflections on Resistance*. Boston, MA: Northeastern University Press, 1988.

Dixon, Melvin. *Ride Out the Wilderness: Geography and Identity in Afro-Americn Literature*. Urbana: University of Illinois Press, 1987.

Doane, Mary Ann. *Femmes Fatales: Feminism, Film Theory, Psychoanalysis*. New York: Routledge, 1991.

Donovan, Josephine. *Feminist Theory: The Intellectual Traditions of American Feminism*. New York: Continuum, 1988.

_____, ed. *Feminist Literary Criticism: Explorations in Theory*. 2nd ed. Lexington: University of Kentucky Press, 1989.

Douglas, Ann. *The Feminization of American Culture*. New York: Knopf, 1977.

Eagleton, Terry. *Literary Theory: An Introduction*. Minneapolis: University of Minnesota Press, 1983.

Elder, Arlene. *"The Hindered Hand": Cultural Implications of Early Afro-American Fiction*. Westport, CT: Greenwood, 1978.

Ellis, John M. *Against Deconstruction*. Princeton, NJ: Princeton University Press, 1989.

Ellison, Ralph. *Shadow and Act* (New York: Vintage), 1972.

Felman, Shoshana, ed. *Literature and Psychoanalysis: The Question of Reading: Otherwise*. Baltimore, MD: Johns Hopkins University Press, 1982.

Felski, Rita. *Beyond Feminist Aesthetics: Feminist Literature and Social Change*. Cambridge, MA: Harvard University Press, 1989.

Fiedler, Leslie. *Love and Death in the American Novel*. New York: Stein & Day, 1960; rpt. New York: Anchor, 1992.

Fisher, Dexter, and Robert Stepto. *Afro-American Literature: The Reconstruction of Instruction*. New York: Modern Language Association, 1979.

Foucault, Michel. *The Archeolgy of Knowledge*. Translated by A. M. Sheridan. New York: Pantheon, 1972.

_____. *The History of Sexuality*. Vol. 1, *An Introduction*. Translated by Robert Hurley. New York: Pantheon, 1978.

_____. *Language, Counter-Memory, Practice: Selected Essays and Interviews*. Edited and with an introduction by Donald F. Bouchard. Ithaca, NY: Cornell University Press, 1977.

Friedan, Betty. *The Feminine Mystique*. New York: Norton, 1963.

Fuss, Diana. *Essentially Speaking: Feminism, Nature, and Difference*. New York: Routledge, 1989.

Gates, Henry Louis, Jr. *Figures in Black: Words, Signs, and the "Racial" Self.* New York: Oxford University Press, 1989.

_____. *The Signifying Monkey: A Theory of Afro-American Literary Criticism.* New York: Oxford University Press, 1988.

_____. *Black Literature and Literary Theory.* New York: Methuen, 1984.

_____. *"Race," Writing, and Difference.* Chicago: University of Chicago Press, 1986.

_____. *Reading Black, Reading Feminist: A Critical Anthology.* New York: Meridian, 1990.

Gayle, Addison, Jr. *The Way of the New World: The Black Novel in America.* Garden City, NY: Anchor/Doubleday, 1976.

Gelfant, Blanche. *Women Writing in America: Voices in Collage.* Hanover, NH: University Press of New England for Dartmouth College, 1984.

Geertz, Clifford. *The Interpretation of Culture.* New York: Basic Books, 1973.

Gibson, Donald B. *The Politics of Literary Expression: A Study of Major Black Writers.* Westport, CT: Greenwood, 1981.

Gilbert, Sandra, and Susan Gubar. *The Madwoman in the Attic: The Woman Writer and the Nineteenth-Century Literary Imagination.* New Haven, CT: Yale University Press, 1979.

Greene, Gayle, and Coppelia Kahn, eds. *Making a Difference: Feminist Literary Criticism.* New York: Routledge, 1988.

Gwinn, Minrose. *Black and White Women of the Old South: The Peculiar Sisterhood in American Literature.* Knoxville: University of Tennessee Press, 1985.

Harper, Michael S., and Robert Stepto, eds. *Chant of Saints: A Gathering of Afro-American Literature, Art, and Scholarship.* Urbana: University of Illinois Press, 1979.

Harris, Trudier. *Black Women in the Fiction of James Baldwin.* Knoxville: University of Tennessee Press, 1985.

_____. *From Mammies to Militants: Domestics in Black American Literature.* Philadelphia, PA: Temple University Press, 1982.

Heilbrun, Carolyn. *Reinventing Womanhood.* New York: Norton, 1979.

Heilbrun, Carolyn, and Margaret Higonnet, eds. *The Representation of Women in Fiction.* Baltimore, MD: Johns Hopkins University Press, 1982.

Hernton, Calvin C. *The Sexual Mountain and Black Women Writers: Adventures in Sex, Literature and Real Life.* New York: Anchor, 1987.

Hirsch, Marianne. *The Mother/Daughter Plot: Narrative, Psychoanalysis, Feminism.* Bloomington: Indiana University Press, 1989.

Hogue, W. Lawrence. *Discourse and the Other: The Production of the Afro-American Text.* Durham, NC: Duke University Press, 1986.

Honey, Maureen, ed. *Shadowed Dreams: Women's Poetry of the Harlem Renaissance.* New Brunswick, NJ: Rutgers University Press, 1989.

hooks, bell. *Feminist Theory: From Margin to Center.* Boston, MA: South End Press, 1984.

_____. *Talking Back: Thinking Feminist, Thinking Black.* Boston: South End Press, 1989.

Howard, Lillie P. *Zora Neale Hurston.* Boston: G. K. Hall, 1980.

Huggins, Nathan. *Harlem Renaissance.* New York: Oxford University Press, 1971.

Hull, Gloria T. *Color, Sex, and Poetry: Three Women Writers of the Harlem Renaissance.* Bloomington: Indiana University Press, 1987.

James, C. L. R. *Notes on Dialectics: Hegel, Marx, Lenin* (1948, 1965; rpt. London: Allison & Bushby, 1980).

Jameson, Fredric. *The Political Unconscious: Narrative as a Socially Symbolic Act.* Ithaca, NY: Cornell University Press, 1981.

Johnson, Abby Arthur, and Ronald Mayberry. *Propaganda and Aesthetics: The Literary Politics of Afro-American Magazines in the Twentieth Century.* Amherst: University of Massachusetts Press, 1979.

Johnson, Barbara. *The Critical Difference.* Baltimore, MD: Johns Hopkins University Press, 1980.

――――. *A World of Difference.* Baltimore, MD: Johns Hopkins University Press, 1987.

Johnson, Charles. *Being and Race: Black Writing Since 1970.* Bloomington: Indiana University Press, 1988.

Jones, Anne Goodwyn. *Tomorrow Is Another Day: The Woman Writer in the South, 1859–1936.* Baton Rouge: Louisiana State University Press, 1981.

Kauffman, Linda, ed. *Feminism and Institutions: Dialogues on Feminist Theory.* New York: Basil Blackwell, 1989.

――――. *Gender and Theory: Dialogues on Feminist Criticism.* New York: Basil Blackwell, 1989.

Kelley, Mary. *Private Women, Public Stage: Literary Domesticity in Nineteenth-Century America.* New York: Oxford University Press, 1985.

Kermode, Frank. *The Classic: Literary Images of Permanence and Change.* New York: Viking, 1975.

Kubitschek, Missy Dehn. *Claiming the Heritage: African American Women Novelists and History.* Jackson: University of Mississippi Press, 1991.

Langbauer, Laurie. *Women and Romance: The Consolations of Gender in the English Novel.* Ithaca, NY: Cornell University Press, 1990.

Leitch, Vincent B. *American Literary Criticism from the Thirties to the Eighties.* New York: Columbia University Press, 1989.

Littlejohn, David. *Black on White: A Critical Survey of Writing by American Negroes.* New York: Grossman, 1966.

Longhurst, Derek, ed. *Gender, Genre and Narrative Pleasure.* Winchester, MA: Pandora, 1989.

McDowell, Deborah E., and Arnold Rampersad, eds. *Slavery and the Literary Imagination.* Baltimore, MD: Johns Hopkins University Press, 1989.

McKay, Nellie, ed. *Critical Essays on Toni Morrison.* Boston, MA: Hall, 1988.

Martin, Wendy, ed. *New Essays on "The Awakening."* New York: Cambridge University Press, 1988.

Meese, Elizabeth A. *Crossing the Double-Cross: The Practice of Feminist Criticism.* Chapel Hill: University of North Carolina Press, 1986.

Meese, Elizabeth A., and Alice Parker, eds. *The Difference Within: Feminism and Critical Theory.* Philadelphia, PA: John Benjamins, 1989.

Miller, Jane. *Women Writing About Men.* New York: Pantheon, 1986.

Miller, Nancy K., ed. *The Politics of Gender.* New York: Columbia University Press, 1986.

Millett, Kate. *Sexual Politics.* New York: Ballantine, 1969.

Minh-ha, Trihn T. *Woman, Native, Other: Writing, Postcoloniality and Feminism.* Bloomington: Indiana University Press, 1989.

Modleski, Tania. *Loving with a Vengeance: Mass-Produced Fantasies for Women.* New York: Anchor, 1982.

Moers, Ellen. *Literary Women: The Great Writers.* Garden City, NY: Doubleday, 1976.

Moi, Toril. *Sexual/Textual Politics: Feminist Literary Theory.* New York: Methuen, 1985.

Nelson, Cary, and Lawrence Grossberg, eds. *Marxism and the Interpretation of Culture*. Urbana and Chicago: University of Illinois Press, 1988.

Newton, Judith, and Deborah Rosenfelt. *Feminist Criticism and Social Change*. New York: Methuen, 1985.

Nicholson, Linda J., ed. *Feminism/Postmodernism*. New York: Routledge, 1989.

Otten, Terry. *The Crime of Innocence in the Fiction of Toni Morrison*. Columbia: University of Missouri Press, 1989.

Palmer, Paulina. *Contemporary Women's Fiction: Narrative Practice and Feminist Theory*. Jackson: University of Mississippi Press, 1989.

Payne, Ladell. *Black Novelists and the Southern Literary Tradition*. Athens: University of Georgia Press, 1981.

Pratt, Annis. *Archetypal Patterns in Women's Fiction*. Bloomington: Indiana University Press, 1981.

Pryse, Marjorie, and Hortense Spillers, eds. *Conjouring: Black Women, Fiction, and Literary Tradition*. Bloomington: Indiana University Press, 1985.

Radway, Janice A. *Reading the Romance: Women, Patriarchy, and Popular Literature*. Chapel Hill: University of North Carolina Press, 1984.

Rainwater, Catherine, and William J. Scheik, eds. *Contemporary American Women Writers: Narrative Strategies*. Lexington: University of Kentucky Press, 1985.

Rigney, Barbara Hill. *Madness and Sexual Politics in the Feminist Novel*. Madison: University of Wisconsin Press, 1978.

Riley, Denise. *"Am I That Name?": Feminism and the Category of "Woman" in History*. Minneapolis: University of Minnesota Press, 1988.

Rooney, Ellen. *Seductive Reasoning: Pluralism as the Problematic of Contemporary Literary Theory*. Ithaca, NY: Cornell University Press, 1989.

Russell, Sandi. *Render Me My Song: African-American Women Writers from Slavery to the Present*. New York: St. Martin's, 1990.

Scott, Bonnie Kime, ed. *The Gender of Modernism: A Critical Anthology*. Bloomington: Indiana University Press, 1990.

Scott, Joan Wallach. *Gender and the Politics of History*. New York: Columbia University Press, 1989.

Shockley, Ann Allen, ed. *Afro-American Women Writers, 1746–1933: An Anthology and Critical Guide*. New York: New American Library, 1989.

Showalter, Elaine. *A Literature of Their Own: British Women Novelists from Brontë to Lessing*. Princeton, NJ: Princeton University Press, 1977.

———, ed. *The New Feminist Criticism: Essays on Women, Literature, and Theory*. New York: Pantheon, 1985.

———. *Speaking of Gender*. New York: Routledge, 1989.

Smith, Sidone. *A Poetics of Women's Autobiography: Marginality and the Fiction of Self-Representation*. Bloomington: Indiana University Press, 1987.

Smith, Valerie. *Self-Discovery and Authority in Afro-American Narrative*. Cambridge, MA: Harvard University Press, 1987.

Spacks, Patricia Meyer. *The Female Imagination*. New York: Avon, 1975.

Spelman, Elizabeth V. *Inessential Woman: Problems of Exclusion in Feminist Thought*. Boston, MA: Beacon, 1988.

Spencer, Jane. *The Rise of the Woman Novelist: From Aphra Behn to Jane Austen*. New York and Oxford: Basil Blackwell, 1986.

Spillers, Hortense, ed. *Comparative American Identities: Race, Sex, and Nationality in the Modern Text*. New York: Routledge, 1991.

Spivak, Gayatri Chakravorty. *In Other Worlds: Essays in Cultural Politics*. New York: Routledge, 1988.

_____. *The Post-Colonial Critic*. New York: Routledge, 1990.

Stepto, Robert. *From Behind the Veil: A Study of Afro-American Narrative*. Urbana: University of Illinois Press, 1979.

Sylvander, Carolyn Wedin. *Jessie Redmon Fauset, Black American Writer*. Troy: Whitson, 1981.

Tate, Claudia. *Domestic Allegories of Political Desire: The Black Heroine's Text at the Turn of the Century*. New York: Oxford University Press, 1992.

Todd, Janet. *Feminist Literary History*. New York: Routledge, 1988.

_____, ed. *Men by Women*. New York: Holmes & Meier, 1981.

Tompkins, Jane. *Reader Response Criticism: From Formalism to Post-Structuralism*. Baltimore, MD: Johns Hopkins University Press, 1980.

_____. *Sensational Designs: The Cultural Work of American Literature*. New York: Oxford University Press, 1985.

Turner, Darwin. *In a Minor Chord: Three Afro-American Writers and Their Search for Identity*. Carbondale: Southern Illinois University Press, 1971.

Vogel, Lise. *Marxism and the Oppression of Women: Towards a Unitary Theory*. New Brunswick, NJ: Rutgers University Press, 1983.

Wade-Gayles, Gloria. *No Crystal Stair: Visions of Race and Sex in Black Women's Fiction*. New York: Pilgrim, 1984.

Walby, Sylvia. *Theorizing Patriarchy*. Oxford: Basil Blackwell, 1990.

Walker, Alice. *In Search of Our Mothers' Gardens*. New York: Harvest, 1984.

Wall, Cheryl, ed. *Changing Our Own Words: Essays on Criticism, Theory, and Writing by Black Women*. New Brunswick, NJ: Rutgers University Press, 1989.

Wallace, Michelle. *Invisibility Blues: From Pop to Theory*. New York: Verso, 1990.

Watson, Carole McAlpine. *Prologue: The Novels of Black American Women, 1891–1965*. Westport, CT: Greenwood, 1985.

Waugh, Patricia. *Feminine Fictions: Revisiting the Postmodern*. New York and London: Routledge, 1989.

Weed, Elizabeth, ed. *Coming to Terms: Feminism/Theory/Politics*. New York: Routledge, 1989.

Weedon, Chris. *Feminist Practice and Poststructuralist Theory*. New York: Basil Blackwell, 1987.

White, Hayden. *Tropics of Discourse: Essays in Cultural Criticism*. Baltimore, MD: Johns Hopkins University Press, 1978.

Williams, Raymond. *Marxism and Literature*. New York: Oxford University Press, 1977.

Willis, Susan. *Specifying: Black Women Writing the American Experience*. Madison: University of Wisconsin Press, 1987.

Wintz, Cardy D. *Black Culture and the Harlem Renaissance*. Houston, TX: Rice University Press, 1988.

Wyatt, Jean. *Reconstructing Desire: The Role of the Unconscious in Women's Reading and Writing*. Chapel Hill: University of North Carolina Press, 1990.

Yellin, Jean Fagan. *The Intricate Knot: Black Figures in American Literature, 1776–1863*. New York: New York University Press, 1972.

HISTORICAL SCHOLARSHIP

Aptheker, Betina. *Woman's Legacy: Essays on Race and Class in American History*. Amherst: University of Massachusetts Press, 1982.

Aptheker, Herbert. *American Negro Slave Revolts*. New York: International Publishers, 1953.

Blassingame, John. *The Slave Community: Plantation Life in the Antebellum South.* New York: Oxford University Press, 1978.

Clark, Kenneth. *Dark Ghetto.* New York: Harper & Row, 1965.

Clinton, Catherine. *The Plantation Mistress: Woman's World in the Old South.* New York: Pantheon, 1982.

Cott, Nancy F. *The Grounding of Modern Feminism.* New Haven, CT: Yale University Press, 1987.

Cott, Nancy F., and Elizabeth Pleck, eds. *A Heritage of Her Own: Toward a New Social History of American Women.* New York: Simon & Schuster, 1979.

Davis, Angela. *Women, Culture, and Politics.* New York: Random House, 1989.

_____. *Women, Race, and Class.* New York: Vintage, 1983.

DuBois, Ellen Carol. *Feminism and Suffrage: The Emergence of an Independent Women's Movement in America, 1848–1869.* Ithaca, NY: Cornell University Press, 1978.

DuBois, Ellen Carol, and Viki L. Ruiz, eds. *Unequal Sisters: A Multi-Cultural Reader in U.S. Women's History.* New York: Routledge, 1990.

Flexner, Eleanor. *Century of Struggle: The Woman's Rights Movement in the United States.* Rev. ed. Cambridge, MA: Harvard University Press, 1975.

Fox-Genovese, Elizabeth. *Within the Plantation Household: Black and White Women of the Old South.* Chapel Hill: University of North Carolina Press, 1988.

Franklin, John Hope, and Alfred E. Moss. *From Slavery to Freedom: A History of Negro Americans.* 6th ed. New York: Knopf, 1988.

Genovese, Eugene. *Roll, Jordan, Roll: The World the Slaves Made.* New York: Vintage, 1976.

Giddings, Paula. *In Search of Sisterhood: Delta Sigma Theta and the Challenge of the Black Sorority Movement in the United States.* New York: Morrow, 1988.

_____. *When and Where I Enter: The Impact of Black Women on Race and Sex in America.* New York: Bantam, 1984.

Harding, Vincent. *There Is a River: The Black Struggle for Freedom in America.* New York: Vintage, 1981.

Harley, Sharon, and Rosalyn Terborg-Penn, eds. *The Afro-American Woman: Struggles and Images.* Port Washington, NY: Kennikat, 1978.

Harris, Michael. *The Rise of Gospel Blues: The Music of Thomas Andrew Dorsey in the Urban Church.* New York: Oxford University Press, 1992.

Harrison, Daphne Duval. *Black Pearls: Blues Queens of the 1920s.* New Brunswick, NJ: Rutgers University Press, 1988.

Hernton, Calvin C. *Sex and Racism in America.* New York: Doubleday, 1966.

Hine, Darlene Clark. *The State of Afro-American History.* Baton Rouge: Louisiana State University Press, 1986.

Hobsbawn, Eric, and Terence Ranger. *The Invention of Tradition.* New York: Cambridge University Press, 1983.

Huggins, Nathan. *Harlem Renaissance.* New York: Oxford University Press, 1971.

Hull, Gloria T., Patricia Bell Scott, and Barbara Smith, eds. *But Some of Us Are Brave: Black Women's Studies.* New York: The Feminist Press, 1982.

Jones, Jacqueline. *Labor of Love, Labor of Sorrow: Black Women, Work, and the Family from Slavery to the Present.* New York: Vintage, 1985.

Jones, LeRoi [Amiri Baraka]. *Blues People: The Negro Experience in White America and the Music That Developed from It.* New York: Morrow, 1963.

Ladner, Joyce. *Tomorrow's Tomorrow: The Black Woman.* Garden City, NY: Doubleday, 1971.

Lerner, Gerda. *The Creation of Patriarchy*. New York: Oxford University Press, 1986.

Levine, Lawrence W. *Black Culture and Black Consciousness: Afro-American Folk Thought from Slavery to Freedom*. New York: Oxford University Press, 1977.

Lewis, David Levering. *When Harlem Was in Vogue*. New York: Knopf, 1979; rpt. New York: Oxford University Press, 1989.

Lieb, Sandra. *Mother of the Blues: A Study of Ma Rainey*. Amherst: University of Massachusetts Press, 1981.

Locke, Alain, ed. *The New Negro*. New York: Boni, 1925; reprinted with an introduction by Robert Hayden. New York: Atheneum, 1986.

Neverton-Morton, Cynthia. *Afro-American Women of the South and the Advancement of the Race, 1895–1925*. Knoxville: University of Tennessee Press, 1989.

Nobel, Jeanne. *Beautiful, Also, Are the Souls of My Black Sisters: A History of the Black Woman in America*. Englewood Cliffs, NJ: Prentice-Hall, 1980.

Okihiro, Gary Y., ed. *In Resistance: Studies in African, Caribbean and Afro-American History*. Amherst: University of Massachusetts Press, 1986.

Osofsky, Gilbert. *Harlem, the Making of a Ghetto: Negro New York, 1890–1930*. New York: Harper & Row, 1963.

Richardson, Marilyn, ed. *Maria W. Stewart, America's First Black Woman Political Writer: Essays and Speeches*. Bloomington: Indiana University Press, 1987.

Rose, Phyllis. *Jazz Cleopatra: Josephine Baker in Her Time*. New York: Doubleday, 1989.

Scott, Anne Firor. *The Southern Lady: From Pedestal to Politics, 1830–1930*. Chicago: University of Chicago Press, 1970.

Scott, James. *Weapons of the Weak: Everyday Forms of Peasant Resistance*. New Haven, CT: Yale University Press, 1985.

Smith-Rosenberg, Carroll. *Disorderly Conduct: Visions of Gender in Victorian America*. New York: Oxford University Press, 1985.

Stanton, Elizabeth Cady, Susan B. Anthony, and M. J. Gage, eds. *History of Woman Suffrage*. Rochester, NY: Fowler & Wells, 1881.

Steady, Filomina Chioma, ed. *The Black Woman Cross-Culturally*. Cambridge, MA: Schenkam, 1981.

Sterling, Dorothy. *Black Foremothers: Three Lives*. 2nd ed. New York: The Feminist Press, 1988.

Strane, Susan. *A Whole-Souled Woman: Prudence Crandall and the Education of Black Women*. New York: Norton, 1990.

Stuckey, Sterling. *Slave Culture: Nationalist Theory and the Foundation of Black America*. New York: Oxford University Press, 1987.

Wallace, Phyllis. *Black Women in the Labor Force*. Cambridge, MA: MIT Press, 1980.

Wells [Barnett], Ida B. *On Lynchings: Southern Horrors; A Red Record; Mob Rule in New Orleans*. New York: Arno Press, 1969.

Welter, Barbara, ed. *Dimity Convictions: The American Woman in the Nineteenth Century*. Columbus: Ohio University Press, 1975.

White, Deborah Gray. *Ar'n't I a Woman? Female Slaves in the Plantation South*. New York: Norton, 1985.

SOCIOLOGICAL AND PSYCHOLOGICAL SCHOLARSHIP

Benjamin, Jessica. *The Bonds of Love: Psychoanalysis, Feminism, and the Problem of Domination*. New York: Pantheon, 1988.

Bernard, Jessie. *Marriage and Family Among Negroes*. Englewood Cliffs, NJ: Prentice-Hall, 1966.

Billingsley, Andrew. *Black Familes in White America.* 1968; rpt. New York: Simon & Schuster, 1988.

Botkin, Benjamin A. *Lay My Burden Down.* Chicago: University of Chicago Press, 1945.

Brown, Teresa, ed. *Between Feminism and Psychoanalysis.* New York: Routledge, 1989.

Butler, Judith. *Gender Trouble.* New York: Routledge, 1989.

Caplan, Pat, ed. *The Cultural Construction of Sexuality.* New York: Tavistock, 1987.

Chodorow, Nancy. *Feminism and Psychoanalytic Theory.* New Haven, CT: Yale University Press, 1989.

———. *The Reproduction of Mothering: Psychoanalysis and the Sociology of Gender.* Berkeley: University of California Press, 1978.

D'Emilio, John, and Estelle B. Freedman. *Intimate Matters: A History of Sexuality in America.* New York: Harper & Row, 1988.

De Rougemont, Denis. *Love in the Western World.* New York: Schocken, 1983.

Frazier, E. Franklin. *The Negro Family in the United States.* Rev. Ed. New York: Holt, Rinehart & Winston, 1948.

Ferguson, Ann. *Blood at the Root: Motherhood, Sexuality and Male Dominance.* Winchester, MA: Pandora, 1989.

Firestone, Shulamith. *The Dialectic of Sex.* New York: Bantam, 1970.

Gallop, Jane. *The Daughter's Seduction: Feminism and Psychoanalysis.* Ithaca, NY: Cornell University Press, 1982.

Gilligan, Carol. *In a Different Voice: Psychological Theory and Women's Development.* Cambridge, MA: Harvard University Press, 1982.

Gutman, Herbert G. *The Black Family in Slavery and Freedom, 1750–1925.* New York: Vintage, 1976.

Herman, Judith Lewis. *Father-Daughter Incest.* Cambridge, MA: Harvard University Press, 1981.

Kristeva, Julia. *In the Beginning Was Love: Psychoanalysis and Faith.* Translated by Arthur Goldhammer. New York: Columbia University Press, 1987.

Ladner, Joyce, ed. *The Death of White Sociology.* New York: Vintage, 1973.

Martin, Emily. *The Woman in the Body: A Cultural Analysis of Reproduction.* Boston: Beacon, 1987.

Moynihan, Daniel Patrick. *The Negro Family: The Case for National Action.* Washington, D.C.: U.S. Department of Labor, 1965.

Otner, Sherry B., and Harriet Whitehead. *Sexual Meanings: The Cultural Construction of Gender and Sexuality.* New York: Cambridge University Press, 1988.

Pateman, Carole. *The Sexual Contract.* Stanford, CA: Stanford University Press, 1988.

Peiss, Kathy, and Christina Simmons, eds. *Passion and Power: Sexuality in History.* Philadelphia, PA: Temple University Press, 1989.

Rich, Adrienne. *Of Woman Born: Motherhood as Experience and Institution.* New York: Norton, 1976.

Rothenberg, Paula, ed. *Racism and Sexism: An Integrated Study.* New York: St. Martin's, 1988.

Smitherman, Geneva. *Talking and Testifying: The Language of Black America.* Detroit, MI: Wayne State University Press, 1986.

Snitow, Ann, Christine Stansell, and Sharon Thompson, eds. *Powers of Desire: The Politics of Sexuality.* New York: Monthly Review Press, 1983.

Staples, Roberts. *The Black Family: Essays and Studies.* 3rd ed. Belmont, CA: Wadsworth, 1986.

Vance, Carole S., ed. *Pleasure and Danger: Exploring Female Sexuality.* Boston: Routledge & Kegan Paul, 1985.

Wallace, Michelle. *Black Macho and the Myth of the Superwoman.* New York: Warner, 1978.
Wilson, William Julius. *The Declining Significance of Race.* Chicago: University of Chicago Press, 1978.
———. *The Truly Disadvantaged: The Inner City, the Underclass, and Public Policy.* Chicago: University of Chicago Press, 1987.

Articles, Essays, and Dissertations

Alexander, Don, and Christine Wright. "Race, Sex and Class: The Clash over *The Color Purple.*" *Women and Revolution* 34 (Spring 1988): 18–22.
Ammons, Elizabeth. "New Literary History: Edith Wharton and Jessie Redmon Fauset." *College Literature* (Fall 1987): 207–18.
Appiah, Kwame Anthony. "The Conservation of 'Race.'" *Black American Literature Forum* 23 (Spring 1989): 37–60.
Awkward, Michael. "Race, Gender, and the Politics of Reading." *Black American Literature Forum* 22 (Spring 1988): 5–27.
Baker, Houston, A., Jr. "In Dubious Battle." *New Literary History* 18 (Winter 1987): 363–70.
———. "The Promised Body: Reflections on Canon in an Afro-American Context." In *The Rhetoric of Interpretation and the Interpretation of Rhetoric*, edited by Raul Hernardi, 87–103. Durham, NC: Duke University Press, 1989.
Barksdale, Richard. "Castration Symbolism in Recent Black American Fiction." *College Language Association Journal* 29 (June 1986): 400–413.
Barrett, Michele, and Mary McIntosh. "Ethnocentrism and Socialist-Feminist Theory." *Feminist Review* 20 (June 1985): 23–47.
Baym, Nina. "Melodramas of Beset Manhood: How Theories of American Fiction Exclude Women Authors." *American Quarterly* 33 (1981): 123–39.
Bennett, Lerone, Jr. "The Roots of Black Love." *Ebony*, August 1981, 31–36.
Butler, Marilyn. "Against Tradition: The Case for a Particularized Historical Method." In *Historical Studies and Literary Criticism*, edited by Jerome J. McGann, 25–47. Madison: University of Wisconsin Press, 1985.
Carby, Hazel. "'It Jus Be's Dat Way Sometime': The Sexual Politics of Women's Blues." In *Unequal Sisters: A Multicultural Reader in U.S. Women's History*, edited by Ellen Carol DuBois and Viki L. Ruiz, 238–49. New York: Routledge, 1990.
———. "Reinventing History/Imagining the Future." Review of *Specifying: Black Women Writing the American Experience*, by Susan Willis. *Black American Literature Forum* 23, no. 2 (Summer 1989): 381–87.
Coleman, Ancilla. "Mythological Structure and Psychological Significance in Hurston's *Seraph on the Suwanee.*" *Publications of the Mississippi Philological Association* (1988): 21–27.
Crews, Frederick. "Whose American Renaissance?" *New York Review of Books*, October 27, 1988, 68–81.
Daniels, Douglas Henry. "The Significance of Blues for American History." *Journal of Negro History* 70 (Winter–Spring 1985): 14–23.
Davis, Thadious M. "Nella Larsen." In "Afro-American Writers from the Harlem Renaissance to 1940," *Dictionary of Literary Biography*, edited by Trudier Harris and Thadious M. Davis, 51:182–92.

Dobson, Joanne. "The Hidden Hand: Subversion of Cultural Ideology in Three Mid-Nineteenth Century American Women's Novels." *American Quarterly* 38 (Summer 1986): 223–43.

Farnham, Christie, "Sapphire? The Issue of Dominance in the Slave Family, 1830–1865." In *"To Toil the Livelong Day": American Women at Work, 1780–1980*, edited by Carol Groneman and Mary Beth Norton, 68–83. Ithaca, NY: Cornell University Press, 1987.

Ferguson, Sally Ann. "Folkloric Men and Female Growth in *Their Eyes Were Watching God*." *Black American Literature Forum* 21, nos. 1–2 (Spring–Summer 1987): 186–97.

Fields, Barbara. "Ideology and Race in American History." In *Region, Race and Reconstruction*, edited by J. Morgan Kousser and James M. McPherson, 143–77. New York: Oxford University Press, 1982.

Finke, Laurie. "The Rhetoric of Marginality: Why I Do Feminist Theory." *Tulsa Studies in Women's Literature* 5 (Fall 1986): 251–72.

Foreman, P. Gabrielle. "The Spoken and the Silenced in *Incidents in the Life of a Slave Girl* and *Our Nig*." *Callaloo* 13 (Spring 1990): 313–24.

Foster, Frances Smith. "Researching and Reinterpreting the Reconstruction of Literature of Frances Ellen Watkins Harper." Paper presented at the annual meeting of the American Studies Association, Costa Mesa, CA, November 1992.

Gates, Henry Louis, Jr. "'What's Love Got to Do with It?': Critical Theory, Integrity, and the Black Idiom." *New Literary History* 18 (Winter 1987): 345–62.

Gilkes, Cheryl Townsend. "Dual Heroism and Double Burdens: Interpreting Afro-American Women's Experience and History." *Feminist Studies* 15, no. 3 (Fall 1989): 573–90.

Harris, Norman. "'Who's Zoomin' Who': The New Black Formalism." *Midwest MLA Journal* 20 (Spring 1987): 37–45.

Hawthorne, Evelyn. "On Gaining the Double-Vision: *Tar Baby* as Diasporean Novel." *Black American Literature Forum* 22 (Spring 1988): 97–107.

Hellenbrand, Harold. "Speech, After Silence: Alice Walker's *The Third Life of Grange Copeland*." *Black American Literature Forum* 20 (Spring–Summer, 1986): 113–28.

Henderson, Mae. "(W)riting *The Work* and Working the Rites." *Black American Literature Forum* 23 (Winter 1989): 631–59.

Henderson, Stephen. "The Blues as Black Poetry." *Callaloo* 5 (October 1982): 22–30.

Hinz, Evelyn J. "Hierogamy Versus Wedlock: Types of Marriage Plots and Their Relationship to Genres of Prose Fiction." *PMLA* 91 (1976): 900–913.

Hogue, W. Lawrence. "Discourse of the Other: *The Third Life of Grange Copeland*." *MELUS* 12 (Summer 1985): 97–114.

———. "History, the Feminist Discourse, and Alice Walker's *The Third Life of Grange Copeland*." *MELUS* 12 (Summer 1985): 45–63.

Homans, Margaret. "Feminist Criticism and Theory: The Ghost of Creusa." *Yale Journal of Criticism* 1 (Fall 1987): 153–82.

Horton, James Oliver. "Freedom's Yoke: Gender Conventions Among Antebellum Free Blacks." *Feminist Studies* 12 (Spring 1986): 51–76.

Hostetler, Ann E. "The Aesthetics of Race and Gender in Nella Larsen's *Quicksand*." *PMLA* 105 (January 1990): 35–46.

Howard, Lillie P. "Marriage: Zora Neale Hurston's System of Values." *College Language Association Journal* 21 (December 1977): 256–68.

———. "Nanny and Janie: Will the Twain Ever Meet? (A Look at Zora Neale Hurston's *Their Eyes Were Watching God*)." *Journal of Black Studies* 12 (June 1982): 403–14.

Irigaray, Luce. "Any Theory of the 'Subject' Has Always Been Appropriated by the 'Masculine.'" In *Speculum of the Other Woman*. Ithaca, NY: Cornell University Press, 1985.

Jameson, Fredric. "The Politics of Theory: Ideological Positions in the Postmodernism Debate." *New German Critique* 33 (1984): 53–65.

Jenkins, Wilbert. "Jessie Fauset: A Modern Apostle of Black Racial Pride." *Zora Neale Hurston Forum* 1 (Fall 1986): 14–24.

Jordan, Jennifer. "Feminist Fantasies: Zora Neale Hurston's *Their Eyes Were Watching God*." *Tulsa Studies in Women's Literature* 7 (Spring 1988): 105–17.

Joyce, Joyce A. "The Black Canon: Reconstructing Black American Literary Criticism." *New Literary History* 18 (Winter 1987): 335–44.

Kamme-Erkel, Sybille. *Happily Ever After? Marriage and Its Rejection in Afro-American Novels*. (Ph.D. diss., Philipps University, 1988.) Frankfurt am Main: Peter Lang, 1989.

Karamcheti, Indira. "Post-Coloniality and the Internationalization of Cultural Studies." Paper presented at the Mainstreams and Margins Conference. University of Massachusetts-Amherst, April 3, 1992.

Kavanaugh, James H. "Marxist Literary Criticism and Theory." *Choice*, October 1981, 203–13.

Keller, Bruce. "Carl Van Vechten's Black Renaissance." In *The Harlem Renaissance: Revaluation*, ed. Amritjit Singh, William S. Shriver, and Stanley Brodwin. New York: Garland, 1989.

King, Deborah K. "Multiple Jeopardy, Multiple Consciousness: The Context of a Black Feminist Ideology." *Signs* 14, no. 1 (Fall 1988): 18–33.

Krasner, James. "The Life of Women: Zora Neale Hurston and Female Autobiography." *Black American Literature Forum* 23 (Spring 1989): 113–26.

Kubitschek, Missy Dehn. "'Tuh De Horizon and Back': The Female Quest in *Their Eyes Were Watching God*." *Black American Literature Forum* 17 (Fall 1983): 109–15.

Larson, Charles. "Heroic Ethnocentrism: The Idea of Universality in Literature." *The American Scholar* 42 (Summer 1973): 463–75.

Larson, Charles R. "Whatever Happened to Nella Larsen?" *Belles Lettres* 4 (Spring 1989): 15.

Lupton, Mary Jane. "Bad Blood in Jersey: Jessie Fauset's *The Chinaberry Tree*." *College Language Association Journal* 27 (June 1984): 383–92.

_____. "Black Women and Survival in *Comedy American Style* and *Their Eyes Were Watching God*." *Zora Neale Hurston Forum* 1 (Fall 1986): 38–44.

_____. "Clothes and Closure in Three Novels by Black Women." *Black American Literature Forum* 20 (Winter 1986): 409–21.

McCredie, Wendy J. "Authority and Authorization in *Their Eyes Were Watching God*." *Black American Literature Forum* 16, no. 1 (Spring 1982): 25–28.

McDowell, Deborah E. "'The Changing Same': Generational Connections and Black Women Novelists." *New Literary History* 18 (Winter 1987): 281–302.

_____. Review of *Specifying*, by Susan Willis. In *Signs* 14 (Summer 1989): 948–52.

Marks, Donald. "Sex, Violence, and Organic Consciousness in Zora Neale Hurston's *Their Eyes Were Watching God*." *Black American Literature Forum* 19 (Fall 1985): 152–57.

Mason, Theodore J. "Between the Populist and the Scientist: Ideology and Power in Recent Afro-American Criticism or The Dozens as Scholarshp." *Callaloo* 11, no. 3 (Summer 1988): 606–15.

Miller, R. Baxter. "Baptized Infidel: Play and Critical Legacy." *Black American Literature Forum* 21, no. 4 (Winter 1987): 391–414.

Morrison, Toni. "Unspeakable Things Unspoken: The Afro-American Presence in American Literature." *Michigan Quarterly Review* 38, no. 1 (Winter 1989): 1–34.

Moses, Wilson J. "The Lost World of the Negro, 1895–1919: Black Literary and Intellectual Life before the 'Renaissance.'" *Black American Literature Forum* 21, nos. 1–2 (Spring–Summer 1987): 61–84.

Mullen, Harryette. "Runaway Tongue: Resistant Orality in *Uncle Tom's Cabin, Our Nig, Incidents in the Life of a Slave Girl*, and *Beloved*. Paper presented at the annual meeting of the American Studies Association, New Orleans, LA, November 1990.

Myers, Linda James. "The Deep Structure of Culture: Relevance of Traditional African Culture in Contemporary Life." *Journal of Black Studies* 18 (September 1987): 72–85.

Naylor, Gloria. "Love and Sex in the Afro-American Novel." *Yale Review* 78, no. 1 (Spring 1989): 19–31.

Newman, Louise. "Ideologies of Womanhood at the Turn of the Century." Paper presented at the annual meeting of the American Studies Association, New Orleans, LA, November 1990.

Newton, Judith. "History as Usual?: Feminism and the 'New Historicism.'" *Cultural Critique* 17 (Spring 1988): 87–121.

Noonan, Paula E. "Women and Love: Feminine Perspectives on Love and Sexuality in the Fiction of 19th and 20th Century Women Writers." Ph.D. diss., University of Denver, 1979.

Ogunyemi, Chikwenye Okonjo. "Womanism: The Dynamics of the Contemporary Black Female Novel in English." *Signs* 11 (Autumn 1985): 63–80.

Palmer, Phyllis Marynick. "White Women/Black Women: The Dualism of Female Identity and Experience in the United States." *Feminist Studies* 9, no. 1 (Spring 1983): 151–70.

Radhakrishnan, R. "Culture as Common Ground: Ethnicity and Beyond." *MELUS* 14 (Summer 1987): 5–19.

Reid, Pamela Trotman. "Feminism Versus Minority Group Identity: Not for Black Women Only." *Sex Roles* 10, nos. 3–4 (1984): 247–55.

Rose, Phyllis. "Exactly What Is It About Josephine Baker?" *New York Times*, March 10, 1991: H31.

Rowell, Charles H. "An Interview with Gayl Jones." *Callaloo* 5 (October 1982): 32–53.

Sadoff, Dianne F. "Black Matrilineage: The Case of Alice Walker and Zora Neale Hurston." *Signs* 11 (Autumn 1985): 4–26.

Skerret, Joseph T. "The Wright Interpretation: Ralph Ellison and the Anxiety of Influence." *Massachusetts Review* 21 (Spring 1980): 196–212.

Spillers, Hortense. "Formalism Comes to Harlem." *Black American Literature Forum* 16 (Summer 1982): 59–63.

Smith, Valerie. "A Self-critical Tradition." *Women's Review of Books* 5 (February 1988): 15.

Tate, Claudia. "*Corregidora:* Ursa's Blues Medley." *Black American Literature Forum* 13 (Winter 1979): 139–48.

_____. "On Black Literary Women and the Evolution of Critical Discourse." *Tulsa Studies in Women's Literature* 5 (Spring 1986): 111–23.

_____. "Pauline Hopkins: Our Literary Foremother." In *Conjouring: Black Women, Fiction, and Literary Tradition*, edited by Marjorie Pryse and Hortense Spillers, 53–66. Bloomington: Indiana University Press, 1985.

_____. "Reshuffling the Deck; Or, (Re)Reading Race and Gender in Black Women's Writing." *Tulsa Studies in Women's Literature* 7 (Spring 1988): 105–32.

Terborg-Penn, Rosalyn. "Black Women in Resistance: A Cross-Cultural Perspective." In *In Resistance: Studies in African, Caribbean, and Afro-American History*, edited by Gary Y. Okihiro, 188–209. Amherst: University of Massachusetts Press, 1986.

Thornton, Hortense. "Sexism as Quagmire: Nella Larsen's *Quicksand*." 16 (March 1973): 285–301.

Tompkins, Jane. "A Short Course in Post-Structuralism." *College English* 50 (November 1988): 733–47.

Wade-Gayles, Gloria. "The Truths of Our Mothers' Lives: Mother-Daughter Relationships in Black Women's Fiction." *Sage* 1 (Fall 1984): 8–12.

Walker, Alice. "In the Closet of the Soul: A Letter to an African-American Friend." *Ms.*, November 1986, 32–35.

Walker, S. Jay. "Zora Neale Hurston's *Their Eyes Were Watching God*: Black Novel of Sexism." *Modern Fiction Studies* 20 (Winter 1974–75): 519–28.

Wall, Cheryl A. "*Mules and Men* and Women: Zora Neale Hurston's Strategies of Narration and Visions of Female Empowerment." *Black American Literature Forum* 23 (Winter 1989): 661–80.

_____. "Passing for What? Aspects of Identity in Nella Larsen's Novels." *Black American Literature Forum* 20 (Spring–Summer 1986): 97–111.

_____. "Poets and Versifiers, Singers and Signifiers: Women of the Harlem Renaissance." In *Women, the Arts, and the 1920s in Paris and New York*, edited by Kenneth W. Wheeler and Virginia Lee Lussier, 74–98. New Brunswick, NJ: Transaction Books, 1982.

_____. "Zora Neale Hurston: Changing Her Own Words." In *American Novelists Revisited: Essays in Feminist Criticism*, edited by Fritz Fleischmann, 371–93. Boston: G. K. Hall, 1982.

Washington, Mary Helen. "Black Women Image Makers." *Black World*, August 1974, 10–18.

_____. "I Sign My Mother's Name: Alice Walker, Dorothy West, and Paule Marshall. *Mothering the Mind: Twelve Studies of Writers and Their Silent Partners*, edited by Ruth Perry and Martine Watson Brownley, 142–63. New York: Holmes & Meier, 1984.

_____. "Nella Larsen: Mystery Woman of the Harlem Renaissance." *Ms.*, December 1980, 44–50.

Watkins, Mel. "Sexism, Racism, and Black Women Writers." *New York Times Book Review*, June 15, 1986, 1, 35.

Waxman, Barbara Frey. "Canonicity and Black American Literature: A Feminist View." *MELUS* 14 (Summer 1987): 87–93.

West, Cornel. "Minority Discourse and the Pitfalls of Canon Formation. *Yale Journal of Criticism* 1 (Fall 1987): 193–201.

Williams, Sherley Anne. "Roots of Privilege: New Black Fiction." *Ms.*, June 1985, 71.

Willis, Susan. "Gender as Commodity." *South Atlantic Quarterly* 86 (Fall 1987): 403–21.
Wolff, Maria Tai. "Listening and Living: Reading and Experience in *Their Eyes Were Watching God*." *Black American Literature Forum* 16 (Spring 1982): 29–33.
Yarborough, Richard. "The Depiction of Blacks in the Early Afro-American Novel." Ph.D. diss., Stanford University, 1980.

Index

AOF-3999